PERSONALITY PSYCHOLOGY IN EUROPE:

Vol. 2

Current Trends and Controversies

PERSONALITY PSYCHOLOGY IN EUROPE:

Volume 2

Current Trends and Controversies

Edited by
A. Angleitner, A. Furnham, and G. Van Heck

Selected Papers from the
Second European Conference on Personality
held at the University of Bielefeld, F.R.G.
May 17-19, 1984

SWETS NORTH AMERICA INC. / BERWYN
SWETS & ZEITLINGER B.V. / LISSE
1986

Library of Congress Cataloging-in-Publication Data
(Revised for vol. 2)

European Conference on Personality.
    Personality psychology in Europe.

    Edited by Han Bonarius and others.
    Vol. 2. has imprint: Lisse : Swets & Zeitlinger ;
Berwyn, PA : Swets North America.
    Includes bibliographies and indexes.
    Contents: [v. 1.] Theoretical and empirical
developments -- v. 2. Current trends and controversies.
    1. Personality--Congresses. 2. Psychology--Europe--
Congresses. I. Bonarius, Han. II. Title.
BF698.E77 1984   155.2   84-187203
ISBN 90-265-0559-0 (pbk. : v. 1)
ISBN 90-265-0597-3 (v. 2)

CIP-GEGEVENS KONINKLIJKE BIBLIOTHEEK, DEN HAAG

Personality

Personality psychology in Europe. - Lisse :
Swets & Zeitlinger
Vol. 2: Current trends and controversies / ed.
by A. Angleitner, A. Furnham, G. van Heck. - Ill.
Met lit. opg., reg.
ISBN 90-265-0597-3
SISO 417 UDC 159.923(4)
Trefw.: persoonlijkheidspsychologie ; Europa.

Cover design: H. Veltman
Printed in the Netherlands by Offsetdrukkerij Kanters B.V., Alblasserdam

© Copyright 1986, A. Angleitner, A. Furnham, G. van Heck and Swets and
Zeitlinger b.v., Lisse

ISBN 90 265 0597 3

CONTENTS

PREFACE

One of the chapters in this book starts with the statement that it is an exciting time to be working in the field of personality psychology. The major reason for excitement is the fact that the field of personality psychology nowadays shows many fresh and innovative approaches. This book informs about some of these developments.

The present volume contains fourteen chapters based on a selection of lectures and papers presented at the Second European Conference on Personality. This conference took place at the University of Bielefeld, May 17-19, 1984.

The editors wish to thank all the conference participants who submitted high quality manuscripts for the present book. The editors felt that the conference was quite succesful in reflecting the current status of personality psychology in Europe and also in indicating future directions of the field. With this in mind, it was decided to select those conference contributions that most clearly articulate trends and controversies in current theorizing and methodology. For that reason not only chapters based on contributions by European participants were included, but also - in contrast to the main title of the book - two chapters by American psychologists. First, these chapters stand in meaningful relationship to the selected European presentations. Second, they provide, in our opinion, new and inspiring answers to some old European questions. All conference contributions were extensively and carefully revised to reflect optimally the aims of the present book.

The fourteen chapters are organised in six parts. The first part includes chapters on a very basic issue in personality psychology. It reflects current thinking and methodological solutions regarding the problem of individuality in personality psychology. *Lamiell* discusses the history of the idiographic-nomothetic debate. He shows how his solution in terms of "idiothetic" studies can reconcile the discipline's idiographic and nomothetic objectives without sacrificing methodological rigor. *Hermans* presents a case-study, thereby illustrating an idiographic approach within the context of self-confrontations and developing valuations.

Part II deals with the vehemently discussed person-situation controversy. However, it gives a fresh approach to this issue in trying to focus on the impact and constraints of situations. *Thomae* treats ways of coping with critical life events in a developmental perspective. Presenting some intriguing results of longitudinal research, he highlights the adaptability and flexibility in handling the challenges and stresses of everyday life. *De Raad* is concerned with a specific type of situations, which occur very frequently in everybody's daily life: conversations. *De Raad* presents scenarios describing the different ways in which participants in conversational encounters orient their activities to each other. *Hettema, Van Heck, Appels,* and *Van Zon* conceptualize the impact of situations in terms of the extent to which situations allow for individual variation. They show convincingly the usefulness of generalizability theory and methodology for an adequate assessment of situational power.

Part III concentrates on the meaning of traits. Within the context of a constructivist view of personality, *Hampson* conceives of traits in a newly way, treating them as cognitive categories. Using the concept of category breadth, she presents empirical data on the hierarchical organisation of personality descriptive terms. *John* considers the features of traits. Based on philosophical reflections and some empirical data, he gives a detailed analysis of the crucial features of one single term, viz. altruism. Finally, *Buss* and *Craik* present their act frequency approach. They make clear how this approach differs from the somewhat related, more European, social constructivist point of view.

Part IV focuses on trait inferences. *Mervielde* distinguishes between different models for representing implicit personality theories. Studies on the relative efficiency of these methods for predicting trait attributions are presented. *Borkenau* presents an empirical study on systematic distortions in the recognition of trait information. In contrast to the more radical view of Shweder, *Borkenau* stresses the view that correlations between trait ratings can be conceived as a compromise between observed and expected co-occurrences of traits. Finally, *Smid* and *Brokken* introduce a Bayesian model for the study of trait inferences, featuring personal stereotypes.

In Part V the biological tradition in personality theory and research is presented. This part contains two chapters. In the first one, *Eysenck* considers the various conditions which have to be fulfilled before a personality model can be accepted as a paradigm. In addition, he considers the degree to which his dimensional model comes up to these standards. The second chapter is by *Przymusiński* and *Strelau*. Within the context of Strelau's regulative theory of temperament they report on a study about the influences of stimulation-seeking and activity on decision-making in gambling situations.

Part VI is based on a symposium on subliminal perception and microgenesis. *Dixon*, *Hentschel*, and *Smith* present a review of typical experiments in this somewhat controversial and probably relatively unfamiliar research tradition.

The editors of the book based on the First European Conference on Personality (Tilburg, The Netherlands, 1982) concluded the preface of that particular book with the statement that, although eleven nationalities were involved, the book could not possibly mirror adequately the full richness of European personality psychology. We agree that this also holds for the present volume. Nevertheless, the fact that the editors now came from three different European countries, seems to reflect current collaboration and hopefully scientific enrichment in European personality psychology.

Alois Angleitner
University of Bielefeld, FRG.
Adrian Furnham
University of London, England
Guus Van Heck
Tilburg University, The Netherlands.

LIST OF CONTRIBUTORS

Marie-Thérèse Appels
Department of Psychology
Tilburg University
Hogeschoollaan 225
Box 90153
NL-5000 LE Tilburg / The Netherlands

Peter Borkenau
Department of Psychology
University of Bielefeld
Universitätsstrasse 1
D-4800 Bielefeld 1 / West Germany

Frank B. Brokken
Institute of Personality Psychology
University of Groningen
Grote Markt 31-32
NL-9712 HV Groningen / The Netherlands

David M. Buss
Department of Psychology
The University of Michigan
580 Union Drive
Ann Arbor, MI 48109-1346 / United States of America

Kenneth H. Craik
Department of Psychology
University of California
Berkeley, CA / United States of America

Boele De Raad
Institute of Personality Psychology
University of Groningen
Grote Markt 31-32
NL-9712 HV Groningen / The Netherlands

Norman F. Dixon
Department of Psychology
University College London
Gowerstreet
London WC1E 6BT / United Kingdom

Hans J. Eysenck
Institute of Psychiatry
University of London
DeCrespigny Park, Denmark Hill
London FC5 8AF / United Kingdom

X

Sarah E. Hampson
Department of Psychology
Birkbeck College
University of London
Malet Street
London WC1E 7HX / United Kingdom

Uwe Hentschel
Institute of Psychology
University of Mainz
Saarstrasse 21
D-6500 Mainz / West Germany

Hubert J.M. Hermans
Psychological Laboratory
Catholic University of Nijmegen
Montessorilaan 3
Box 9104
NL-6500 HE Nijmegen / The Netherlands

Joop Hettema
Department of Psychology
Tilburg University
Hogeschoollaan 225
Box 90153
NL-5000 LE Tilburg / The Netherlands

Oliver P. John
Oregon Research Institute
1899 Willamette Street
Eugene, OR 97401 / United States of America

James T. Lamiell
Department of Psychology
Georgetown University
Washington, D.C. 20 057 / United States of America

Ivan Mervielde
Department of Psychology
State University of Ghent
H. Dunantlaan 2
B-9000 Ghent / Belgium

Ryszard Przymusiński
Academy of Catholic Theology
University of Warsaw
Stawki 5/7
PL-00183 Warsaw / Poland

Nico G. Smid
Institute of Personality Psychology
University of Groningen
Grote Markt 31-32
NL-9712 HV Groningen / The Netherlands

Gudmund J.W. Smith
Department of Psychology
Lund University
Paradisgatan 5
S-22 350 Lund / Sweden

Jan Strelau
Department of Psychology
University of Warsaw
Stawki 5/7
PL-00183 Warsaw / Poland

Hans Thomae
Langemarckstrasse 87
D-5300 Bonn 3 / West Germany

Guus L. Van Heck
Department of Psychology
Tilburg University
Hogeschoollaan 225
Box 90153
NL-5000 LE Tilburg / The Netherlands

Ine Van Zon
Department of Psychology
Tilburg University
Hogeschoollaan 225
Box 90153
NL-5000 LE Tilburg / The Netherlands

PART I

THE STUDY OF INDIVIDUALS IN PERSONALITY PSYCHOLOGY

EPISTEMOLOGICAL TENETS OF
AN IDIOTHETIC PSYCHOLOGY OF PERSONALITY*

James T. Lamiell

Georgetown University
Washington, D.C.
United States

Several years ago, Donald W. Fiske argued that

> ... A thorough reexamination of the personality field is imperative. The need is evident from an unprejudiced appraisal of the limited progress made in recent decades and of the nature of that progress. The assumptions underlying the study of personality must be made explicit and critically reviewed. What have we been doing? Where are we? What can we do about our situation? (1978, p. 3).

One who would dismiss these concerns as isolated and merely idiosyncratic crankiness will find little solace in such other analyses as provided by Conley (1983), DeWaele and Harré (1974), Rorer and Widiger (1983), Rychlak (1976, 1981a), and Sechrest (1976). And while these critics clearly disagree with one another (and I with them) in many important respects, they nevertheless converge on at least one point: The vast bulk of empirical research that has been conducted in the name of "personality" over the past several decades has failed to advance personality *theory* in any significant and enduring way.

Out of concern for this very basic problem, I suggested several years ago in the pages of the *American Psychologist* that personality investigators adopt an "idiothetic" approach to their subject matter (Lamiell, 1981). My original intent in coining this rather awkward neologism was to highlight both the possibility and necessity of reconciling the study of individuals - personality psychology's so-called "idiographic" task - with the search for general principles of human psychological functioning - the discipline's overriding "nomothetic" mission.

In the limited space allotted to me for this contribution, I would like to focus on the epistemological considerations that gave rise to and nourish my "idiothetic" proposal. Just why I think it important to discuss such matters at all is something that I hope to make clear as the discussion proceeds.

---

*) This chapter is adapted from material written for a book by the same author, tentatively entitled *The psychology of personality:An epistemological inquiry* (Columbia University Press, in preparation). I would like to thank the following individuals for the many hours of stimulating discussion both during and after the Second European Conference on Personality: Jean Pierre DeWaele, Rom Harré, Lieve Van Den Brande, Luk Van Langenhove, Ulrich Schweiker, and Hannelore Weber.

PERSONALITY PSYCHOLOGY'S EPISTEMOLOGICAL PROBLEM

In textbook discussions of the psychology of personality, it is virtually *de rigueur* to begin by posing some variant of the discipline's most basic ontological question: What is personality? Predictably, however, the author moves rapidly to a discussion of the fact that, as familiar and useful as the concept seems to be in everyday discourse, psychologists have yet to settle on any single definition of personality that is at once substantive, precise, and generally agreed upon (see, e.g., Hall & Lindzey, 1978, p. 9).

It is significant, however, that despite our continuing inability to agree on what it is that we are studying, we have had little trouble maintaining broad consensus on the matter of how to go about studying it. Dating at least to 1918, when R.S. Woodworth formally imposed the techniques of intelligence testing onto the systematic assessment of (other?) personality characteristics, it has been generally understood – indeed adamantly insisted – that "the study of personality is essentially the study of individual differences" (Wiggins, Renner, Clore, & Rose, 1976, p. 4).

Whatever other difficulties the psychology of personality might have, it is my abiding conviction that this unwavering commitment to individual differences research is *the* single greatest impediment to theoretical advances within the field. Pared to its logical essentials, the argument here is both simple and straightforward:

> (1) A theory of personality – any theory of personality – is a conceptual framework designed to provide explanations for and hence an understanding of *individual* behavior/psychological functioning (Levy, 1970).

> (2) The empirical findings generated by individual differences research have no legitimate translation whatsoever at the level of the individual.

> (3) Knowledge of the sort contained in the empirical findings generated by individual differences research is therefore ill-suited to the task of advancing a theory of personality, however useful that same knowledge might be for other purposes.

Unfortunately, the illusion that the empirical findings generated by individual differences research can be meaningfully interpreted at the level of the individual is as compelling as it is pervasive, and it is likely to endure for as long as the subtle but critical errors of reasoning in which it subsists elude our grasp and/or our concern. It is here, then, where personality psychology's most fundamental epistemological problem lies. But before discussing some specific manifestations of this problem in the contemporary literature, let us orient ourselves with regard to historical context.

Some historical perspective

Unquestionably, the argument that I have sketched out above revisits in certain respects the so-called "nomothetic vs. idiographic" controversy that has festered periodically within the discipline throughout the present century. Although the American psychologist Gordon Allport is usually credited with having initiated and fueled this controversy (cf. Allport, 1937a, 1937b, 1961, 1962, 1966, 1967), it is clear that his own thinking was greatly influenced by (among others) the German philosopher Windelband (from whose 1921 treatise Allport borrowed the terms "nomothetic" and "idiographic") and by the German psychologist William Stern, of whose personalistic psychology Allport was greatly enamored (see esp. Allport, 1937b). Both in the European and American literature, therefore, this controversy has had a long history indeed.

This being the case, and since to many the nomothetic vs. idiographic controversy has never seemed terribly fruitful (cf. Holt, 1962), the reader is entitled to wonder what could possibly be gained by resurrecting that controversy here. Skepticism on this count is only increased when one considers the white flag raised by Allport himself as he concluded one of his last (non-posthumous) contributions to the personality literature:

> Nevitt Sanford (1963) has written that by and large psychologists are 'unimpressed' by my insisting on the (nomothetic-idiographic) distinction. Well, if this is so in spite of 4 decades of labor on my part, and in spite of my efforts in the present paper - I suppose I should in all decency cry 'uncle' and retire to my corner. (Allport, 1966, p. 107, parentheses added)

With the most visible and trenchant critic of strict adherence to the traditional "nomothetic" research paradigm thus dispatched, we should not be surprised to find that paradigm continuing to dominate the thinking of contemporary personality investigators. As Sechrest (1976), Rorer and Widiger (1983) have pointed out, and as no one familiar with the field's current literature could fail to see, the assessment and study of individual differences remains the *sine qua non* of empirical personality research. Morover, Allport's ignominious denoument has undoubtedly only reinforced the conviction, long shared by the vast majority of those who have historically animated this field, that all is just as it should be; that Feshbach's very recent assertion (1984, p. 451) that "fundamental to a personality perspective is a concern with individual differences" is as valid now as ever.

Yet as indicated above, I am persuaded that this paradigmatic conviction is impeding rather than facilitating the scientific study of personality. Indeed, I would argue that a viable science of personality could exist if another piece of individual differences research was never conducted. As for Sanford's observation that most personality investigators have been "unimpressed" by the arguments mounted by Allport and other previous critics of the prevailing orthodoxy, I would suggest that the latter actually failed in this regard because they did not press their epistemological case against the dominant paradigm far enough, and so in the end left themselves with scarcely any case at all.

In defense of this view, I would begin by emphasizing that at no point in the nomothetic vs. idiographic controversy has it been seriously disputed that, from the standpoint of personality theory, "the objects of study are individual organisms and not aggregates of organisms" (Murray, 1938, p. 127). Undoubtedly, the reason for widespread consensus on this basic point is that one would be hard-pressed indeed to articulate in any coherent fashion what the entities of focal concern to a theorist of *person*-ality would otherwise be. Where but at the level of the individual would one expect to explore personality - however theoretically conceived - as an instrument of psychological theory?

The point here is that the notion that "the study of personality is essentially the study of individual differences" rose to and maintains the status of dogma among empirically oriented personality investigators *not* out of any opposition to or rejection of the theoretical concern for individual behavior/psychological functioning, but rather out of the conviction that individual differences research is uniquely suited to the task of *reconciling* that very theoretical concern with (a) the concern for methodological rigor and (b) the quest for general laws or nomothetic principles of personality functioning.

Nor, it must be emphasized, did Allport or those in his patrimony reject this conviction categorically. Rather, spokespersons for the idiographic point of view have historically argued against *strict* reliance on the dominant paradigm, and have done so on the grounds that the knowledge about any given individual yielded by research conducted within that paradigm - i.e., knowledge of the sort Allport labeled "nomothetic" - would inevitably have to be *supplemented* by knowledge gained in some other way(s) - i.e., by knowledge of the sort Allport labeled "idiographic." The operative term here is "supplement," because this argument rejects neither the notion that certain nomothetic aspects of personality exist nor the notion that individual differences research is logically suited to the discovery of some. Thus did Allport (1961) explicitly admonish his readers to

> ... bear in mind that we are not condemning the common trait (i.e., "nomothetic") approach. Far from it. When we wish to compare people with one another, it is the only approach possible. Furthermore, the resulting scores, and profiles, are up to a point illuminating. We are simply saying that there is a second, more accurate way, of viewing personality: namely, the internal patterning (the morphogenesis) of the life considered as a unique product of nature and society. (p. 360, latter parentheses in original)
> ... Personality exists only at a postelementary state; it exists only when the common features of human nature have already interacted with one another and produced unique, self-continuing, and evolving systems. This is not to say that the search for common elements or common human functions is undesirable. For the most part the science of psychology does this and nothing else. I insist only that if we are interested in *personality* (emphasis in original), we must go beyond the elementaristic and reach into the morphogenic (i.e., idiographic) realm. (p. 361, parentheses added)

Now as a manifesto for the traditional idiographic position, the most serious problem with the above is that it contains little if anything that doctrinaire "nomotheticists" cannot reconcile with their own views, and whatever might remain seems dismissable on grounds that it is incompatible with a scientific approach to the study of personality. In particular, adherents to the traditional individual differences paradigm have never viewed themselves as foreclosing in principle on the need to explore how the common or universal elements of personality function "morphogenically" in causing an individual's behavior to take on a particular pattern or style. The argument has simply been that the first order of business must be to identify the common or universal elements, and those who have sought to accommodate Allport's concerns within the mainstream have emphasized just this point (see, e.g., Beck, 1953; Falk, 1956; Franck, 1982; Harris, 1980).

But on this view, Allport's insistence that inquiry must move beyond the search for common elements reduces to mere impatience, born of an unwillingness to accept the fact that idiographic/morphogenic inquiry, while ultimately necessary, would be premature in the absence of a viable nomothetic foundation (cf. Beck, 1953, p. 359). And as for Allport's suggestion that the pattern or style that a particular person's behavior does assume in a "postelementary state" might literally be unique - as opposed to merely individual in the sense of being *his/her own* - the response within the mainstream has always been that there is no scientific way to resolve the question of uniqueness one way or the other, and so it is simply moot (cf. Levy, 1970; Sanford, 1963).

When all is said and done, therefore, it would appear that the difficulties Allport encountered in carrying the idiographic message to mainstream personality investigators can be summed up as follows: He could never alter the collective perception among his intellectual adversaries that an "idiographic" approach to the study of personality was and is either (a) wholly compatible with and subsumable by traditional "nomothetic" methods after all, and hence valid but superfluous (e.g., Eysenck, 1954, p. 340), or (b) ultimately incompatible with prevailing methods, but in that event non - or even anti-scientific (see esp. Nunnally, 1967, p. 472). Either way, Allport ends up in his corner.

What is nomothetic about the "nomothetic" paradigm?

As paradoxical as it may seem, I would argue in light of the above that the continuing domination of empirical personality psychology by individual differences research is not wholly or even primarily attributable to idiographists' lack of persuasiveness in matters where they deviated from the mainstream. Instead, the resilience of the traditional paradigm has much more to do with an assumption that the idiographists *granted* - indeed shared with - adherents to the prevailing paradigm, namely, the assumption that individual differences research is logically suited to the discovery of whatever general laws or nomothetic principles scientific personality psychology might have to offer. In granting this assumption, Allport and his (relatively few) sympathizers surrendered their only real leverage against the received view, and in the process sealed their own fate.

Contrary to the traditional idiographic thesis, the major problem with individual differences research as a framework for the scientific study of personality is not that such research fails to yield knowledge that is sufficiently individualized or "idiographic" in nature - although this is quite true. Rather, the most serious and irremediable problem with the so-called "nomothetic" paradigm is that it does not yield knowledge that is *nomothetic* in nature either, at least not in any sense that a personality theorist would be compelled to take seriously.

Whenever the issue of establishing a general law or nomothetic principle is raised, one of the most fundamental questions is: What are the entities over which generality is being sought in the search for such laws or principles? From an epistemological standpoint, the answer to this question dictates the level of analysis at which the hypothesized law or principle must be tested, and at which empirical evidence of putative relevance to that hypothesis must be interpretable.

Since a personality theory is designed to provide explanations for and hence a way of understanding individual behavior/psychological functioning, individual persons constitute the entities over which generality must be sought in the search for nomothetic principles of personality. That is, any such principle would properly be thought of as one that is found to hold *for each of many individuals.* Quite obviously, therefore, empirical findings generated by research undertaken in the quest for such principles must be interpretable at the level of the individual. Short of arguing that the assertions of a theory of personality are not really meant to apply to persons after all, there is simply no other logically viable way in which the search for general or nomothetic principles of personality can proceed, and this is true no matter what theory of personality one might happen to endorse or wish to test.

It is here, then, where the problem arises, because as noted at the outset of this chapter, empirical evidence of the sort that is generated by individual differences research has *no* legitimate interpretation whatsoever at the level of the individual. This being the case, we are entitled to wonder just how such research comes by and manages to carry the mantle "nomothetic." How can empirical research the findings of which are interpretable for *no* individual possibly yield knowledge about what holds for *individuals in general?* And if individual differences research does not yield such knowledge, then in what sense is it suited at all – let alone "uniquely" – to scientific personality psychology's nomothetic objectives?

The answers to these questions reside, of course, in the fact that for some seven decades now, empirical personality psychology has indulged on a rather massive scale superficially different versions of what William James (1890) once identified as the *psychologist's fallacy*. More specifically, knowledge about *variables* in terms of which persons have been differentiated normatively for purposes of quantitative analysis has been and is being routinely translated as if it constituted knowledge about the *persons* who have been so differentiated. As long as the errors of reasoning that infect the translation process remain obscured (or simply ignored) the entire enterprise seems perfectly reasonable, and the illusion that individual differences research logically serves the quest for nomothetic principles of individual behavior/psychological functioning is maintained.

ERRORS OF REASONING IN THE PSYCHOLOGY OF IMPERSONALITY:
SOME SPECIFIC EXAMPLES

The consistency-vs.-inconsistency controversy

In evidence of the errors of reasoning to which I have been alluding, one especially telling example is provided by the dispute over temporal and transsituational (in)consistency in behavior, a dispute that has occupied center stage in the literature of the field for well over a decade now.

As is well known, that dispute was sparked by the publication in 1968 of Walter Mischel's *Personality and Assessment*. In that work, Mischel was concerned to empirically evaluate a "critical assumption" supposedly inherent within the very concept of personality, i.e., the assumption of "consistency of particular predispositions *within any given individual*" (p. 9, emphasis added). Having discovered in his archival inquiry into this matter that correlations were routinely quite low between measures of individual differences in personality characteristics on the one hand, and of behavioral differences that should have been predictable from such measures on the other hand, Mischel suggested that the assumption of any appreciable degree of consistency in the putatively important theoretical sense just indicated was, at the very best, in need of serious reexamination.

For all of the time, effort, and journal space that has been devoted to the consistency-vs.-inconsistency controversy, it is terribly unfortunate that the empirical evidence over which it has been waged has been (and continues to be, cf. Mischel, 1984) completely misinterpreted by disputants on all sides. More specifically, as concerns the question of the "consistency of particular predispositions within any given individual," the fact of the matter is that both the "low" correlations cited by Mischel (1968) and the "high" correlations that have since been reported by others (e.g., Epstein, 1979, 1980; Gormly, 1984; McGowan & Gormly, 1976) mean exactly the same thing: that the individuals assessed were *not equally* (in)consistent in their respective manifestations of the measured attributes. This logical fact is amply illustrated in Figure 1.

The data shown in Figure 1 were obtained in an actual study the details of which have been discussed elsewhere (Lamiell, 1982; Lamiell, Trierweiler, & Foss, 1983a) and need not concern us here. It is sufficient merely to note that in each panel of Figure 1, z-scores for each of 19 individuals on a personality variable have been plotted for two measurement occasions. Thus, each line in the figure represents a single individual, and the slope of a line reflects the degree to which an individual's location within the distribution of scores shifted from the first measurement occasion to the second (left panel), and from the second measurement occasion to the third (right panel). For the data in the left-hand panel of Figure 1, the Pearson product-moment correlation (i.e., the average of the cross-products of z-scores) equals, 60, while the correlation for the data in the right-hand panel equals -.01.

Quite obviously, the most striking feature of these data is that the 19 individuals assessed were not equally (in)consistent in their relative manifestations of the measured attribute over either of the temporal

J.T. Lamiell

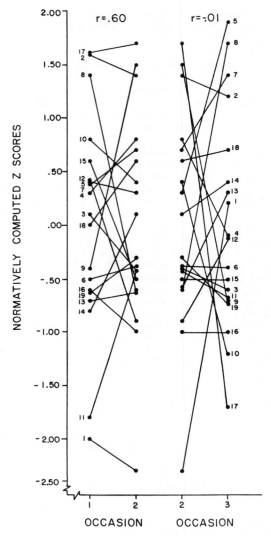

Figure 1: *A "microscopic picture" of data underlying two "stability coefficients."*
(Adapted with permission of publisher from Lamiell, 1982).

intervals investigated. In point of fact, therefore, the "low" correlation of -.01 obtained for the Occasion 2 - Occasion 3 time interval does *not* mean that *in general* the individuals were inconsistent in their respective manifestations of the attribute in question. Nor does the "high" correlation of .60 obtained for the Occasion 1 - Occasion 2 time interval mean that *in general* the individuals were highly consistent in this regard. The only interpretation that can legitimately be placed on either correlation is that the individuals assessed were not equally (in)consistent, in which case there is no generalization about the degree of consistency manifested by the individuals in the sample that could possibly be valid.

The only instance in which a conventional reliability or validity coefficient could support a generalization about the degree of consistency with which a particular attribute or predisposition has been manifested by individuals is when the correlation in question is perfect, because that is the one instance in which what has been found to hold for persons *in the aggregate,* i.e., as a group, also holds for persons *in general,* i.e., for each of the individuals in the group. Unfortunately, the distinction between what is truly general and what is merely aggregate has become completely obscured within contemporary personality psychology (cf. Bakan, 1966), and it is precisely for this reason that the consistency-vs.-inconsistency debate has foundered epistemologically.

The error of reasoning here consists in the notion that if a perfect correlation means that in general the individuals in one's sample were perfectly consistent in their relative manifestations of the measured attribute - which is true - then "high" correlations must mean that in general the individuals were "highly" consistent in this regard - which is not true - and "low" correlations must mean that in general the individuals were inconsistent in this regard - which is not true either. In short, neither the "low" nor the "high" correlations over which legion investigators have been bickering for some 15 years now enable one to tell whether or not, or to what degree, *any* one individual was consistent in his/her manifestation of a putative predisposition. This is to say that with respect to the specific theoretical controversy spawned by Mischel's work, such correlations are simply uninterpretable.

It is not irrelevant to point out here that although Mischel's highly influential findings were published after Allport had died, evidence virtually identical to that which Mischel produced, and conclusions virtually identical to those he drew, had appeared several decades earlier (see, e.g., Hartshorne, May, & Shuttleworth, 1930; Lehmann & Witty, 1934; Symonds, 1931). Moreover, not only was Allport aware of this earlier work, he was also aware of the fact that the low correlations reported therein did not establish that "in general" people were inconsistent. Instead, Allport argued, such correlations could just as readily be interpreted as evidence that individuals are not consistent in the same ways, or in ways that an investigator can expect to discern simply by imposing his/her own trait concepts onto all of them simultaneously (cf. Bem & Allen, 1974). But again, Allport either failed to see or chose not to pursue the logical fact that even if the above-cited investigators had reported "high" correlations, the very same conclusions would have been mandated.

What is so ironic about this is that if Allport had pursued this latter point, he might actually have come closer to achieving his larger objective of drawing personality investigators out of or away from the individual differences paradigm. In any event, and in light of the rebuke that has been heaped upon Allport over the years by personality psychology's would-be "nomotheticists", it seems only fair to point out this much: If with respect to the specific theoretical issue Mischel raised, his findings had been properly interpreted at the time either by himself or by the field at large, then his book *Personality and Assessment* would have been written and/or received as the massive empirical vindication of Allport's views on the matter that in fact it is, rather than as a challenge to the concept of personality that it neither was nor ever will be. The same holds for all of the empirical evidence that has since been brought to bear on the controversy – including, I should note, the omega-square ratios and coefficients of generalizability that are sometimes reported instead of conventional reliability and validity coefficients (cf. Golding, 1975).

The search for basic human tendencies

In recent years, there has been a resurgence of interest among personality investigators in matters taxonomical; i.e., in the problem of establishing a kind of periodic table of personality "elements" in terms of which "the" basic human tendencies – and thus any given individual's tendencies – can be described and catalogued. I am referring here to such programs of research as are currently being conducted by Bem (1983), Buss and Craik (1983a, 1983b, 1984), and Wiggins (1979), to cite just a few examples.

Of course, the empirical foundation of all such efforts consists of the patterns of intercorrelations between individual differences variables that an investigator has deemed worthy of consideration for possible inclusion in the taxonomy. With respect to our present concerns, the critical epistemological problem with these efforts is that the *empirical* "tendencies" reflected in less-than-perfect correlations between variables are being interpreted as if they revealed something about the *psychological* "tendencies" within each of the different individuals observations on whom have been used to define those variables.

Given a correlation of magnitude r between two individual differences variables X and Y, one might reasonably assert: "There is a tendency (of strength or magnitude r) for high Xs to be paired with high Ys, and for low Xs to be paired with low Ys." Worded just so, there is nothing at all wrong with such a statement from an epistemological standpoint. That is, the statement says what data of the sort decribed would actually show. Note, however, that from the standpoint of a theory of personality there is really nothing informative about the statement either.

The reason for this is that the referent for the term "there" in the above assertion is and could only be the array of data on which the assertion is based. That is, the tendency being referred to would be *there in the data array,* and since a data array of the sort described could not be defined for persons-as-persons but only for persons-as-group, the tendency revealed by such a data array could not possibly constitute knowledge about the tendencies of the individuals represented by discrete data points therein.

The problem, of course, is that personality theorists *qua* personality theorists do not theorize about empirical tendencies within collections of data points. Instead, they theorize about psychological tendencies of individual persons, and there is simply nothing in the tendencies revealed by correlations between two (or more) individual differences variables that can legitimately be said to inform that theoretical concern at all.

To be sure, matters can be and usually are made to seem otherwise, but this is only accomplished by a bit of semantic legerdemain according to which data of the sort described would be cited as evidence that "people" – i.e., those persons – high on variable X *have* a tendency to be high on variable Y, while "people" (those persons) low on variable X *have* a tendency to be low on variable Y. Worded thusly, this latter statement sounds relevant to the concerns of personality theory precisely because it asserts that some bit of knowledge about the psychological or behavioral tendencies of persons-as-persons has been discovered in the data. But it is also true that, as worded, the statement would no longer have any logical connection at all to the data on which it would putatively be based.

If the term "tendency" can be logically grounded at all to data of the sort on which traditional "nomotheticists" predicate their collective quest for basic human tendencies, it can be so only by virtue of its reference to the magnitude of the correlation (simple or multiple) between the individual differences variables in question. But *individual differences variables* are literally and necessarily *undefined for individuals*, as is the correlation between those variables. Stated otherwise, the "tendencies" revealed by individual differences research cannot even be coherently discussed at the level of discrete data points, and in data of the sort wherein such "tendencies" are discovered, it is only in terms of discrete data points that persons are represented. It follows that there is no logically coherent way to "discover" in the tendencies revealed by the correlations between individual differences variables any tendencies – psychological, behavioral, or otherwise – in any of the persons who have been studied.

Obviously, empirical findings that do not reveal the tendencies of *any* person cannot sensibly be said to yield knowledge about the tendencies of *persons in general*. That is, such findings cannot possibly be said to yield knowledge about basic human tendencies that is nomothetic in the only sense of that term to which a theory of persons – individual behavior/psychological functioning – would ever be compelled to bow.

Knowledge about psychological tendencies and their role in the production of the behavior of persons is not contained in and hence cannot possibly be extracted from knowledge of intercorrelations between individual differences variables. It does not matter how the variables are labeled, how many of them are taken into consideration, how large or small the obtained correlations are, or how long we persist in gathering them. Knowledge about basic human tendencies is simply not there, and to continue to pretend otherwise is to foster a way of thinking that is merely *scientistic* in just that sense that some critics (e.g., Giorgi, 1970) have claimed it to be.

The prediction of individual behavior

Yet another cherished tenet of traditional "nomotheticism" is that the findings yielded by individual differences research can advance the practical objective of predicting individual behavior, and in the process serve the more theoretical objective of demonstrating both that and how behavior is systematically related to underlying qualities or attributes with which individuals' respective personalities are endowed in varying amounts. Appended to this notion is the belief that insofar as the construct validity (Campbell & Fiske, 1959) of individual differences variables intended to represent such qualities or attributes can be established, the empirical findings generated by research employing those variables provide, if properly cross-validated, grounds for articulating the "nomothetic laws" of personality functioning. In fact, within the individual differences paradigm, the concept of *law* really has no meaning other than this.

In dealing with these notions, it is necessary to begin by pointing out that when a personality investigator speaks of "predicting an individual's behavior" on the basis of findings generated by individual differences research, all that can really be meant is that s/he can *formulate* a prediction *about* that individual's behavior. Since the accuracy of a prediction necessarily remains open to question when the basis for the prediction is a less-than-perfect correlation (be it single or multiple), and since for all intents and purposes predictions of this sort are always based on less-than-perfect correlations, claims to be "predicting an individual's behavior" really should not be made. Having established this much, the fallacious reasoning embedded in traditional conceptions of the personality-and-prediction enterprise begins to surface.

Consider the fact that one can formulate a prediction about an individual's behavior without benefit of the knowledge yielded by individual differences research (or any other kind of research, for that matter). One can simply decide to formulate a prediction "out of the blue," and then proceed to do so. This being the case, systematic empirical research can scarcely be regarded as special in the sense of enabling one to do something that one could otherwise not do. What then, we may ask, is special about research-based predictions?

If one puts this question to advocates of conventional "nomotheticism", the answer is routinely and inevitably of a form that can be paraphrased as follows:

> Well, yes, one can formulate a prediction about an individual's behavior without benefit of the knowledge yielded by systematic empirical research. But one who formulates his/her prediction 'out of the blue' is in no position to say anything about the accuracy of that prediction. On the other hand, one whose prediction is informed by empirical research can address the question of accuracy, and in comparison with 'out-of-the-blue' predictions, this is what is special about predictions based on the findings of individual differences research.

From an epistemological standpoint, the most serious problem with this view is that when a prediction about a person's behavior is "informed" by the findings of individual differences research, one *cannot*, in fact, specify ahead of time the accuracy of that prediction. As regards the issue of predictive accuracy, what the empirical findings of individual differences research entitle one te speak about is the *average* of the (squared) errors of prediction *in the long run*, i.e., across individuals. Table 1 may help to clarify this point.

TABLE 1: *Schematic for errors of prediction in individual differences research*

Hypothetical three-variable regression equation:

$$Y^1 = a + b_1 (X_1) + b_2 (X_2) + b_3 (X_3)$$

	A posteriori Error of prediction	A priori Value
Person 1	$(Y - Y^1)$	Unspecifiable
2	$(Y - Y^1)$	Unspecifiable
3	$(Y - Y^1)$	Unspecifiable
4	$(Y - Y^1)$	Unspecifiable
5	$(Y - Y^1)$	Unspecifiable
6	$(Y - Y^1)$	Unspecifiable
7	$(Y - Y^1)$	Unspecifiable
8	$(Y - Y^1)$	Unspecifiable
9	$(Y - Y^1)$	Unspecifiable
10	$(Y - Y^1)$	Unspecifiable
GROUP	*Average* of squared $(Y - Y^1)$ values	*Average* of squared $(Y - Y^1)$ values (on cross-validation)

Note: Y^1 Represents the predicted criterion value for a given person based on the regression equation, while Y represents the actually obtained criterion value for that person. The variables X_1, X_2, and X_3 represent individual differences variables used as predictors. The values b_1, b_2, and b_3 represent partial regression coefficients, and a represents the additive constant.

Symbolizing an individual's predicted status on the criterion as Y^1 and his/her actual status on the criterion as Y, the statement just made means that a competently executed correlation/regression analysis enables one to specify the *mean* value of $[(Y - Y^1)$ squared] for a *group* of individuals. It does not enable one to specify $(Y - Y^1)$ for any one individual, i.e., the accuracy of or degree of error in one's prediction about any person. Indeed, if it were possible to specify the value of $(Y - Y^1)$ on a case-by-case basis, then there would no longer *be* any "error of prediction". One would by definition be in a position to account for "error" ahead of time - the very phrase is oxymoronic - and hence to insure that all subsequent predictions were perfectly accurate!

This last point draws attention to the only condition under which the knowledge yielded by individual differences research does in fact enable an individual differences investigator to specify ahead of time the accuracy of his/her prediction about any given individual. That condition is met when the correlation (simple or multiple) on the basis of which the prediction equation has been derived is unity (i.e., +/- 1.00). In that and only that instance, the error of prediction for any given individual can be known ahead of time precisely because it is by definition zero for each and every individual.

When the correlation is less than unity, however, the error of prediction is *by definition indeterminate* at the level of the individual and hence *unspecifiable for each and every individual*. In fact, for any given individual, the error of prediction can take on any value permitted by the scale on which the criterion variable has been defined. No greater precision than this can legitimately be claimed given the kind of knowledge yielded by individual differences research, and this much "precision" can legitimately be claimed without benefit of any research knowledge at all. And so we are right back where we started.

Beyond its implications vis-a-vis behavioral prediction *per se,* it should be clear from the above that there is really nothing left of the notion that individual differences research can yield nomothetic laws of relevance to personality theory. It has already been noted that within the traditional paradigm, the very concept of "lawfulness" is tied directly to knowledge concerning the predictability of behavior. But since the knowledge yielded by individual differences research concerning behavioral predictability is actually knowledge about *no* person, it cannot possibly be knowledge about *each of many* persons, and this latter is the only meaning that attaches to the term "nomothetic" from the point of view of personality theory. Hence, such "laws" as individual differences research might legitimately be said to yield are, from the perspective of the personality theorist, quite irrelevant.

Because the empirical findings generated by individual differences research cannot legitimately be interpreted at the level of the individual, it is not at all unwarranted to view such research as providing us with what is, in effect, a psychology of *impersonality*. Obviously, this view is utterly antithetical to some very deeply entrenched beliefs. But is seems to me that wherever we find tradition and logic on a collision course - and there should be no doubt that that is what we are finding here - it is tradition rather than logic that must give way.

FROM INDIVIDUAL DIFFERENCES TO PERSONAL EPISTEMOLOGY

From all that has been said to this point it should be clear that, far from undermining the search for general laws or nomothetic principles of personality, the study of individuals is epistemologically central thereto. By the same token, however, the argument thus far provides no clear indication of how to proceed beyond this point, as it fails to address the question of just what it is about individuals that theoretically-driven personality research would investigate.

As a point of departure for our consideration of this question, it is instructive to bear in mind that if the conduct of theoretically relevant personality research were simply a matter of undertaking functional analyses of the behavior of individual organisms, then the logic and methods of radical behaviorism as bequeathed to scientific psychology by such as J.B. Watson and B.F. Skinner would have defined an adequate paradigm for personality research long ago. Perhaps, therefore, the fact that personality investigators have not widely embraced the tenets of radical behaviorism is itself of some significance in the quest for a viable alternative approach to empirical personality research.

Consider, for example, the words of I.E. Farber (1964), who in arguing for a psychology of personality that would be "coterminous with the study of behavior" stated that

> (O)ne may anticipate that as behavior theories become more precise and more comprehensive they will encompass more and more phenomena now referred to under the rubric of 'personality.' I, for one, look forward to the day, which I do not expect to see myself, when personality theories are regarded as historical curiosities. (p. 37)

If Farber's vision of personality psychology's future was less than sagacious, his implication that the functional analysis of behavior has no real need for a concept of personality was not (cf. Lamiell, 1984; Rychlak, 1976). In the present context, the most important ramification of this point is that for the purposes of a scientific psychology of personality, not just any old sort of "$N = 1$ research" is going to suffice.

On the contrary, the search for a viable alternative to the traditional individual differences paradigm requires above all else a preparedness to take seriously Levy's (1970) deceptively simple insight that "the concept of personality *owes its existence* to (the) psychological tendency to seek *meaning* in (one's) experience (p. 19, parentheses and emphasis added). From my own perspective, the single most important implication of this point is that, in the final analysis, a theory of personality is concerned not with behavior *per se* - and certainly not with the mere tracking of individual differences therein - but rather with the *meaning* of behavior as framed - consciously or otherwise - within the mind or "psyche" of the behaving individual.

Note that there is nothing in what has just been said that denies the clear and substantial differences that do exist between the various extant schools of thought within personality theory (psychoanalytic, cognitive-social learning, phenomenological, humanistic, existential, etc.). It merely suggests that those differences are best viewed as the reflection of divergent assumptions about *how* individuals frame meaningful ideas in the first place, rather than disagreements over (a) whether or not such ideas *are* framed, or (b) whether or not they function as psychological determinants of an individual's behavior.

When personality psychology's pan-theoretical agenda is viewed in this way, one can scarcely avoid the conclusion that basic research within the discipline must address itself ultimately and as fully as possible to questions concerning (a) the grounds on and reasoning processes by which individuals frame those meaningful ideas that constitute their own knowledge - broadly defined - and (b) the nature of the relationships between such knowledge and overt action. In effect, this view asserts that personality psychology's focal subject matter is nothing other than subjective or *personal epistemology,* and I would suggest that theoretically driven personality research should be designed and carried out with this in mind.

In this connection, it is worth noting that when the term

"idiothetic" is defined with reference to its linguistic roots, it literally means "of or pertaining to *one's own* (idio-) point of view, knowledge, or *thesis* (thetic)." It is this definition that reflects the alternative approach to the study of personality that I envision; an approach whereby the substantive individuality of personal knowledge is respected (cf. Tyler, 1978) without undermining the search for general or nomothetic principles. The latter would be sought, on this view, through studies of the *processes* by which personal knowledge is framed by an individual and then extended – or not – into behavior.

Unfortunately, space limitations prevent me from discussing at any length here the sort of empirical research to which I have thus far been led by these general yet very basic considerations. For this reason, I must refer the reader to other recent articles where some relevant empirical work is discussed and defended in detail (Lamiell, Foss, Larsen, & Hempel, 1983; see also Conger, 1983; Lamiell, Foss, Trierweiler, & Leffel, 1983; Lamiell, Trierweiler, & Foss, 1983a, 1983b; Woody, 1983), and conclude the present discussion by briefly commenting on the relationship between this proposal and other emergent trends within contemporary personality research.

There are those who will conclude from what has been said above that in calling for systematic, theoretically guided inquiry centered around questions concerning the nature of personal epistemology, I am merely trumpeting by a different tune a kind of cognitive psychology of personality, and there is certainly a sense in which this is true. For it seems to me that if we are to take up the challenge of explaining behavior in terms of its meaning to the behaving individual, then questions concerning the psychological processes by which such meanings are framed and in turn acted on (or not) are of truly fundamental theoretical significance, and it is difficult to see how an investigator can approach such questions without adopting a more "cognitive" orientation. In this respect, my "idiothetic" proposal is solidly aligned with the emergent cognitivism in personality psychology and, for reasons discussed at length earlier in this chapter, I am convinced that Bem (1983) is greatly mistaken when he argues that this movement is diverting attention away from what he is pleased to regard as "the study of personality itself" (p. 575).

But having said this much, I should hasten to add that I have not settled idly on the term "personal epistemology". Rather, I invoke it here because there are some important respects in which my view of what a cognitive psychology of personality entails differs from much of what is currently recognized as such (see, e.g., Cantor & Kihlstrom, 1981; Cantor & Mischel, 1979; Forgus & Shulman, 1979; Higgins, Kuiper, & Olson, 1981; Mischel, 1979).

For one thing, my conception of what is involved in the study of personal epistemology is much better captured by the term *human judgment* – and all that that implies – than by the term "information processing." What *is* "information" anyway? How – that is, on what grounds – does information *become* information to a *person*? How is that which one *knows* (consciously or otherwise) related to that which one *does* – and does not do? What sorts of causal concepts do we as personality psychologists need in order to coherently explain or even discuss behavior in these terms (cf. Rychlak, 1981a, 1981b)? All of these questions, and many more like them, are of central and enduring relevance to a viable psychology of personality, and with Rorer and Widiger (1983) I am convinced that we can no longer afford to look past them.

Secondly, and appropos of the argument developed earlier, I am concerned by the fact that, at present, empirical research in cognitive personality psychology is on the verge of being, if it has not already become, dominated by the traditional individual differences paradigm no less than have been other more conventional programs of research (see references cited above). Thus do we now find investigators abandoning the study of individual differences variables conceived as traits and types for the study of individual differences variables conceived as scripts, schemas and prototypes. So long as this trend continues, the still-burgeoning movement toward a cognitive psychology of personality is going to be undermined by the very same epistemological problems discussed earlier. The alternative is to embrace - and where necessary create - methods of inquiry that enable us to address theoretically relevant questions concerning human cognition in a way that does not depend on the assessment and study of individual differences, and I would direct the reader once again to the previously-cited articles for concrete examples of efforts that have been made along these lines to date.

If I have accomplished nothing else in the present chapter, I do hope to have explained why knowledge of the sort yielded by the study of individual differences variables cannot advance theoretical conceptions of individual psychological functioning, no matter what sorts of labels are attached to those variables. In the process, I hope to have provided some very good reasons for redirecting basic research in the field away from technically sophisticated but theoretically uninformative pursuits, and toward inquiry that is at least in principle capable of reconciling the discipline's idiographic and nomothetic objectives. Long-dominant convictions to the contrary notwithstanding, individual differences research serves neither of these objectives, however useful it might be for other purposes.

Through empirical research to which I have referred the reader above, I have sought to illustrate (among other things) how "idiothetic" studies in personal epistemology can address questions of fundamental significance to personality theory in a way that does reconcile the discipline's idiographic and nomothetic objectives without sacrificing methodological rigor. To be sure, such efforts are merely preliminary, and many, many issues remain to be resolved.

But I am no less certain for this that, as personality investigators, we must confront the conceptual and technical difficulties these issues entail. Nor does the spectre of such difficulties mitigate in the least my conviction that so long as the notion that "the study of personality is essentially the study of individual differences" prevails, there simply will not be any genuine theoretical progress in this field.

REFERENCES

Allport, G.W. (1937a). *Personality: A psychological interpretation.* New York: Holt, Rinehart & Winston.

Allport, G.W. (1937b). The personalistic psychology of William Stern. *Character and Personality, 5,* 231-246.

Allport, G.W. (1961). *Pattern and growth in personality*. New York: Holt, Rinehart & Winston.

Allport, G.W. (1962). The general and the unique in psychological science. *Journal of Personality, 30,* 405–422.

Allport, G.W. (1966). Traits revisited. *American Psychologist, 21,* 1–10.

Allport, G.W. (1967). *The person in psychology*. Boston: Beacon Press.

Bakan, D. (1966). The test of significance in psychological research. *Psychological Bulletin, 66,* 423–437.

Beck, S.J. (1953). The science of personality: Nomothetic or idiographic? *Psychological Review, 60,* 353–359.

Bem, D.J. (1983). Constructing a theory of the triple typology: Some (second) thoughts on nomothetic and idiographic approaches to personality. *Journal of Personality, 51,* 566–577.

Bem, D.J., & Allen, A. (1974). On predicting some of the people some of the time: The search for cross-situational consistencies in behavior. *Psychological Review, 81,* 506–520.

Buss, D.M., & Craik, K.H. (1983a). The act frequency approach to personality. *Psychological Review, 90,* 105–126.

Buss, D.M., & Craik, K.H. (1983b). The dispositional analysis of everyday conduct. *Journal of Personality, 51,* 393–412.

Buss, D.M. & Craik, K.H. (1984). Acts, dispositions, and personality. In B.A. Maher & W.B. Maher (Eds.), *Progress in experimental personality research* (Vol. 13, pp. 241–301). New York: Academic Press.

Campbell, D.T., & Fiske, D.W. (1959). Convergent and discriminant validation by the multitrait-multimethod matrix. *Psychological Bulletin, 56,* 81–105.

Cantor, N., & Kihlstrom, J.F. (Eds.) (1981). *Personality, cognition, and social interaction*. Hillsdale, NJ: Erlbaum.

Cantor, N., & Mischel, W. (1979). Prototypes in person perception. In L. Berkowitz (Ed.), *Advances in experimental social psychology*, (Vol. 12, pp. 3–52). New York: Academic Press.

Conger, A.J. (1983). Toward a further understanding of the intuitive personologist: Some critical evidence on the diabolical quality of subjective psychometrics. *Journal of Personality, 51,* 248–258.

Conley, J.J. (1983). Theoretical nihilism in personality psychology. *Personality Forum, 1,* 8–11.

DeWaele, J.P., & Harré, R. (1974). The personality of individuals. In R. Harré (Ed.), *Personality* (pp. 189–246). Oxford, England: Basil Blackwell.

Epstein, S. (1979). The stability of behavior: I. On predicting most of the people much of the time. *Journal of Personality and Social Psychology, 37,* 1097–1126.

Epstein, S. (1980). The stability of behavior: II. Implications for psychological research. *American Psychologist, 35,* 790–806.

Eysenck, H.J. (1954). The science of personality: Nomothetic! *Psychological Review, 61,* 339–342.

Falk, J. (1956). Issues distinguishing idiographic from nomothetic approaches to personality theory. *Psychological Review, 63,* 53–62.

Farber, I.E. (1964). A framework for the study of personality as a behavioral science. In P. Worchel & D. Byrne (Eds.), *Personality change* (pp. 3–37). New York: Wiley.

Feshbach, S. (1984). The "personality" of personality theory and research. *Personality and Social Psychology Bulletin, 10,* 446-456.

Fiske, D.W. (1978). *Strategies for personality research.* San Francisco, CA: Jossey-Bass.

Forgus, R., & Shulman, B.H. (1979). *Personality: A cognitive view.* Englewood Cliffs, NJ: Prentice-Hall.

Franck, I. (1982). Psychology as a science: Resolving the idiographic-nomothetic controversy. *Journal for the Theory of Social Behaviour, 12,* 1-20.

Giorgi, A. (1970). *Psychology as a human science: A phenomenologically based approach.* New York: Harper & Row.

Golding, S.L. (1975). Flies in the ointment: Methodological problems in the analysis of the percentage of variance due to persons and situations. *Psychological Bulletin, 82,* 278-288.

Gormly, J. (1984). Correspondence between personality trait ratings and behavioral events. *Journal of Personality, 52,* 220-232.

Hall, C.S., & Lindzey, G. (1978). *Theories of personality* (3rd ed.). New York: Wiley.

Harris, J.G., Jr. (1980). Nomovalidation and idiovalidation: A quest for the true personality profile. *American Psychologist, 35,* 729-744.

Hartshorne, H., May, M.A., & Shuttleworth, F.K. (1930). *Studies in the organization of character.* New York: Macmillan.

Higgins, E.T., Kuiper, N.A., & Olson, J.M. (1981). Social cognition: A need to get personal. In E.T. Higgins, C.P. Herman, & M.P. Zanna (Eds.), *Social cognition: The Ontario Symposium* (pp. 395-420). Hillsdale, NJ: Erlbaum.

Holt, R. (1962). Individuality and generalization in the psychology of personality. *Journal of Personality, 30,* 377-404.

James, W. (1890). *Principles of psychology.* New York: Henry Holt.

Lamiell, J.T. (1981). Toward an idiothetic psychology of personality. *American Psychologist, 36,* 276-289.

Lamiell J.T. (1982). The case for an idiothetic psychology of personality: A conceptual and empirical foundation. In B.A. Maher & W.B. Maher (Eds.), *Progress in experimental personality research* (Vol. 11, pp. 1-64). New York: Academic Press.

Lamiell, J.T. (1984). Personality: The individual in a scientific psychology. In W.N. Dember, J.J. Jenkins, & T.J. Teyler, *General psychology* (2nd Ed., pp. 635-677). Hillsdale, NJ: Erlbaum.

Lamiell, J.T., Foss, M.A., Larsen, R.J., & Hempel, A. (1983). Studies in intuitive personology from an idiothetic point of view: Implications for personality theory. *Journal of Personality, 51,* 438-467.

Lamiell, J.T., Foss, M.A., Trierweiler, S.J., & Leffel, G.M. (1983). Toward a further understanding of the intuitive personologist: Some preliminary evidence for the dialectical quality of subjective personality impressions. *Journal of Personality, 53,* 213-235.

Lamiell, J.T., Trierweiler, S.J., & Foss, M.A. (1983a). Detecting (in) consistencies in personality: Resolving intuitions and empirical evidence. *Journal of Personality Assessment, 47,* 380-389.

Lamiell, J.T., Trierweiler, S.J., & Foss, M.A. (1983b). Theoretical vs. actuarial analyses of personality ratings, and other rudimentary distinctions. *Journal of Personality, 51,* 259-274.

Lehman, H.C., & Witty, P.A. (1934). Faculty psychology and personality traits. *American Journal of Psychology, 44,* 490.

Levy, L. (1970). *Conceptions of personality: Theories and research.* New York: Random House.

McGowan, J., & Gormly, J. (1976). Validation of personality traits: A multicriteria approach. *Journal of Personality and Social Psychology, 34,* 791-795.

Mischel, W. (1968). *Personality and assessment.* New York: Wiley.

Mischel, W. (1979). On the interface of cognition and personality: Beyond the person-situation debate. *American Psychologist, 34,* 740-754.

Mischel, W. (1984). Convergences and challenges in the search for consistency. *American Psychologist, 39,* 351-364.

Murray, H.A. (1938). *Explorations in personality.* London: Oxford University Press.

Nunnally, J.C. (1967). *Psychometric theory.* New York: McGraw-Hill.

Rorer, L.G., & Widiger, T.A. (1983). Personality structure and assessment. In M.R. Rosenzweig & L.W. Porter (Eds.), *Annual Review of Psychology* (Vol. 34, pp. 431-463). Palo Alto, CA: Annual Reviews, Inc.

Rychlak, J.F. (1976). Personality theory: Its nature, past, present and - future? *Personality and Social Psychology Bulletin, 2,* 209-224.

Rychlak, J.F. (1981a). *Introduction to personality and psychotherapy* (2nd Edition). Boston: Houghton-Mifflin.

Rychlak, J.F. (1981b). *A philosophy of science for personality theory* (2nd Edition). Malabar, FL: Kreiger Publishing Co.

Sanford, N. (1963). Personality: Its place in psychology. In S. Koch (Ed.), *Psychology: A study of a science* (Vol. 5, pp. 488-592) New York: McGraw-Hill.

Sechrest, L. (1976). Personality. In M.R. Rosenzweig & L.W. Porter (Eds.), *Annual Review of Psychology* (Vol. 27, pp. 1-27). Palo Alto, CA: Annual Reviews, Inc.

Symonds, P.M. (1931). *Diagnosing personality and conduct.* New York: Appleton-Century-Crofts.

Tyler, L. (1978). *Individuality: Human possibilities and personal choice in the psychological development of men and woman.* San Francisco, CA: Jossey-Bass.

Wiggins, J.S. (1979). A psychological taxonomy of trait descriptive terms: The interpersonal domain. *Journal of Personality and Social Psychology, 37,* 395-412.

Wiggins, J.S., Renner, K.E., Clore, G.L., & Rose, R.J. (1976). *Principles of personality* (2nd Edition). Reading, MA: Addison-Wesley.

Windelband, W. (1921). *An introduction to philosophy* (translated by J. McCabe). London: Unwin.

Woodworth, R.S. (1918). *Dynamic psychology.* New York: Columbia University Press.

Woody, E.Z. (1983). The intuitive personologist revisited. A critique of dialectical person perception. *Journal of Personality, 51,* 236-258.

STABILITY AND CHANGE IN THE PROCESS OF VALUATION:
AN IDIOGRAPHIC APPROACH

Hubert J.M. Hermans

Catholic University of Nijmegen
The Netherlands

The science of personality is sometimes said to comprise the study of individual consistencies across time and activities. As Shontz (1965) says, this statement is appealing in its simplicity but it is inadequate as an identification of the scope of personality theory. It fails to recognize how often personologists, more than most, have acknowledged the importance of inconsistency and change in human behavior (Lazarus, 1963, pp. 37-45). This acknowledgment is reflected in their emphasis upon processes of development, their stress on the importance of conflict and ambivalence in the determination of behavior, their concern with the efficacy of psychotherapy, and their recurrent recognition of the fact that growth toward complete integration is a never-ending process.

Neither consistency nor inconsistency of behavior can be ignored. They are the phenomena which personality theories are designed to explain. Such theories specify what will remain constant, what will change and how these changes will manifest themselves. They provide a frame of reference which leads to the identification and prediction of specific changes, and state the rules by which predictions may be made. They deal with the meaning of relationships within a particular set of relevant variables.

This is a lot to ask of any theory, and it is far more than is provided by most current theories of personality. It is a goal; and as such it serves as an organizing principle for discussion and gives direction to continued theoretical endeavours.

The present paper deals with the question of how constancy and change can be distinguished and identified in the valuation process of the individual person. First, I give an outline of the theoretical background which enables the distinction to be made between stability and change in a person's valuation system. Second, an idiographic method of study is shortly described which enables us to study the valuation system as it develops through time. Third, the constant and the changing parts in the valuation system are identified and analyzed in a case-study. Fourth, the results of this study give rise to a discussion of the relationship between stability and change in the study of the individual.

Essentials of valuation theory

Valuation theory (Hermans, 1974, 1976, 1981) was originally formulated as a reaction against the dominant position of nomothetic research in the field of personality, which by its nature should be the first to concentrate on the historical life of the individual person. The theory's underlying view of Man is inspired by philosophical-phenomenological thinking (Merleau-Ponty, 1945, 1948) and conceives of personality as an *organized process*. The process aspect refers to the historical nature of human experience. The experiential process implies a spatio-temporal orientation: the person lives in a present situation and is - from a specific point in space and time - oriented to the past and the future. The organizational aspect points to the fact that the person not only orients successively to different aspects in his spatio-temporal situation, but also brings those aspects together in a structure. In this structure the several experiences are placed as parts in a composite whole, in which one experience is given a more important position than an other. This means that the experiential process is conceived of as an organized whole of historical events.

The central concept *valuation* refers to anything which the person finds to be of importance in his or her life-situation. It is anything which has a positive (pleasant), negative (unpleasant), or ambivalent (both pleasant and unpleasant) personal value or meaning. A broad range of phenomena are potentially included: a dear memory, a difficult problem, a beloved person, a relevant goal, an unreachable ideal, a disturbing dream, an influential talk with a friend, etc. Since the person is differentially oriented to the immediate, present situation, to the past and to the future, different valuations emerge. By the capacity of self-reflection these several valuations are concentrated and organized in a valuation system.

The personal importance of a valuation is always current. As the experiencing process moves from one point to an other, or from one phase to an other, so the spatio-temporal orientation shifts, with the result that the valuation system changes to a larger or smaller extent. Some valuations, which lose their relevance, are excluded; other valuations, which are elicited by the change in situation, are taken up into the system. Besides this change element in the system, there is an element consisting of constant valuations. Depending on interaction with the situation and on the number of valuations concerned in this interaction, the changing element will be larger or smaller.

A valuation can be considered as an internally differentiated and externally delimited meaning. For this reason also the term "value area" can be used. Like areas, valuations have boundaries which guarantee the internal unity of a differentiated meaning structure and by which it can be distinguished from the meaning structure of another valuation. The boundaries of different value areas differ in strength: those with weaker boundaries can more easily be influenced by other parts of the system than those with stronger boundaries.

An essential feature of the theory is the assumption that each valuation has an affective connotation. In more specific terms, each valuation involves an affective modality, i.e., a pattern of affects which is characteristic for this specific valuation. When we know which affects are characteristic for a valuation, we know something about the valuation itself. The affective meaning of the valuation cannot be separated from it and reveals properties of the valuation itself. Therefore, the study of affective modality is necessary for understanding the valuation. By distinguishing valuations as cognitive meanings and affective modalities as affective meanings, the theoretical framework provides an opportunity to study cognitive and affective changes in their interconnectedness.

The theory assumes that people develop and organize their valuation system in such a way that it implies a certain level of well-being. In the interaction with the situation, positive (pleasant) and negative (unpleasant) experiences emerge. In general, people try to develop a system containing more positive than negative valuations. The valuation system leads a person to select situations, and to interact with them in such a way that a satisfactory level of well-being is maintained.

Comparison with other approaches

The specific position of our theory can be clarified by comparing it with other psychological approaches. For example, the system of valuations does have some similarity with Kelly's system of constructs; and the person organizes, extends and reorganizes a system of valuations in the course of time. The difference, however, is that a valuation is not the same as a construct. For Kelly (1955) a construct is a way in which two or more things are alike and *thereby* different from a third or more things. A construct is a discrimination. A valuation on the other hand is not typically a discrimination, but an experience, which as a relevant personal meaning is part of the valuation system. Although Kelly has an eye for the affective domain of personality, in our approach this domain is more central. *Each* valuation has an affective component, which is indicated by a pattern of affects specific for that valuation and reflecting its personal meaning. Well-being is included in that pattern and is expressed by the balance of positive and negative affects. This gives one the possibility of considering the contribution of each valuation to the well-being of the organized system as a whole.

As in the Rogerian approach, the importance of the experiential life of the person is stressed. But in our case valuation system is different from self-concept. In this respect we agree with Akaret (1959) who suggested that the individual may not have a unified Gestalt of himself: rather he may have a high opinion about himself in some areas, but not in others. We would like to stress that a person can include positive and negative valuations about himself in the system even when they are conflicting with each other. So a Head of Department may consider himself simultaneously a good leader and a bad professional. These two valuations can conflict with one another when he asks himself if he is doing his job well enough. Moreover, valuation system has a broader theoretical scope than self-concept. A valuation emerges from interaction with the situation and can refer to situational aspects which do not belong to the self-concept in the strict sense of the word. Thus, somebody can be concerned about the sickness of a friend or about the divorce of two people whom he knows very well, not because this is of central importance in his self-concept, but because it is for him a relevant aspect of his interaction with a situation which has its own history. In this sense a valuation is a cognitive orientation to a personal, relevant aspect of that interaction.

The emphasis on the positive-negative dimension in the affective domain corresponds with the pleasure-pain principle in Freudian psychology. However, valuation theory is not an instinct-theory and is not based on the assumption of tension reduction. Some valuations impress one by reason of their search for tension and avoidance of rest: as, for example, in certain sport situations where a thrill is derived from danger or striving for the unknown. Valuations are not derived from some kind of biological energy or inner determinant; but, rather, are the result of interactions in which *the person himself* is the organizing agency. In our thinking the principle of *self-organization* plays a central role. In self-organization valuations referring to past, present and future are, in principle, of equal importance.

The self-confrontation method: Self-investigation of developing valuations

The method of self-confrontation was deduced from valuation theory. It was designed as a means of studying the relationship between valuations and affects and the way in which both variables are organized in a structured whole (Hermans, 1976).

The method contains two parts: the construction of valuations, and the connection of each valuation with a standard set of affect-denoting terms. This results in an affect-matrix, filled in by the person, in which each cell represents the extent to which according to the person a specific affect is characteristic for a specific valuation. This procedure is typically repeated two or more times, with several weeks or months between occasions, in order to study changes and constancies in the valuations and in the corresponding affective modalities.

The valuations are elicited by a series of open questions (Table 1). The main questions are those which ask for relevant issues in the past, present and future. They invite persons to reflect upon their life-situation in such a way that they are as free as possible to mention those concerns which are relevant from the perspective of the present situation. Persons are encouraged to phrase the valuations in their own terms so that the formulation is as much as possible in agreement with the intended meaning. The typical grammatical expression is the sentence, which provides a broad range of syntactic possibilities for the expression of meanings. When persons are not able to phrase a valuation in a sentence, they are permitted to express it in just a few words or in one word.

The method is made up of 12 sets, each set having two or three questions. Each group of questions points more or less in the same direction. There is no requirement that each question should result in an answer. Within any one set the person concentrates on that question which has the most eliciting quality for him or her. It is possible that such a question leads to more than one valuation. The questions are not devised on a stimulus-response basis. They are not supposed to lead to a quick answer, and there is no one-to-one relationship between question and answer. They invite the person to reflect upon his life situation, with the help of a trained interviewer.

To ensure an optimally favorable attitude towards the self-confrontation envisaged in this method, the helper (interviewer) impresses on the client the need to be completely frank in each and every part of the investigation and explains that nothing is taboo. The

TABLE 1: *The questions of the self-confrontation method*

Please read the questions below at your leisure before formulating an answer. If you concentrate on the points they raise, you will find a response readily forthcoming.

set 1: *The Past*
These questions are intended to guide you to one or more aspects of your past life that may have been of great importance to you.
-- Is there something in your past that has been of major importance or significance for your life and which still plays an important part today?
-- Has there been, in the past, a person (or persons), an experience, or a circumstance that greatly influenced your life and still appreciably affects your present existence?
   You are free to go back into the past as far as you think fit.
(Strikingly, this set often elicits negative valuations. The questions provide a 'way into' areas which are located in the past, exert a continuing influence and have not yet been 'got out of the system').

set 2: *The Present*
This set again comprises two questions which will lead you, after a certain amount of reflection, to formulate a response:
-- Is there in your present life something that is of major importance for, or of great influence on, your existence?
-- Is there in your present life a person(s) or a circumstance which exerts a significant influence on you?

set 3: *The Future*
The following questions will again be found to guide you to a response:
-- Do you foresee something that will be of great importance for, or of major influence on, your future life?
-- Do you feel that a certain person(s) or circumstance will exert a great influence in your future life?
-- Is there a future goal or object which you expect to play an important role in your life?
   You are free to look as far ahead as you wish.

set 4: *Activity*
-- What is the work or the field of study in which you normally engage?
(This question aims to elicit the major activity with which persons occupy themself in daily life. This will mostly be a job or program of studies. If it is opportune, the question can also be made to read: "What is normally your main occupation?").

set 5: *Enjoyment*
-- What is the main thing in your life from which you derive great enjoyment?
-- What more than anything else causes you moments of great enjoyment?
(This set may elicit many varying responses. If this is the case, the area selected should be the one which the client regards as relatively the most important.)

TABLE 1 (Continue):

set 6: *Thinking*
-- Is there something which you think about a great deal?
-- Is there something which frequently exercises your mind?
(Unlike sets 4 and 5, this set characteristically comprises questions
which elicit problem areas).

set 7: *Person: antagonistic*
-- Which person in your life particularly arouses antagonistic feelings
   in you?
-- Which person in your life are you particularly at odds with?
-- Is there a person in your life who is in some way or other
   important to you, but with whom you feel you cannot satisfactorily
   relate?
(Practice has shown that, to many people, the tenor of the third
question differs considerably from that of the first two. The merit of
the third is that if no answer is forthcoming in response to the other
two, the client may still suggest a person. This observation applies
likewise to the third question in set 8, 9 and 10. Sets 7-10 mostly
elicit names or descriptions of people. However, the method aims
primarily at meanings. These are realized when the helper asks an
additional question: how do you experience this person (those people)?
When the person is not able to do so, it is enough to mention a name).

set 8: *Group: antagonistic*
-- What group of people or what type of people particularly arouses
   antagonistic feelings in you?
-- What group of people or what type of people do you feel particularly
   compelled to defy?
-- Is there in your life a group of people or a type of people who are
   in some way or other important to you but with whom you feel you
   cannot satisfactorily relate?

set 9: *Person: unity*
-- With which person in your life dou you identify most easily?
-- Which person in your life do you particularly feel at one with?
-- Is there someone who is important in your life and to whom you feel
   closely allied?

set 10: *Group: unity*
-- With which group of people or what type of people do you identify
   most easily?
-- What group of people or what type of people do you particularly
   feel at one with?
-- Is there a group of people or a type of people that is important in
   your life and to whom you feel closely allied?

set 11: *Society*
-- Is there an aspect of society which is of importance or influential
   for you?
-- What do you think of your position in society?

TABLE 1 (Continue):

set 12: *Additional valuations*
-- Is there anything else which is important for, or of influence on, your present life and which is not covered by one of the preceding labels?
-- Will you please go through the labels to make sure nothing has been forgotten that is in some way or other important to you. If you can name other significant aspects, we will formulate additional labels together.
(These final questions seek to ensure the completeness of the client's system of valuations. When 11 sets have been dealt with, the client has become thoroughly attuned to the method. He can now suggest additions, realizing that this part of the procedure serves to ensure that all the important aspects of his present life are as fully represented as possible in the system.)

---

client, sitting next to the helper, looks over the first set of questions. He thinks for a while. Certain associations occur to him, varying from clear mental images to blurred chaotic memories. "Something" is going on in his mind. If his silent reflections are protracted and apparently inconclusive, the helper will invite him to think aloud. As the client verbalizes the mental processes touched off by the questions, the helper jots down notes on matters which are brought up. When the client's flow of associations stops, the helper takes over the initiative and proceeds to reformulate succinctly the various points which have arisen. The client thus gets an abridged and focussed playback of his own associations. This will assist him in ordering and structuring his associations. The client, when listening to the helper's recapitulations, will very likely embark on a fresh round of association hunting, because he senses something more fundamental still than what he has just said. The process, interspersed with feedback from the helper's recapitulations, may continue for a while. When the associations have come to an end, the client has to formulate *in his own words* a summary description that the helper can set down on a label card. This finalized response is to be formulated as a word, word cluster or preferably as a sentence. The process between the initial question and the final answer has the character of an *approximation process* between formulation and intended experience (for further details of the method see Hermans, 1976).

   The questions and the subsequent approximation process lead to a variety of valuations. The aim is to arrive at an *exhaustive* survey of relevant concerns. At the end of the investigation the person is asked if the valuation system contains all the concerns which he considers important from his present perspective. If something is missing, he or she can add this in the form of an additional valuation (set 12, Table 1). At the end of this procedure people may have differing numbers of valuations; but in most of the cases the total is between 20 and 40.

   Next, a standard list of affect terms is provided to the person. Concentrating on the first valuation, he indicates on a five-points scale to what extent he or she experiences each of the affects in relation to this specific valuation. All valuations are successively described with the same list of affect terms. This relating of valuations and affect is done by the person alone, without the presence of the helper. The rationale underlying this procedure is that certain psychological concepts, which are part of the theory, are to be translated into corresponding affect-scales. From the perspective of these scales and combination of scales the valuation system can be investigated and clarified. In the course of time and over several investigations different lists of affects have been used. The list applied in the study described here is the most recent one (Hermans, Hermans-Jansen, & Van Gilst, 1985) and contains 30 affects terms (Table 2). With the resulting matrix of Valuations (rows) x Affects (columns) a variety of computations is possible. The indices revelant to the present study are summarized below.

(1) index P is the sum score of 10 positive (pleasant) affects: nrs. 1, 5, 9, 16, 19, 20, 23, 27, 29, and 30.
(2) index N is the sum score of 10 negative (unpleasant) affects: nrs. 2, 4, 6, 8, 12, 15, 18, 21, 24, and 28. For each valuation the $P:N$ ratio can be studied. This indicates the well-being which the person experiences in relation to the specific concern of this valuation. Well-being is positive when $P > N$, negative when $N > P$, and ambivalent when $P = N$.
(3) index S is the sum score of four affect-terms expressing self-enhancement: nrs. 3, 7, 17, and 26. Comparable theoretical concepts are Angyal's (1965) "autonomy" and Bakan's (1966) "agency".
(4) index O is the sum score of four affect-terms expressing contact and union with the other (i.e., other people or the surrounding world): nrs. 10, 11, 14, and 22. This concept corresponds with Angyal's "homonomy" and Bakan's "communion". For each valuation the $S:O$ ratio can be determined. When the experience of self-enhancement is stronger than the experience of contact with the other, then $S > O$. When the contact with the other prevails, then $O > S$. When both kinds of experience coexist, then $S = O$.
(5) index r represents the extent of correspondence between the affective modality of two valuations, i.e., the correlation between the valuations in any two rows. This correlation gives an indication of the similarity between the affective meanings of two valuations. Index r can also be computed when affective modality is compared across two points in time. In this way constancy or change in the modality of a valuation can be studied.

TABLE 2: *Affect-terms of the self-confrontation method*

1. Joy	11. Love	21. Inferiority
2. Powerlessness	12. Self-alienation	22. Intimacy
3. Self-esteem	13. Unhappiness	23. Security
4. Anxiety	14. Tenderness	24. Anger
5. Happiness	15. Guilt	25. Despondency
6. Worry	16. Solidarity	26. Pride
7. Strength	17. Self-confidence	27. Energy
8. Stress	18. Loneliness	28. Disappointment
9. Enjoyment	19. Inner warmth	29. Inner calm
10. Carefulness	20. Trust	30. Freedom

The correlations between the indices P, N, S, and O and their reliabilities, computed separately for a group of students and for a group of clients, are presented in Table 3. As expected, the indices are not statistically independent. Nevertheless, we see that S and O affects can be differentiated from each other. The correlation between S and O is (more for the students than the clients) far below their respective reliabilities. This finding, in combination with the high correlations of S and O with P, allows one to conclude that S and O represent distinguishable sub-dimensions of the broader P dimension. Validation studies of the four indices are discussed by Hermans et al. (1985).

The second investigation, after some weeks or months, consists of the same stages as the first; but there is an important difference in the valuation-construction phase. This time the person does not start by formulating valuations. Instead he is confronted by the value statements which he himself constructed in Investigation 1. Again the helper reads the questions together with the person; but after each question he will now produce the value statement which the person regarded as adequate in Investigation 1. The person is instructed to consider, for each statement separately, whether he can still "go along" with its content, i.e., whether in his new situation he would still come up with the same answer to the question. The helper explains that, if this is not the case, the person has various options available:
- an old valuation may be reformulated (label modification);
- an old valuation may be replaced, with the new one setting out the person's answer to the same question as the old valuation purported to answer. The new label takes the place of the old one (label substitution);
- an old valuation may be discarded altogether (label elimination);
- a quite new valuation may be added (label supplementation).

In this way the person has considerable freedom to point to the constant and changing parts of the valuation system. This is in line with the expertise of the person concerning the content of his personal experiences.

TABLE 3: *Product-moment correlation-coefficients between indices P, N, S, and O and reliability-coefficients (Cronbach's α) for a group of 43 students (20 males, 23 females) and a group of 40 clients (20 males, 20 females)*

	students					clients				
	P	N	S	O	α	P	N	S	O	α
P	–				.90	–				.95
N	-.75	–			.90	-.59	–			.93
S	.59	-.47	–		.83	.82	-.68	–		.83
O	.62	-.24	.27	–	.86	.79	-.31	.64	–	.89

P = positive affect   S = affect referring to self-enhancement
N = negative affect   O = affect referring to contact with the other.

In essence, the self-confrontation method represents a dialogical model between psychologist and person. Both are seen as experts, each with their own specific expertise. The person is an expert in the knowledge he has concerning experiences in his particular life situation. He has the largest data-bank available about his own life, and is uniquely able to communicate about those things which he considers as relevant in his *local* situation. The psychologist is primarily an expert with respect to general concepts and theories, and their corresponding methodology; he has insight into phenomena and processes at the level of *general* relevance.

The self-confrontation method creates a platform on which these two expertises meet each other with intent to cooperate. The person presents his or her valuation system; the psychologist offers a series of affect-terms, selected on the basis of general concepts. These affects and their combinations permit a new perspective on the valuation system, and can, in principle, detect its hidden or implicit aspects. The person can use this perspective to look at his valuation system anew, and to develop it further. In his turn, the psychologist can see what kinds of experience and process correspond with his scales, concepts and theories. He proceeds by means of an idiographic study in which standardized scales facilitate both the comparison of valuations within a system at one point in time, and also the change of valuations in the course of time. By performing a number of idiographic studies he can move gradually in the direction of more general findings.

The self-confrontation method can also be understood as a process in the intersection of two kinds of dialogue. In an internal dialogue the person interrogates and investigates himself. In an external dialogue he communicates with the psychologist, and thus permits a new view on his valuation process. Because this happens several times with intervals of weeks or months, the person has the opportunity to think about the results of each stage of the investigation and to relate them to his daily experiences. Such a procedure is, for the person, an elaborate and intensive experience of repeated self-reflection. At the same time it enables the psychologist to study constancy and change.

Introduction of the case-study and procedure

The case-study described here concerns a woman, Irene, who was 44 years old at the time when she did the first self-investigation. She was reared in a very restrictive home, and after secondary school entered a convent. After 15 years of spiritual life she resigned; and has since worked as an economist in a school. She asked for psychotherapeutic assistance after a period of heavy and disturbing headaches. She consented to self-investigation as a means of looking at the organization of her life.

The first self-investigation was done with the help of a professional psychotherapist (not the author). The results, i.e., the content and organization of the valuation system and its affective properties, were fully discussed with her. In a subsequent series of weekly sessions her everyday experiences were clarified by close reference to the valuation system. The goal of the sessions was to reorganize the valuation system in such a way that the restrictive burden of the past was loosened and more self-expansion and well-being was realized.

Seven months after the first investigation, both person and helper felt that relevant parts of the valuation system had changed. This was a reason for doing a second self-investigation which would give an opportunity to revise the valuation system in the light of the present situation and to study the changes. In the same way as before the second investigation was followed by weekly sessions. These talks were necessary because the valuation system was judged by person and helper at the time of the second investigation as too far from the desired goal. They resulted in a third self-investigation, 11 months after the second. (The counselling is still being continued at the moment).

The two successive time periods of 7 and 11 months are rather long, and are not equal. The reason for their lenght is that in this case, in comparison with other clients, there is a rather slow movement in the valuation system. It was decided to do the next investigation when helper and person both had the feeling that there was enough change in the valuations to justify a new inspection of the total system. This impression of change was stronger in the first period than in the second; that is why the latter period was longer. The joint decisions of helper and person in the planning of the investigations is theoretically in agreement with the collaborating relationship between psychologist and person.

The results of these three investigations together form a model of the laborious struggle of a person who within a period of 18 months maintains the identity of some valuations and changes others.

Affective properties of constant valuations

In the first self-investigation Irene constructed 17 valuations, in the second 30, and in the third also 30. In order to give a closer look at the constant part of the valuation system, we present in Table 4 the valuations which remained the same between the first two investigations. Remember that in the second investigation the person is completely free to give the same formulations as before or to change them, more or less. In the case of Irene, we find that 9 of the 17 original valuations are identical after a period of seven months. The stability (r) of the corresponding affective modalities is remarkably high. The correlations range between .98 and .77, with a median correlation of .90.

The index r, as a measure of the similarity of the affective modality between Investigations 1 and 2, can be seen as a test-retest coefficient for a particular valuation by a particular person. We see that this coefficient can be very high (r = .98 equals 96% common variance), in a situation in which we give the person the opportunity to formulate his valuations in his own terms and to keep the formulation constant if no part of it gives rise to modification. The valuations which remained constant do show some variation on the indices which we referred to. Six are accompanied mainly by negative, and three mainly by positive affects. The positive valuations have high levels both for self-enhancement and for contact with the other.

The results are further corroborated when we compare Investigations

34 H.J.M. Hermans

TABLE 4: *Value statements persisting in Investigation 1 and 2, their scores on indices P, N, S, and O, and the extent of stability (r) of their affective modality*

No.	Value statement	P^2	N^2	S^2	O^2	r
1	I got it from home: you've got to do it that way, that's the way it is	7	38	0	2	.90
2	In the convent I had even less space than at home	1	35	0	0	.96
5^1	I don't say what I think really clearly enough	3	29	0	0	.86
6^1	I have a few friends whom I can always go to	35	5	10	13	.85
8^1	I'm able to enjoy flowers and plants	36	0	13	11	.86
9^1	I'm able to enjoy water (water = peace and space)	37	0	12	13	.77
12^1	I don't give myself easily	0	28	0	0	.97
13	Tension	0	33	0	0	.98
14^1	I find conflict terrible	0	31	0	0	.98

1. Value statements persisting in Investigation 1, 2 and 3.
2. P = positive affect   S = affect referring to self-enhancement
    N = negative affect   O = affect referring to contact with the other.

2 and 3. Of the 30 valuations of the second investigation 12 remain constant in the third. Their content and stability are presented in Table 5. The median test-retest correlation is between .90 and .87. Here again the constant valuations are partly positive and partly negative.

Finally, those valuations were examined which received an identical formulation in all three investigations, that is, remained unchanged over a period of 18 months. There are 6 of the 17 valuations in the first investigation which are repeated in the second and third investigations (they are specially marked in Table 4). The levels of coefficient *r* (over a period of 18 mounths) are, from high to low: .98, .92, .91, .91, .87, and .83. The median correlation is .91. These valuations are once again partly positive and partly negative.

Summarizing, we see a high stability over a period of 18 months in the affective pattern of identically formulated valuations, with a median correlation approaching .90. In the case of certain valuations a test-retest reliability is found which approaches perfect stability (*r* = .99).

TABLE 5: *Value statements persisting in Investigation 2 and 3, their scores on indices P, N, S, and O, and the extent of stability (r) of their affective modality*

No.	Value statement	P	N	S	O	r
4.	Now and then I'll dare to take the space I'm given; then, I want to know from the other if it's right or not	14	0	5	1	.82
5.	I have such doubts about myself that I first think: what does the other make of me, how do I come across	0	28	0	0	.97
7.	I want to get clearer about what I do and what I actually want myself	6	22	2	0	.44
11.	I don't say what I think really clearly enough	0	26	0	0	.97
14.	I have a few friends whom I can always go to	34	3	9	6	.87
16.	I want to talk more	11	15	3	0	.64
18.	I am able to enjoy flowers and plants	32	0	11	3	.90
19.	I am able to enjoy water (water = peace and space	30	0	11	0	.82
21.	I have real difficulties with the "captain" [nickname for the prioress of the convent]	0	38	0	0	.99
24.	I don't give myself easily	0	26	0	0	.94
25.	I find conflict terrible	0	31	0	0	.98
27.	Gymnastics	18	0	7	0	.83

P = positive affect   S = affect referring to self-enhancement
N = negative affect   O = affect referring to contact with the other.

Affective properties of changing valuations

As has been said, there are four kinds of change in valuations: *label modification*, *label substitution*, *label elimination* and *label supplementation*. These options offer the person a variety of means for changing the valuation system in such a way that it contains those concerns which are of *current* importance to him or her.

When one's aim is to study the development of the system, one of the four types is of prime importance, viz., the label modification. It concerns valuations which, while changing in formulation in the course of time, can nevertheless be identified as the same. They express new aspects of meaning. Persons who experience a problem and expressly wishes to find a way of escaping it, will include this problem as a part of their valuation system. As they try different solutions, the valuation concerned will take on additional or new meanings, depending on the success or failure of the attempts. These meanings manifest themselves as *changes of the same* and can be categorized as *label modifications*.

In the case of Irene, there were three label modifications which reflected changes in valuations or in affective modality from Investigation 1 to 2 and from Investigation 2 to 3. They concerned three problems which were central in the talks between her and the helper. They also played a central role in her interaction with the present situation. We will now discuss the development of these problems.

Development of Problem 1: From being stuck to movement, and from movement to stabilization

One of the problems which hindered Irene in her contact with the helper, and also with other people, was that she found it extremely difficult and embarrassing to talk about her past, although the past was always in her mind. In Investigation 1 she forced herself to talk about it. But such a self-imposed duty had the same affective connotation as the restrictive duties and morals of her past. In Investigation 2 "talking more" changes from a duty to a choice (Table 6). This cognitive shift produces a different affective pattern. This is expressed in the low correlation ($r = .32$) between V_1 and V_2. The difference is further revealed by the decrease of negative affects, and an increase of positive ones. From Investigation 2 to 3, however, there is no further development. There is a stabilization of the content (formulation) of the valuation and of the corresponding affective modality ($r = .64$). We see here a valuation which, within the period under study, does not have the capacity to lead to a reversal in the ratio of positive and negative affects. In this sense, it does not contribute much to well-being.

TABLE 6: *Extent to which initial change persists*

	Value statement	P	N	S	O	
V_1	I must talk more	3	26	3	0	
V_2	I want to talk more	11	15	3	0	$r = .32$ $r = .64$
V_3	I want to talk more	7	20	3	0	

Development of Problem 2: From being stuck to strong movement, and from movement to stabilization

The same pattern as in Problem 1 was found in Problem 2 (Table 7): an initial shift which later stabilized. The difference, however, is that the change between V_1 and V_2 is now more remarkable than in the case of Problem 1. The restructuring is manifest both in the

TABLE 7: *Extent to which a strong initial change persists*

	Value statement	P	N	S	O
V_1	I don't dare take the space I'm given; I'm still afraid it isn't right	1	35	0	0
V_2	Now and then I'll dare to take the space I'm given; then I want to know from the other if it's right or not	14	0	5	1
V_3	Now and then I'll dare to take the space I'm given; then I want to know from the other if it's right or not	20	4	6	2

$r = -.64$ (between V_1 and V_2)

$r = .82$ (between V_2 and V_3)

valuational and the affective perspective. In V_1 Irene expressed not having the courage to "take space" and avoiding opportunities offered; in V_2 she indicates a move toward approach-behavior. This change in valuation is accompanied by a strong affective change: the affective modality of V_2 takes the shape of a reversal ($r = -.64$) of the modality of V_1. This reversal is also manifest in the P : N ratio: while V_1 was characterized by a dominance of negative affects, V_2 is exclusively accompanied by positive affects. There is also a slight increase in S-affects, suggesting a growing self-enhancement.

The revision from V_1 to V_2 is followed by a stabilization from V_2 to V_3. The V_2-formulation is identical with the V_3-formulation and the modalities have a high similarity ($r = .82$). The stability, however, is not complete. We see that the increase in positive affects which started in the first period, is continued in the second. This suggests the further establishment of this valuation, which seems to be very relevant for Irene's well-being.

Development of Problem 3: From external to internal attribution

The third problem concerns the work-situation (Table 8). In V_1 Irene describes this in terms of an external attribution, in V_2 in terms of an internal attribution. In V_3 she maintains the internal attribution, but changes the content of the problem. The drastic changes in the valuation, however, contrast with the relative stability of the affective modality (respectively, $r = .88$ and $r = .60$). The reversal of the direction of attribution is not accompanied by a synchronic change in the modality: she develops a new insight, but to a large extent feels the same about it. This discrepancy shows that change of valuation and change of affect are not necessarily parallel processes. This does not mean that there is no affective development at all. The attentive reader could see a gradual and systematic decrease in the negative affects from V_1 to V_2 and from V_2 to V_3. In spite of this decrease, the ratio of this valuation leans to the negative side in all three investigations.

TABLE 8: *Strong cognitive and slight affective change*

	Value statement	P	N	S	O
V_1	Work: I get a particular schedule, dreamed up by someone who doesn't have to do it themselves. Someone else decides how I have to do the domestic jobs. That gives me the feeling that I can't do it	0	32	0	0
V_2	Work: I used to let the other take the initiative. I found that wasn't so good and now see that it's up to me. I used to be inaccessible for the other	0	25	0	0
V_3	At work: if anything was said, it was very threatening – I used to resist in anticipation. I now notice if I do that, and I try to change. Now I can discuss matter	6	18	3	0

$r = .88$

$r = .60$

Summarizing, Irene tackles three problems which represent three changing valuations in her system. Although she is in a period of gaining a new perspective on several aspects of her life-situation, it is striking that none of the three problems shows continuous and pervasive change. In the first and second problem an initial change is followed by stabilization, although these problems have not been fully solved. In the third problem a radical restructuring of the valuation co-exists with relative stability in the affective modality. These observations suggest that, insofar as we see change in the valuation system, it has a partial and differential nature. First, in a period in which person and helper work to develop the system in the direction of increased well-being and self-enhancement a substantial part of the system remains unchanged. Second, the part which does move in the desired direction shows a change-process which is either periodically different or different as between the valuational and affective components.

Constancy and change are simultaneous and successive

In this section we follow Shontz's (1965) advice that personality should be studied from the perspective both of constancy and change. When we concentrate on the valuation-process of an individual as it develops over time, a rather complicated picture arises. The person under study demonstrated that constancy and change are simultaneous *and* successive.

The simultaneity became apparent when we observed that some part of the valuation system were identical over time, while *in the same period* other parts of the system (the three problems) showed considerable and meaningful modifications. This simultaneity of stability and instability could also be observed in the affective domain. There was in the first period a sharp contrast between the very high stability-coefficient of the modality of some valuations (as high as r = .98) and the drastic reversion of the modality of another valuation (r = -.64 in the case of the second problem). It is to be noted that this change cannot be accounted for in terms of the "unreliability" of classical test-theory. The systematic change in the content of the valuations indicates that the person was shifting to another approach to her situation.

Obviously the person, being in a psychotherapeutic kind of relationship, did not change her total valuation system. She did not change all her valuations a little; on the contrary, she modified only some of them, and kept other valuations, both positive and negative, highly constant. These results can be better understood when we realize that the personality-process needs some continuity. On the basis of this proposition, one does not expect the total valuation system to develop over a given time. Rather, the development of some parts of the system is possible as a result of stability in other parts.

In this case-study the simultaneity of constancy and change does not exclude their succession. In the Problems 1 and 2 there was change between Investigations 1 and 2; stabilization between Investigations 2 and 3. This initial change and later stabilization was apparent both in the content of the valuation and in the affective modality. This result indicates that changing valuations are not continuously in movement. Further it suggests that when the person has partially developed one part of the system she may leave it to stabilize, and shift to another part to concentrate the change process there.

With regard to the process of change, we see in our case-study that change in valuation and affective change are not always synchroneous. Although synchronicity is apparent in the Problems 1 and 2, there is a remarkable achronicity in the development of Problem 3. The content of the second valuation (V_2) is quite different from that of the first (V_1): the initial external attribution was exchanged for an internal attribution. However, the affective modality was highly similar for both valuations (r = .88). This means that a strong change in valuation was accompanied by high stability of affective meaning. This implies that valuational and affective change *can* occur together, but do not do so necessarily.

Idiography and nomothesis as related to stability and change

In the tradition of personality psychology it is striking that the coincidence of stability and change has had the attention of authors who were also interested in the combination of a nomothetic and an idiographic approach. In this section we mention only three of them, although more examples could be given.

Thomae (1968) points to the misconception underlying a lot of research, that constancy and change exclude each other. He agrees with Yarrow et al. (1964) that many researchers have worked on the basis of alternative hypotheses which considered constancy and change as mutually exclusive aspects of personality. This conception has the disadvantage that attention is directed only to radical change and not to microvariation which can be of equal relevance. Thomae gives an extensive treatment of relationships between the nomothetic and the idiographic approach, and objects to those investigators who treat them as absolutely different ways of looking at personality. Between the type of study which tries to describe all the details of individual behavior and the type which searches for general behavior characteristics, there are manifold transitions (p. 21).

Another example can be found in the research program of Cattell (1963). This reflects several initiatives which are directed at identifying and measuring dimensions of intraindividual change or *states* (e.g., affective dimensions, dynamic aspects of motivation, and processes), as well as more stable personality characteristics or *traits*. Three of Cattell's data box techniques bear directly on the nomothesis-idiography distinction: R-technique, dR-(or differential) R-technique, and P-technique. R-technique involves the cross-sectionnally based examination of covariance relationships among a set of measures as they are correlated over a sample of people assessed on one occasion of measurement. The second, dR-technique, also cross-sectional in nature, involves the analysis of covariance relationships among change or difference scores (e.g., occasion-2 minus occasion-1 scores) derived from two measurements of a sample of persons on a number of variables. P-technique involves the longitudinally-based examination of covariance relationships among multiple measures as they vary over an extended succession of measurement occasions for an individual subject. Both dR- and P-techniques have been developed and used explicitly for the purpose of identifying change structures (Cattell, 1963). P-technique, in particular, emphasizes the individual and the thorough study of intraindividual change as a preliminary step to the development of nomothetic relationships (Nesselroade, 1984).

A third example is the theoretical analysis of goal-oriented behavior presented by Pervin (1983). He states that the patterned, organized quality of behavior suggests that it is directed toward end-points or goals. In this goal-orientation there is a rhythm or pattern to behavior which can only be appreciated by the study of behavior across diverse situations and over extended periods of time. If we look at processes over time we observe both constancy and change, recurrent patterns and variations on themes, changes in forms or outer appearances and the maintenance of inner structures (p. 3). Pervin describes some distinguishing features of the research which has emanated from the conceptualization of human behavior as purposive and organized. One of them is an effort to be both idiographic and nomothetic; that is, to develop generalized principles of understanding through the analysis of data on individual subjects. In this research it is typical that more data are gathered on individual subjects than would ordinarily be the case. Furthermore, in analyzing these data attention is paid not only to robust regularities and confirmed predictions but also to potentially enlightening deviations and rare but significant phenomena (p. 33).

Both the literature cited above and our own case study, give reason enough for studying the issue of stability and change in an idiographic way. It is this particular type of study which is so well suited to throwing light on the complexities of stability and change in the individual. Such a study may show regularities or significant phenomenal characteristics for this particular life. Furthermore, one can investigate whether such regularities or phenomena exist also in other people. If one moves to the investigation of several cases within a certain class of people, one is shifting to a nomothetic type of study with the possibility of general findings (Bakan, 1969). (See also Block, 1971, for the construction of a typology of persons).

The person as a self-investigator in a collaborative relationship: A perspective on future personality research

It is a common feature of all kinds of idiographic studies that they are concerned with what is particular to the individual (Runyan, 1983). Because of the complexities of the individual world, it is a tremendous task for psychology to construe concepts, taxonomies and methods which must take into account the large number of variables and their interaction and development in the life of the individual. This seems to be a task which is too much for the psychologist alone. A more active role on the part of the subject in psychological research is required. In this respect we do not mean persons as cooperative objects of study, but as subjects capable of studying themself and their situation. In the position of self-investigators they have the opportunity to point us to those aspects of their life-situation which are relevant to them from their point of view. This implies that they *select* certain phenomena as important; on the basis of this selection these are worth being studied by the psychologist. I expect that idiographic studies will actually benefit from the person's role of self-investigator; and in the long run so also will nomothetic studies. When the psychologist accepts the person as somebody who is able to self-reflect and to communicate about significant experiences, then he or she will be able to listen to the person as carefully as possible and to develop free-response methods which enable him to have his own say. The frequent objection to such a position is that human judgement is full of shortcomings. Even when one assumes that this is the case, it is no valid argument against the self-investigator role in psychological research. An analogy would be the claim that a short-sighted person is blind. When there are shortcomings in the person as self-investigator it is the task of the psychologist to check them and, when possible, to provide means of improving the quality of the person's contribution.

Ideally the person plays his or her role in a collaborative relationship with the psychologist. Such a relation has the promise that the two contributions will compensate for their individual limitations and profit from their specific expertise. In my view the core of the body of psychological knowledge rests in human characteristics and processes *in general*. The limitation of such a general approach lies in its shortcomings with respect to insight into the peculiar world of the individual. The strength of the individual lies in the fact that he has the most direct access to his experiences, to the meanings he gives them in interaction with his naturalistic situation and with the historical aspects of his life. His limitation is that he is heavily bound up in the phenomena of his own life and is not well able to generalize (Fischhoff, 1976; Hermans et al. 1985; Hoekstra, 1978). It is a challenge for the personality psychology of the future to find ways of combining the specific capacities of psychologist and person in fruitful dialogical models.

ACKNOWLEDGEMENT

For his advices and help in the translation of this work, the author is indebted to Peter Stringer; and to Els Hermans-Jansen who placed all the data of the case study at his disposal.

REFERENCES

Akaret, R.U. (1959). Interrelationships among various dimensions of the self-concept. *Journal of Counseling Psychology, 6,* 199–201.
Angyal, A. (1965). *Neurosis and treatment: A holistic theory.* New York: Wiley.
Bakan, D. (1966). *The duality of human existence.* Chicago: Rand McNally.
Bakan, D. (1969). *On method: Toward a reconstruction of psychological investigation.* San Francisco, CA: Jossey-Bass.
Block, J. (1971). *Lives through time.* Berkeley, CA: Bancroft.
Cattell, R.B. (1963). The structuring of change by P-technique and incremental R-technique. In C.W. Harris (Ed.), *Problems in measuring change* (pp. 167-198). Madison: University of Wisconsin Press.
Fischhoff, B. (1976). Attribution theory and judgment under uncertainty. In J.H. Harvey. W.J. Ickes, & R.F. Kidd (Eds.), *New directions in attribution research* (Vol. 1, pp. 421-452). Hillsdale, NJ: Erlbaum.
Hermans, H.J.M. (1974). *Waardegebieden en hun ontwikkeling* [Value areas and their development]. Amsterdam: Swets & Zeitlinger.
Hermans, H.J.M. (1976). *Value areas and their development.* Amsterdam: Swets & Zeitlinger.
Hermans, H.J.M. (1981). *Persoonlijkheid en waardering* [Personality and valuation] (3 Vols.). Lisse: Swets & Zeitlinger.
Hermans, H.J.M., Hermans-Jansen, E., & Van Gilst, W. (1985). *De grondmotieven van het menselijk bestaan; Hun expressie in het persoonlijk waarderingsleven* [The basic motives of human existence; Their expression in personal valuation]. Lisse: Swets & Zeitlinger.
Hoekstra, H.A. (1978). Waarderingstheorie en attributietheorieën: verenigbaar? [Valuation theory and attribution theories: compatible?]. *Nederlands Tijdschrift voor de Psychologie, 33,* 463-471.
Kelly, G.A. (1955). *The psychology of personal constructs.* (2 Vols.). New York: Norton.
Lazarus, R.S. (1963). *Personality and adjustment.* Englewood Cliffs, NJ: Prentice Hall.
Merleau-Ponty, M. (1945). *Phénoménologie de la perception*

[Phenomenology of perception]. Paris: Gallimard.

Merleau-Ponty, M. (1948). *Sens et non-sens* [Sense and nonsense]. Paris: Nagel.

Nesselroade, J.R. (1984). Concepts of intraindividual variability and change: Impressions of Cattell's influence on lifespan developmental psychology. *Multivariate Behavioral Research, 19,* 269-286.

Pervin, L.A. (1983). The stasis and flow of behavior: Toward a theory of goals. In M.M. Page (Ed.), Nebraska Symposium on Motivation. *Personality: Current theory & research* (pp. 1-53). Lincoln, NE: University of Nebraska Press.

Runyan, W.M. (1983). Idiographic goals and methods in the study of lives. *Journal of Personality, 51,* 413-437.

Shontz, F.C. (1965). *Research methods in personality.* New York: Appleton-Century-Crofts.

Thomae, H. (1968). *Das Individuum und seine Welt* [The individual and his world]. Göttingen: Hogrefe.

Yarrow, L.J., Bayley, N., et al. (1964). Symposion on personality consistency and change. *Vita Humana, 7,* 65-146.

PART II

IMPACT AND CONSTRAINTS OF SITUATIONS IN
PERSONALITY FUNCTIONING

RESPONSE HIERARCHIES RELATED TO DIFFERENT AREAS OF LIFE STRESS

A CONTRIBUTION TO THE PERSON-SITUATION ISSUE

by

Hans Thomae

University of Bonn, FRG

Lazarus and his co-workers (Lazarus & Launier, 1980) have questioned the value of trait-centered conceptualizations of coping with stress and have emphasized process-centered approaches. When discussing findings on gender differences, however, Folkman and Lazarus (1980) are referring to trait-like coping patterns. An ambivalence regarding process- and trait-orientation can be found in almost all approaches to the classification and measurement of responses to stress (e.g., Haan, 1977; Pearlin & Schooler, 1978; Shanan, 1983; Vaillant, 1977). For instance, Laux and Vossel (1982) ask for a joint consideration of trait- and process-centered approaches in order to find innovative ways to the study of stress and coping.

There is therefore a close relationship between personality theory on the one hand, and research on stress and coping on the other. Stress models as the transactional model of Lazarus and Launier (1980) or the model of Mason (1975) may also be related to general psychology. As soon as problems of coping are discussed, main issues of personality psychology become salient.

TOWARD A TAXONOMY OF RESPONSES TO STRESS

One of the main obstacles to the study of coping is the definition of the term *coping* itself. Authors like Haan (1977) use coping as a synonym for "successful problem-solving," whereas Lazarus and Launier (1980) use the same term for any activity elicited by the perception of threat or challenge. Therefore, we suggest the introduction of a neutral term like *response* when dealing with stress defined by *critical life events* or by one of those *daily* hassles Lazarus is referring to.

From biographical studies done during the last thirty years (e.g., Hambitzer, 1962; Kipnowski, 1980; Lehr, 1969; Thomae, 1953, 1968, 1984) and from other sources which will be reported later, we conclude that the most adequate approach to the study of complex problem-solving, such as to be observed in natural situations, is defined by the assessment of response hierarchies. These response hierarchies may be applied by different persons in similar situations or by the same persons in different situations. Therefore, personality theories applied to this area are influenced by *theories of action*, which integrate cognitive structures as well as processes, on the one hand, and motivational-emotional processes and structures, on the other. According to this action-oriented theorizing any response to stress is goal-directed, more or less guided by plans, and controlled by conscious thought.

The structure of a response hierarchy, however, is not only determined by cognition-motivation interactions as defined by goals and plans, but also by available response patterns and their reinforcement histories. From this point of view our approach includes learning theory principles. We are referring explicitly to Hull (1952) and his concept of response hierarchy with its implication of different reaction- and inhibition-potentials. The main difference between Hull's approach and ours primarily concerns our non-mechanistic, cognitive orientation and our focus on complex human behaviour as studied in real life situations.

Our taxonomy of responses to stress was critically derived. Instead of evaluating the reports given by our respondents in neo-psychoanalysis categories like Haan (1977), or super-imposing a logical-deductive frame of reference like Lazarus & Launier (1980), we tried to preserve the *semantics* of the reports on dealing with stress. By definition, any taxonomy has to reduce the countless person- and situation-specific responses, for instance, to problems concerning own family, health, housing, or income. This abstraction is accomplished in our studies by a process of abstraction. In doing this we tried to trace the general behavioural pattern which became manifest in the concrete actions, thoughts, and/or emotions in the reports. General behavioural patterns similar to these were defined already by Murray (1938) in his list of criteria for needs. For instance, in our criteria for the response pattern *achievement related behaviour* we directly applied Murray's definition when mention must be made of accomplishing something difficult, mastering, manipulating or organizing physical objects, human beings or ideas.

Most of our analyses of reports on responses to stress resulted in a taxonomy of 20 - 28 behavioural patterns. These analyses also showed that the *same* stress situation usually is approached by an individual with a *variety* of responses. From strictly empirical analysis of biographies we concluded also that the complexity of responses to stress cannot be ordered along a few dimensions. The only adequate approach consists of the definition of response hierarchies as applied by *different* people in *different* situations. The hierarchy can be operationalized by the mean rating scores of frequency and intensity of the response classes as included in the classification system.

It is not possible to explain the very complex procedure necessary for these ratings in the space available. However, I will attempt to demonstrate this approach by discussing different response hierarchies related to the same or similar stressful experiences as reported by different groups of people. Secondly, I shall compare the response hierarchies as reported by the same group of people for dealing with different stressors. In this way, I will demonstrate situation-specific orders in response hierarchies. Finally, I shall present longitudinal data to compare the response hierarchies of the *same* group of people to the *same* stress area at *different* times (between 5 and 11 years). In doing so, I shall highlight a high degree of person-specific consistency in the structure of response hierarchies.

RESPONSE HIERARCHIES RELATED TO CONFLICT AND STRESS IN THE FAMILY AS REPORTED BY DIFFERENT SAMPLES

As a first example of our comparative studies on response hierarchies we must refer to a study of Fester-Waltzing (1983) on coping with the conflict and stress of a divorce. The response hierarchies as reported by her respondents (age 20-55 years) were compared with those of the participants of the Bonn Longitudinal Study of Aging (BOLSA) with respect to their perceived problems in their relationships with spouse, children, and grandchildren (see Fig. 1).

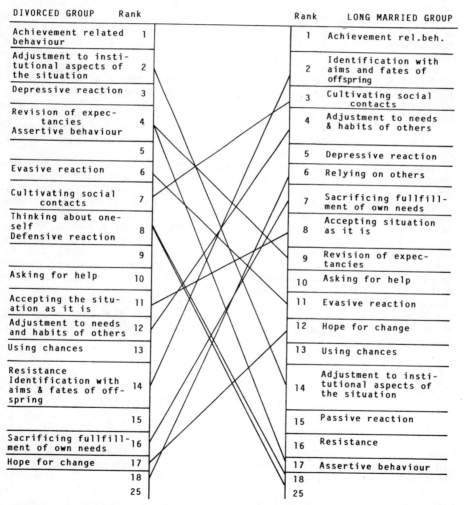

Figure 1: *Response hierarchies related to conflict and stress in the family reported by divorced and long-married women and men.*

Although there are some problems regarding the comparability of these two samples we can define the main difference between them by the duration of their marriage. In the divorced group the mean duration of marriage was 8.9 years, in the BOLSA-sample it was longer than 25 years. From this point of view the samples differ in the outcome of the adjustment process to problems of marriage and family life.

As can be seen in Fig. 1 this difference in duration was associated with decisive differences in the response hierarchies to family problems. The ten most dominant behaviour patterns in the divorced group included *assertive behaviour, emphasizing ego control*, and *adjustment to the institutional aspects of the situation*, e.g., by consulting a lawyer. A common denominator for these behaviour patterns may be labeled *tendency to self-defence, self-protection, and control*. Cooperative, prosocial behavioural patterns were not represented among the ten most dominant response patterns in these groups.

These cooperative, prosocial response patterns had very high ranks in the response hierarchies of the long-married group as indicated by the position of the categories *cultivating social contacts, adjustment to the needs and habits of others, sacrificing*, e.g., by *renouncing the satisfaction of own needs in favour of the partner or the children*. Another way of solving conflicts in the family consists of *identification with the aims and fates of offspring* which may result in caring for the other, etc.

Aside from the differences some communalities in the dominant response hierarchies were found. *Achievement related behaviour*, including efforts to take care for the other, as well as for oneself, belonged to the behavioural devices most often mentioned in both groups. Also *depressive reactions* received a high rank not only in the divorced but also in the group of long married persons. Due to differences in the marriage outcomes, however, the response hierarchies of the divorced group emphasized self-protection, defence and control, whereas in the long-married group cooperation and caring tended to be more emphasized. It would be misleading, if these differences in response hierarchies were explained by reference to personality variables. It is the situation, defined by failure in the own marriage or the intervention of a third person in the one group and the absence of this failure or intervention in the other group which is most decisive.

RESPONSE HIERARCHIES OF DIFFERENT GROUPS OF PATIENTS REGARDING THEIR HEALTH SITUATION

Psychosomatic studies point to the interaction between certain response patterns and the etiology of some diseases, for instance, Rosenman's (1974) hypothesis of a close association between Type A behaviour and high risk for heart infarction. Yet, in a study using a personality inventory Stocksmeier (1976) did not find differences in the psychological reactions of samples with different forms of disease. Type A behaviour is regarded by him as a response pattern related to the high degree of *severity* of illness rather than its *quality*.

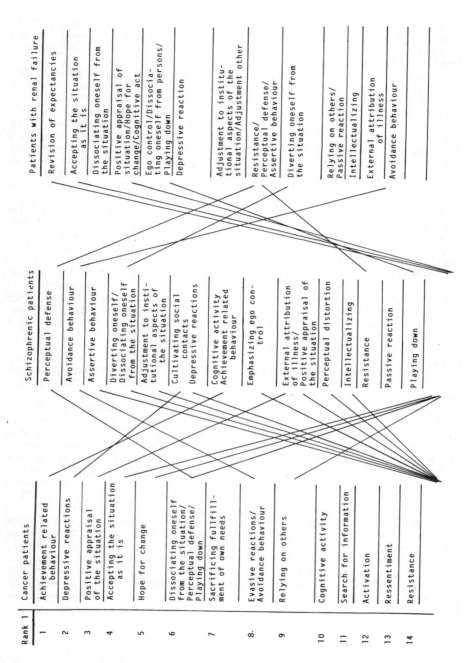

Figure 2: *Response hierarchies of patients with different medical diagnoses regarding their health situation.*

From diploma theses like those of Diehl (1984), Scharnweber (1982), Schaub (1984), and Van De Loo (1983) we are able to compare the response hierarchies of three groups of patients related to the present stage of illness (see Fig. 2).

From the objective quality of the diseases we might expect that patients suffering from a life threatening illness like cancer or renal failure would manifest more *perceptual defence, avoidance reactions* or *perceptual distortions* than schizophrenic patients. However, the two groups with a somatic diagnosis showed more responses indicating active coping like *achievement related behaviour* in the cooperation with the clinic staff or cognitive control of the situation like *revising expectancies* regarding own health or *accepting the situation as it* is or *positive appraisal of the situation* by reference to the treatment they received. Contrary to expectations the schizophrenic patients were responding mainly in a defensive or avoidant way.

One explanation for this finding might be related to the psychological impact of the medical treatment as offered to these patients. For the cancer group it consisted in the usual aftercare in a Department of Oncology (Medical School of Bonn University). The renal patients received a limited care programme training. In terms of the transactional model (Lazarus & Launier, 1980) it may be argued that these patients received information and training, respectively, which increased the own practical and psychological coping resources in dealing with their critical health status. This way the *secondary appraisal* of the situation was changed and a process of *re-appraisal* may have been initiated.

The schizophrenic patients were treated mainly by drugs. Even if psychological treatment would have been applied it would probably not have had beneficial effects in the short time since their hospitalization. Thus, it seems unlikely that their secondary appraisal of their health situation was influenced by their treatment.

There exists an alternative explanation for the differences in the response hierarchies of the two groups of somatic patients and the group of psychiatric patients. The third highest rank in the response hierarchy of the psychiatric patients was *assertive behaviour*, which involves trying to find ways to protect the own self-concept against any detrimental effects of being a schizophrenic patient. Due to widespread stereotypes regarding mental illness the diagnosis implicates adverse changes in the self-concept of the schizophrenic patient. This is less likely for patients with somatic diagnoses.

From this point of view comparisons of response hierarchies contribute much to the social-psychological view of illness. In terms of the person–situation issue of contemporary personality theory, however, these findings underline very clearly the close interaction between person and situation. In particular implicit aspects of the situation, like the social stigmatisation associated with a psychiatric diagnosis, are stronger in determining and structuring the response hierarchy than more explicit ones.

ANOTHER LOOK AT THE PERSON–SITUATION ISSUE

The person–situation issue is discussed in a more systematic way in the final stage of our analysis. Now, the response hierarchies of a longitudinal sample at different measurement points, 10 to 12 years apart, will be compared. The response hierarchies in the first section of this final stage are related to the same problem areas, viz. housing, income, health problems, and conflict and stress in the family. The second section of this final stage consists of an analysis of the response hierarchies of the same sample, assessed at identical measurement points, but related to different situations (problem areas).

If the person is the decisive variable in determining human behaviour there should not be any major differences between the response hierarchies as assessed at different measurement points and with respect to different problem areas. On the other hand, if the situation is the decisive variable we have to expect larger differences between the response hierarchies with respect to the same problem areas assessed at different measurement points (10 - 12 years apart). From a situationistic point of view we also have to expect larger differences between the response hierarchies related to different problem areas.

For the long-term aspect of the consistency-change problem the response hierarchies of 81 subjects of the *Bonn Longitudinal Study of Aging* (BOLSA; Thomae, 1976, 1983) will be compared. The measurement points (*Mp*'s) are *Mp*2 (1966) and *Mp*6 (1977). At *Mp*1 (1965) perceived stress in the health area and responses to health problems had not been assessed. Aside from health problems those concerning housing, family, and income were assessed at each of the *Mp*'s on the basis of interviews of three to four hours.

As shown in Table 1 (columns 1 - 4, boxes 1966 vs. 1977) the ranks of the different response patterns related to the same problem area differed only slightly at the two measurement points. The consistency in responding to identical problem areas is especially evident in the highest ranking response classes. In dealing with housing problems *achievement related behaviour*, *adjustment to institutional aspects of the situation*, *cultivating social contacts*, and *relying on others and adjustment to needs and habits of others* belonged to ranks 1 - 5 at both measurement points. There were also major divergencies between the ranks of some items at the two measurement points. Due to the fact that the team of the BOLSA had changed completely from 1966 to 1977 and due to other factors *only a shift by at least four ranks will be regarded as significant*.

The largest shift in the response hierarchy related to housing problems was concerned with the item *revision of expectancies* which moved to a higher rank in all four problem areas. This change may be due to rater bias or a developmental process implicit in moving from 'young old' to 'old old'. *Delay of gratification* may be due to the awareness that some disadvantages of the own apartment cannot be changed. Therefore, need for more quieteness and privacy has to be sacrificed for the advantage of having a nice family (unfortunately with three very active children) in the neighbourhood. This may explain the higher rank for this response pattern at *Mp*6. This interpretation is supported by the decrease in the rank order of *hope for change*. On the other hand, the lower rank of *resistance* at *Mp*6 can be understood only by the regulation as existing formerly in some West German companies from which part of our sample was drawn. These companies requested their workers to leave the homes they had

TABLE 1: *Ranks of 17 Response Patterns Related to Four Problem Areas at Two Measurement Points*

Response patterns	Columns										
	1		2		3		5		5	6	7
	Problem Areas										
	Housing		Income		Family		Health				
	Mp2	Mp6	Mp2	Mp6	Mp2	Mp6	Mp2	Mp6			
1. Achievement related behaviour	1	1	1	1	2	1	2	1	0	0	0
2. Adjustment to institutions	5	6	2	3	13	13	1	2	0	38	35
3. Adjustment to others	3	2	5	5	1	4	12	13	0	31	23
4. Using chances	12	8	10	7	13	14	10	10	0	6	20
5. Asking for help	9	7	14	17	17	9	10	6	12	27	32
6. Cultivating social contacts	2	3	5	5	2	3	6	16	10	14	37
7. Delay of gratification	16	11	13	11	8	8	16	15	5	27	18
8. Relying on others	3	4	7	11	8	7	5	6	4	12	19
9. Revision of expectancies	16	10	15	9	15	11	17	9	24	0	0
10. Resistance	6	10	6	9	6	15	6	5	13	0	30
11. Aggressive assertiveness	15	17	14	17	12	17	15	16	5	6	0
12. Accepting the situation	6	9	7	12	6	9	3	4	5	10	24
13. Passive reactions	15	15	16	17	15	15	8	13	5	22	4
14. Hope for change	10	14	13	14	10	13	8	13	9	11	0
15. Depressive reactions	10	12	9	13	4	6	4	3	4	22	35
16. Identification with offspring	6	5	3	2	4	2	12	11	0	26	30
17. Evasive reactions	11	12	12	16	11	13	14	13	4	6	10

Note: Mp2 = 1966; *Mp6* = 1977.

Column 5 shows the total of significant differences between *Mp2* and *Mp6*.

Column 6 shows the total of significant differences between the four problem areas at *Mp2*.

Column 7 shows the total of significant differences between the four problem areas at *Mp6*.

rented from the company after retirement. Due to their resistance which contributed to the high rank of this response pattern at *Mp2* most of them were permitted to stay in their homes. Therefore, resistance was less salient in the following years.

Some differences between the response hierarchies of 1966 and 1977 existed also regarding *income problems* (see Table 1, column 2). There were three major decreases in the ranks. *Relying on others* (Item No. 8) dropped from the seventh to the eleventh rank, *accepting the situation as it is* from the seventh to the twelfth position. Other decreases referred to *depressive reactions* and *evasive reactions*. All these changes can be explained by the decreasing salience of income problems as pensions rose during the sixties and early seventies for the majority of our subjects. In the response hierarchy related to housing problems the response patterns with the highest ranks like *achievement related behaviour, adjustment to institutional aspects of the situation, identification with the aims and fates of children and grandchildren* and *the cultivation of social contacts* did not show large changes between 1966 and 1977.

The same was true for the dominant response classes which were adopted in coping with *family problems*. Aside from *achievement related behaviours* prosocial responses like the *cultivation of social contacts, identification with the aims and fates of children and grandchildren,* and *adjustment to the needs and habits of others* kept their positions among the highest ranking reactions. One of the greatest shifts from *Mp2* to *Mp6* in the *family* response hierarchy was related to *revision of expectancies* moving from the lower to medium ranks. Even larger was the change of *asking for help,* a response practically non-existing at *Mp2* and attaining a medium rank in 1977. Before attributing this shift to the increasing age of the sample, I should like to emphasize an increase of conflicts and problems in several of the families which may have initiated a greater readiness to ask for help, a response pattern formerly tabooed by some social norms. On the other hand, *aggressive assertiveness* as well as *resistance,* showing large drops, may have been replaced by help-seeking behaviours.

Regarding *health problems* the response hierarchies included four major shifts from *Mp2* to *Mp6*. *Revision of expectancies* and *asking for help* again became more salient in 1977. *Cultivating social contacts* and *passive reactions* received lower scores at that time. The first two shifts can be understood by the very old age of most of our subjects in 1977 and hence by increasing health problems. The lower ranks of *cultivating social contacts* and *passive reactions* may be due to a learning process by which quite a few of these women and men became aware of the inefficiency of these responses in coping with health problems. The highest ranking response patterns showed a high degree of consistency also in the health related response hierarchy which diverge from each other just by one rank in the 10 to 11 years between *Mp2* and *Mp6*. Also response patterns with medium ranks in these hierarchies remained in these positions over a ten year span. *Adjustment to the needs and habits of others* and *using chances* belonged to this group.

Summarizing, this analysis of response hierarchies from two measurement points of the BOLSA, 10 to 11 years distant from each other, it seems that there is consistency as well as change in the ranks of response patterns dealing with the same problem area (see Table 1, column 5). Consistency was prevailing in the high ranking response classes like *achievement related behaviour,* and *adjustment,* whereas change was observed in some of the responses holding medium and lower ranks. These changes were discussed within the context of the biological and social processes affiliated with the transition into old age. From this point of view they emphasize the impact of the *situation* on the selection of responses to life stress. The high degree of consistency in the ranks of the dominant response classes shows the role of the *person* in structuring human behaviour. Consistency in response to the same problem area, i.e., to similar situations is becoming evident, too, from column 5 of Table 1, which summarizes all significant shifts in the rank order of 17 response classes from *Mp*2 to *Mp*6. Twelve response patterns showed a total rank difference up to five ranks, four changed by 5 to 13 ranks, and only *revision of expectancies* moved up from lower to medium ranks in all problem areas.

Before looking out for trait names which might account for these long-term consistencies one should remember that each of the women and men who coped with problems in housing, income, health, and family was performing certain social roles in the selection of responses to conflict and stress. We shall try to clarify this very briefly regarding the consistencies in the response hierarchies regarding problems in the family. The prosocial behavioural patterns dominant in this context are aspects of the role of a nice grandparent. Therefore, the observed consistencies point to the adherence to a social role. Variations in the performance of these roles may be due to personality variables. This may be also true for those response patterns which are not in conformity with the social role of a good grandparent like *resistance, aggressive assertiveness,* or *evasive reaction.* The influence of social roles can be demonstrated also in the consistently low ranks of *passive reaction* in the response hierarchies related to life stress in housing, due to income or to conflicts and worries in the own family. Whereas in these situations active dealing with the problem is required by society this norm is less clear for health problems, at least in cohorts like those covered by the BOLSA.

RESPONSE HIERARCHIES RELATED TO DIFFERENT PROBLEM AREAS

The final step of our analysis is defined by the analysis of response hierarchies to *different* problem areas as assessed in 1966 and 1977.

From logical-deductive classifications of coping classes like that of Lazarus we might expect that in the response hierarchies related to housing or income problems, emotion-toned responses and reactions directed to the control of these emotions would have a lower rank compared with those of asking for information or of direct action. According to hypotheses as formulated by these authors the response patterns related to problems in the family and regarding health should be dominated by emotional reactions. Neither direct action nor searching for information should get higher ranks.

There were, however, many similarities in the response hierarchies related to *housing and income problems* at *Mp*2 as well as at *Mp*6 (see Table 1, columns 1 and 2). Ten out of 17 response patterns did not differ in a decisive way regarding their ranks in the response hierarchies. There were striking differences between these two hierarchies, too. *Adjustment to institutional aspects of the situation* ranked higher in dealing with income problems, whereas the same was true regarding *asking for help* in response to housing problems. Even more important is the fact that contrary to expectations there were high ranking emotional responses included in both response hierarchies, such as *relying on others, identification with the aims and fates of children and grandchildren,* or the *cultivation of social contacts.* Unexpected, too, were the very high, respectively, high ranks of *adjustment to the needs and habits of others* which do not include necessarily any direct action. In response to housing problems this kind of adjustment may consist of changes in the own needs or emotions if the problems are caused by the noise of the children of some very nice neighbours who very often are helpful. Another emotional response ranking especially high in dealing with income problems was labeled as *identification with the aims and fates of children and grandchildren.* It is a cognitively structured emotion verbalized in a classical way by one of our poorest subjects: "Well, I always had bad luck in my life, but my son, he made it!" Identifying with the (enhanced) success of a child or grandchild helps to stabilize the emotional state. It apparently is effective in both of these problem areas, but especially preferred in dealing with income problems.

Some of the items differed between these areas only at one of the two measurement points (see, e.g., *hope for change, the cultivation of social contacts,* or *evasive reactions*). The decreasing rank of *evasive reactions* in dealing with income problems at *Mp6* certainly points to some learning process by which the ineffectiveness of this response pattern was perceived, at least in this context. The same may be true for the decrease in the rank of *hope for change* in dealing with housing problems.

The main conclusion to be drawn from this comparative analysis of the response hierarchies as related to housing and income problems is the complexity of these hierarchies. Action as well as thought, emotion as well as cognitive control, are included. The similarities as well as the differences between these two response hierarchies point to a high degree of situation-specific selectivity in human coping with life stress.

This will become even more evident by our comparative analysis of the response hierarchies related to conflict and stress in ones' own *family* on the one hand, and to *health problems* on the other hand. Contrary to the expectations, 14 out of 17 response patterns differed in these two hierarchies by more than two ranks, at least at one of the two measurement points (see Table 1, columns 3 and 4). The largest differences were found in the ranks of adjustment to *institutional aspects of the situation* (No.2), which belongs to the leading responses in dealing with health problems whereas the same way of responding was far less preferred in coping with conflict and stress in the own family. On the other hand, *adjustment to the needs and habits of others* ranked very high in the family related hierarchy. It belonged to the medium or lower ranks in dealing with health problems. To solve conflicts and other problems this prosocial kind of adjustment certainly was preferable, whereas it would not help to cope with health problems. For taking preventive measures in health care adjustment to institutions like insurance agencies, doctors, and hospitals was needed, an adjustment including search for information and availability of information. The appeal to institutions like *Counseling Services for Family and Marriage* would have violated very strict social norms requiring to handle family matters confidentially.

Two other major differences between the family and health related response hierarchies became evident especially at *Mp6*. One of these refers to Item No. 6 *(Cultivating social contact)*. Whereas this response pattern was helpful in solving intra-family problems, it seemed not very efficient in dealing with health problems. The decreasing rank of this kind of response in the health related hierarchy points to a learning process. The second response pattern with a different rank for dealing with health problems compared to coping with family conflicts is labeled as *resistance*. Whereas the low value of this way of responding apparently is learnt during the 11 years from $Mp2$ to $Mp6$ in meeting family problems this is not true for the health related hierarchy. *Resistance* in this context consisted mainly in disregard of the doctor's advice for diet control, stopping to smoke, or other aspects of the life style. The high rank of this response pattern at both measurement points shows some problematic aspects of some of our subjects' habits.

Another example of the great divergencies between family- and health-related response hierarchies is Item 16, that is, *identification with the aims and fates of children and grandchildren*. Its consistently high rank in the family related hierarchy may be explained by the instrumentality of this kind of identification which creates a social climate helpful in solving intergenerational conflicts. The same response pattern is of little value in meeting health problems which is demonstrated by its lower rank at both measurement points.

Space does not permit a full description of the details of the other differences between the family- and health-related response hierarchies. Hopefully, these become evident from the columns 3 and 4 of Table 1, showing how situation-specific these elderly people selected their responses, thus disconfirming common stereotypes about a homogeneous depressive, evasive, or aggressive response pattern in the aged.

CONSISTENCY VERSUS CHANGE IN RESPONSE HIERARCHIES

The last three columns (5-7) of Table 1 can be useful in answering the question of whether the information of response hierarchies is more generally dependent on the person or the situation. For this evaluation we calculated any significant differences to the same problem area between $Mp2$ and $Mp6$ (column 5 of Table 1). Furthermore, we calculated any differences between the ranks of each of the 17 items in the four different response hierarchies for each of the two measurement points, provided this difference was larger than two ranks (columns 6 and 7). The significant differences between the ranks of the response patterns related to the same problem at $Mp2$ and at $Mp6$ add up to 100, whereas the significant rank differences of the 17 response classes in the four problem areas amount to 258 in 1966 and to 317 eleven years later. This confirms previous statements regarding a high degree of consistency in responding to similar situations over time and a high degree of situation-specific selectivity in dealing with different kinds of problems.

One should not forget, however, some special aspects in this research problem. There exist not only differences between persons in degree of consistency and selectivity of the response patterns

(Thomae, 1983), but also differences in the consistency and selectivity of different response classes. The 'universality' of *achievement related behaviour* as indicated by the high rank of this response pattern in all four problem areas may be due to its broad definition. On the other hand, this 'universality' reflects the high value of achievement in our society. The high ranks of *adjustment to the needs and habits of others* and *cultivating social contacts* in three of the four problem areas point to the important role of the social environment for dealing with major life stresses. This social environment has contributed to the development of the response patterns and their hierarchical order. As shown in our analysis of the rank orders of these socially integrative behaviours, this social environment is used by the person in coping with his or her problems. Consistency in dealing with similar problems over time and selectivity in choosing responses to different areas of problems demonstrates the active role of the person. This activity is aiming to meet the special challenges and tasks of the situation to be handled. The degree of the person – situation fit attained will be determined by the available behavioural and cognitive competencies (Mischel, 1973) and by state-dependent variables like activation, anxiety, or confidence. From this point of view the integration of process-centered and trait-centered approaches to the study of stress and coping is highly recommended.

CONCLUSION

The construct *response hierarchy* as developed in research on coping with stress highlighted the complexity and selectivity of human behaviour. From the substantial differences between response hierarchies as they related to different problem areas strong support was provided for theories emphasizing the situation-specific structuration of human behaviour such as that of Mischel (1973), and others. Adaptability and flexibility rather than consistency enables man to survive the challenges and stresses of everyday life.

The resources available for this aim would be exhausted very soon if consistency in the structuration of response hierarchies to similar situations would not supplement the flexibility principle. Consistencies in this hierarchy are dependent on their instrumentality, but also on social norms associated with some social roles and the degree in which these norms are perceived and evaluated.

Findings of this kind should be considered in the discussion between action theory and personality theory. For the prediction and understanding of human behaviour the study of goals, norms, and plans as emphasized by action theory is of great value. The differences in the structuration of response hierarchies directed toward different problem situations, such as defined by differences in spouse relationship by different social labels of medical diagnoses and different life areas such as housing, family, or health, supports the hypothesis that goals as well as norms determine the adjustment of persons in everyday life. The consistency of response hierarchies directed toward similar situations even over a longer time demonstrates an economic principle in the structuration of human behaviour by the application of

formerly 'reinforced' response patterns. It also points to some
motivational effects of these learning processes which make some
response classes more attractive than others. Action theory suggests
an equal probability of any response class at any choice point being
elicited - provided that this way of responding corresponds with the
goals, norms, and plans of an individual in his/her social setting. The
consistency of *resistance* in dealing with health problems as shown in
the BOLSA gives an example for some irrational aspects of human
behaviour which sometimes are overlooked by modern action or
cognitive theorists. Because *resistance* as a response to health
problems consists mainly in resistance to doctor's advice to change the
own life style, the impact of motivation and habits is highly stressed.
We expect that younger samples, if followed long enough, will show
similar consistencies.

It would be wrong to conclude from these remarks that the
classification of response patterns into 'rational' and 'irrational' ones
would be an adequate approach for a theory of personality based on
the study of consistency and flexibility of response hierarchies.

A point to be considered, however, refers to the "functional
autonomy" (Allport, 1937) of acquired response classes and some of
their hierarchical structures the study of which might contribute to
the progress of action theory, as well as of personality theory.

REFERENCES

Allport, G.W. (1937). *Personality: A psychological interpretation*. New
    York: Holt.
Diehl, M. (1984). *Die Krebsdiagnose als kritisches Lebensereignis.
    Formen der Auseinandersetzung mit einer lebensbedrohlichen
    Erkrankung* [The diagnosis 'cancer' as a critical life event. Ways of
    coping with a lethal disease]. Unpublished diploma thesis,
    Department of Psychology, University of Bonn, Bonn, FRG.
Fester-Waltzing, H. (1983). *Scheidung - eine psychologische Analyse*
    [Divorce - a psychological analysis]. Frankfurt/M.: Lang.
Folkman, S., & Lazarus, R.S. (1980). An analysis of coping in a
    middle-aged community sample. *Journal of Health and Social
    Behavior, 21*, 219-239.
Haan, N. (1977). *Coping and defending. Processes of self -
    environment organization*. New York: Academic Press.
Hambitzer, M. (1962). *Schicksalsbewältigung und Daseinsermöglichung
    bei Körperbehinderten* [Psychological control and ways of coping in
    handicapped persons]. Bonn: Bouvier.
Hull, C.L. (1952). *A behavior system*. New Haven: Yale University
    Press.
Kipnowski, A. (1980). *Formen der Daseinsermöglichung bei chronischer
    Krankheit. Eine Untersuchung an erwachsenen Hämophilen* [Ways of
    coping in chronic disease. A study of adult hemophiliac patients].
    Unpublished doctoral dissertation, University of Bonn, Bonn, FRG.
Laux. L., & Vossel, G. (1982). Paradigms in stress research:
    Laboratory versus field and traits versus processes. In. L.

Goldberger & S. Breznitz (Eds.), *Handbook of stress: Theoretical and clinical aspects*. New York: The Free Press.

Lazarus, R.S., & Launier, R. (1980). Stress-related transactions between person and environment. In L.A. Pervin & M. Lewis (Eds.), *Perspectives in interactional psychology* (pp. 287-327). New York: Plenum Press,

Lehr, U. (1969). *Frau und Beruf. Eine psychologische Analyse der weiblichen Berufsrolle* [Woman and job. A psychological analysis of the female role]. Frankfurt/M.: Athenaeum.

Mason, J.W. (1975). Emotion as reflected in patterns of endocrine integration. In L. Levi (Ed.), *Emotions - their parameters and measurement*. New York: Raven Press.

Mischel, W. (1973). Toward a cognitive social learning reconceptualization of personality. *Psychological Review, 80,* 252-283.

Murray, H.A. (1938). *Explorations in personality*. Cambridge, MA: Harvard University Press.

Pearlin, L., & Schooler, C. (1978). The structure of coping. *Journal of Health and Social Behavior, 19,* 2-21.

Rosenman, R.H. (1974). The role of behavior patterns and neurogenic factors in the pathogenesis of coronary heart disease. In R.S. Eliot (Ed.), *Stress and the heart* (pp. 123-141). New York: Futura.

Scharnweber, H.A. (1983). *Formen der Auseinandersetzung von Nierenpatienten mit der Dialyse* [Ways of coping with dialysis in patients with a renal disease]. Unpublished diploma thesis. Department of Psychology, University of Bonn, Bonn, FRG.

Schaub, S. (1984). *Bewältigungsstrategied bei schizophrenen Patienten* [Strategies of coping in schizophrenic patients]. Unpublished diploma thesis. Department of Psychology, University of Bonn, Bonn, FRG.

Shanan, J. (1983). *Beyond zenith. The role of personality and cultural background in patterns of transition from middle to later adulthood*. Final research report to the Volkswagen Foundation. Department of Psychology, Hadassah University, Jerusalem, Israel.

Stocksmeier, U. (1976). *Medizinisch - psychologische Aspekte koronarer Herzkrankheit* [Medical-psychological aspects in coronary heart disease]. Unpublished medical Habilitation Thesis. University of Mainz, Mainz, FRG.

Thomae, H. (1953). Über Daseinstechniken sozial auffälliger Jugendlicher [Coping patterns in maladjusted youth]. *Psychologische Forschung, 24,* 11-33.

Thomae, H. (1968). *Das Individuum und seine Welt. Eine Persönlichkeitstheorie* [The individual and his world. A theory of personality]. Göttingen: Verlag für Psychologie Dr. Hogrefe.

Thomae, H. (Ed.) (1976). *Patterns of aging. Findings of the Bonn Longitudinal Study of Aging*. Basel, New York: Karger.

Thomae, H. (1983). *Alternsstile und Alternsschicksale. Ein Beitrag zur differentiellen Gerontologie* [Life styles of elderly persons and life events. A contribution to differential gerontology]. Bern: Huber.

Thomae, H. (1984). Reaktionen auf gesundheitliche Belastung im mittleren und höheren Erwachsenenalter [Reactions to health problems in middle and old age]. *Zeitschrift für Gerontologie, 17,* 186-197.

Vaillant, G.E. (1977). *Adaptation to life*. Boston: Little, Brown and
    Company.
Van De Loo, J. (1983). *Bewältigungsstrategien bei Dialysepatienten*
    [Strategies of coping in dialysis-patients]. Unpublished diploma
    thesis, Department of Psychology, University of Bonn, Bonn, FRG.

PRAGMATICS OF UTTERANCES ABOUT PERSONALITY:
EVERYDAY LIFE SCENARIOS

Boele De Raad

University of Groningen
The Netherlands

This chapter aims at a taxonomy of conversations in which conceptions of personality come into being and are verbally expressed. These conversations pertain to two-turn interactions of a short duration, initiated by a speaker who makes an utterance about personality, and appropriately terminated by an addressee. The specific concern is how to account systematically for the ways speakers and addressees pragmatically deal with the expressed conceptions.

Personality in Everyday Life

The predicate *everyday* in the title of this text is used to indicate interactions in ordinary life. Such interactions provide a basis for socialization (Cicourel, 1978). According to Berger and Luckmann (1966) the primary feature of this process is the acquisition of "conceptual machineries" by which people make plausible the world around them and their experiences in it. Part of this process is the development of a common set of understandings of the social meanings of peoples' behaviours. Everyday interactions can thus be considered as the stage where conceptions about people come into being, are maintained, and are changed in an orderly manner, especially with respect to these peoples' personality or character.

The approach to personality presented here, partly follows the *constructivist position* advocated by Hampson (1982, 1984). This position holds that personality is found in the social process that takes place *between* individuals, and not, as is traditionally assumed, *within* individuals. Personality, in this view, is conceived of as a social artifact, namely as a set of categories for making sense of the variety of impressions of peoples' behaviours (Smid, 1984). The usual semantic categories for summarizing and communicating these meanings are traits. For example, instead of saying that a person gives money to charity, remits someone a debt, and manages matters for someone else, we say that this person is *generous* (Buss & Craik, 1983; Hampson, 1984). Although *generosity*, in this context, can be used for descriptive purposes, it has not the status of an explanation (Kouwer, 1973). Its only status is that of a category located in a social process between individuals, from which process the category draws its meaning. To study personality from the constructivist point of view therefore means studying the process of categorizing the meanings of behaviours at the level of everyday interaction.

If, however, in an everyday situation someone actually expresses the utterance "this person is generous", it is not at all clear from the expression itself what the purpose of the speaker is. Apart from abstract descriptive purposes, the speaker might on the basis of the single observation that that person had once remitted a debt to him or her, for instance, suggest to an addressee to ask that person to become a supporter of some union. Or, once having knowledge of the kind of behaviours the category *generous* refers to, a speaker might, in order to get some money from the partner, appeal to a sense of generosity by calling this person generous. And the speaker might do so without any previous observation of that person's behaviour at all. Everyday interactions are dominated by such pragmatic motives (Berger & Luckmann, 1966).

So, the meanings that people construct for other persons' personalities, whether these meanings are based on observations or not, may be a function of the purposes these people have in the ongoing interaction (Cantor, 1981; Smid, 1984).

Pragmatics

The pragmatics of utterances about personality cannot simply be understood from their content. The pragmatics can only be understood contextually, through a recourse to the relation between the content of the utterances and the *intentions* of the communicators. The intentions, and particularly the enactments of the intentions, have implications for the nature of the relationship between the communicators (Watzlawick, Beavin, & Jackson, 1967).

Part of the categorization of meanings involves the processing of the ways the categories are used, viz., their pragmatics. A prominent place in the social stock of knowledge that is developed in the social process, is accordingly occupied by such pragmatic knowledge. This kind of knowledge has not yet been a major topic of research. The constructivist position should be extended to encompass a specific account of the pragmatic aspects of the social process referred to above. This extension means that the study of how the meaning of a personality category such as *generosity* is negotiated between individuals, should also incorporate the intentions and actions of these individuals, as well as those features of the situational context that are important for the understanding of these intentions and actions.

Person-talk

The present research aims at a taxonomy of conversations in which both the utterances about personality and the intentions of the speakers, as well as the actions performed by the involved individuals, are accounted for.

Although different types of taxonomies have already been developed, both for personality-type categories (John, Goldberg, & Angleitner, 1984) and for situations (Van Heck, 1984), not much is yet known about the way personality construction is contingent upon the pragmatics of everyday interactions. The present research is concentrated on one of the most frequent activities in everyday life, namely "talk" (Douglas, 1971), particularly talk about persons, or person-talk. The analysis of talk is pre-eminently suited for studying the pragmatic impact of personality-type categories (Cicourel, 1978).

To describe talk activities with emphasis on pragmatics is to describe what Austin (1962) called "speech acts" (Searle, 1969). The speech-act theory aims to bring talk events under the rubric of a general theory of action, and it provides a coherent description of some important parameters of person-talk situations. Of particular interest in the present context is Searle's (1969) distinction between the so-called "illocutionary acts" and "propositional acts". Illocutionary acts are the acts performed *in* saying something, such as *seducing* the addressee (to give money), or *asserting* the truth of what is said, for example, of the utterance "You are generous". Which illocutionary act is performed may be inferred from word-order, intonation, gesture, etc. (Watzlawick et al., 1967). Propositional acts represent the content of talk, i.e., the utterances made about persons. A propositional act involves *reference* and *predication*. Reference means that a speaker refers to a specific person (e.g., You). Predication means that the speaker assigns something, viz., a predicate, to this person (e.g., "generosity").

Special attention should be given to the reference part of propositions. De Raad (1984) showed that it makes much difference to the talk-situation whether the talking is about the speaker (I am....), about the addressee (You are....), or about a third party (He/She is....). These three forms are called first-person-, second-person-, and third-person-utterances, respectively. It can be argued that these three person-forms are not learned simply to refer to the persons involved, but that they are learned as a system involving different schemes for action.

First-person utterances, for instance, usually have a managerial character. They are used to create an atmosphere of intimacy (Cozby, 1973), to restore a threatened identity (Hewitt & Stokes, 1975; Scott & Lyman, 1968), or to gain information or behavioural compliance from another by creating a false sense of frankness or intimacy (Miller & Steinberg, 1975). They are also used to present and stage a social self for inspection and acceptance by the co-actors (Goffman, 1959).

Second-person utterances usually imply a direct break into the addressee's concept of being an *agent* of behaviour, and they are often used to evoke a response from the addressee, such as perseverance, doing something, or a change of behaviour, attitude, feeling, or opinion (Abelson & Miller, 1967).

The use of third-person utterances usually implies a situation in which people talk about a person who is not present at the moment of talk, such as in gossip (Fine & Rosnow, 1978). This kind of utterances may serve as a device for indicating group-distinctiveness with respect to this third person (Elias & Scotson, 1965).

To conclude, the study of personality boils down to the study of person-talk in everyday life, in which the person-form, the predicate, the intention, the reactions, and the acts performed by the speaker and the addressee deserve separate attention. With respect to the relatedness of these different aspects, person-form is expected to fulfil a structuring function.

The Organization of Person-talk

Everyday talk concerns free-floating interactions, progressing through incomplete and dangling sentences, allusions, digressions, sentence fragments, etc. The talking is usually only loosely interconnected to surrounding events. This is not to say that such talk lacks an organization. On the contrary, people usually tacitly adhere to the implicit knowledge, distilled in the course of everyday interaction. The sediment of this knowledge operates as taken-for-granted and trustworthy recipes for handling things and people. The maintenance of this tacit knowledge is expressed by Grice's (1975) conversational rule: "Make your conversational contribution such as required, at the stage at which it occurs, by the accepted purpose or direction of talk exchange in which you are engaged". Grice named this rule the *cooperative principle*. Accordingly, verbal exchanges should not be considered as series of disconnected remarks, but as organized sequences of utterances achieved through the cooperation of the involved parties. The present research is restricted to single action-reaction sequences in person-talk situations (Stech, 1979).

Aiming at a taxonomy of person-talk situations thus implies a search for recurring patterns of such sequences in person-talk, which is tantamount to searching for *scenarios* (Kouwer, 1973). A scenario is defined here as a sequence of scenes in which the scenes represent the respective parties' enactments. These enactments are referred to as "moves" (Goffman, 1976; Grimshaw, 1982), interactional units in which cues of intention, content, and context are incorporated into a single act such as seducing, asserting, challenging, or defending. The ultimate goal is a set of scenarios in which the emergence of personality plays a prominant role. In accordance with the amplified constructivist position personality-type categories can then be properly located in the social process between persons. The expected result will be descriptions of the conversational structure of, for instance, "generosity". Such scenarios can be used as key situations for the understanding of (the emergence of) different kinds of personalities (Kouwer, 1973).

Some Examples

How do concrete instances of person-talk situations look like? Below, three examples are given from a stock of 244 descriptions of such situations. These descriptions had been collected in an earlier study by means of a questionnaire (De Raad, 1984, 1985). Subjects had been asked to reconstruct one person-talk situation that had occurred in the last one or two days, and in which they had themselves been involved. Some subjects had refused to fill out the questionnaire. The reasons they provided for their refusal are attended to in the discussion section. About half of the subjects were students, mainly from the departments of social sciences. The other half were local citizens representing a broad variation of occupations. For both of these groups there were about the same number of females and males. The subjects had made literal reports about the propositional acts that were performed, and they had produced an objective account of the context, the intention of the speaker, and the reaction by the addressee to the utterance. The three examples are:

After a divorce a man had to move out of his house under a
judicial sentence. He refused. Therefore, his former wife had
asked her son-in-law to fit the doors with new locks. The man
reproached his son-in-law with evicting him from "his" house.
The son-in-law then made the (person-) utterance: "You are a
fool, a big fool". His intention was to have some peace between
the divorced couple. The man, who was very upset, tormentedly
reacted by saying: "You just let yourself deceive and belie by
your mother-in-law".

A young woman told her boy-friend about her relationship to her
sister and said: "I have a sense of inferiority with respect to my
sister". The boy hardly reacted, just intimated to her that he
had heard the utterance.

Two psychologists were talking about people they had met at a
party. With respect to one of these people the speaker said:
"That woman has a tongue in her head. She has got guts". The
addressee reacted by saying: "I agree with you, but she is not
always nice to everybody.

The propositional acts, i.e., utterances about personality, in the
examples, like "You are a fool, a big fool" or "I have a sense of
inferiority ..." are embedded in strips of activity which can be
conceived of as slices from the flow of ongoing interaction. These
propositional acts are considered as the most elementary expressions of
conceptions about personality.
    Common to all of the 244 descriptions is that they are characterized
by a propositional act containing a particular person-form and a
predicate, an intention (for space-saving purposes only in the first
example the intention of the speaker is given), a reaction by the
addressee, and a description of the situational context.

Person-talk Scenarios

Since the actions performed by the speaker and the addressee, or
their respective moves, occur chronologically, the first part of such a
sequence of moves may establish a *conditional relevance* for anything
that occurs in the slot that follows (Sacks, 1973).
    The way in which the involved parties act out their respective
moves is guided by the semantic knowledge of the world and the
pragmatic knowledge of roles with which they are equipped. This
knowledge is supposed to be sedimented into *scripts*, i.e., recipes by
which the parties can carry out reciprocal activities on that world
(Goffman, 1959; Harré, 1972; Schank & Abelson, 1977). A person-talk
situation is structured by the co-enactment of the involved parties'
scripts. The term "scenario" is used here for the description of this
joint production.
    An important question to be answered in this respect is whether
there is a certain compulsion for a script to be enacted. According to
Abelson (1980), script entry is contingent upon satisfaction of an
action rule attached to the script representation. It is argued here
that the performing of propositional acts takes place if a breach of

expectations is experienced. It appeared that the reported propositional acts refer almost without exception (99 %) to how the speaker copes with his experiences. These experiences are of different kinds. They concern untoward behaviour of self or others, emotional piques (irritation), feelings of pleasure, unusual behaviours or impressions, being disappointed, being offended, deviance, etc. These are all situations involving experiences apparently disturbing the involved parties' conceptions of smoothly progressing events. More generally, such experiences disrupt the tacitly maintained meanings with respect to these conceptions. The propositional acts in this respect can be said to fulfil a restoration function, involving aiming at a change or assurance of feelings, attitude, behaviour, thoughts, opinions of self or other. Thus, when during a conversation, communication or social propriety suddenly breaks down, pointed effort will likely follow to set matters right. This presupposes a shared script that may be named the *cooperation script*. Since this script may involve different variants which have the same "redressive" function, the cooperation-script is best conceived of as a meta-script, and the sub-categories can be called *redressive scripts*.

The enactment of the script provides the apparently beset addressee an opportunity to terminate the enacted episode in a complementary way. Although this is often the case, it also often happens that the addressee rejects the definition of the situation offered by the speaker. If this is the case, assertions can be followed by direct denials, question by questioning the questioner, accusation by counteraccusation, disparagements by insults, threats by taunting their realization, and so on. Such uncalled-for actions by the addressee are script-enactments that should be considered in their own right. Maybe, as seems often to be the case in person-talk, the speaker's action itself is seen as untoward with respect to the cooperation-rules by the addressee, and evokes a redressive script to match. Thus, for the involved parties the enactment of scripts may or may not result in interaction that is in accordance with the *cooperation script*.

METHOD AND RESULTS

How can the aim of person-talk scenarios be achieved? First, the features characterizing the speaker's move in the interaction on the one hand, and on the other the features characterizing the addressee's move, should be extracted from the 244 person-talk situations and be properly described. Second, the contiguities between the two sets of features should be investigated.

To this end, each of the propositional acts was coded for first-, second-, or third-person form (in fact, there were about 80 of each). Both the predicates and the intentions, as well as the reactions were separately described and judged on certain properties. This resulted in sets of variables for each of these four features. Each person-talk situation was thus characterized in terms of four sets of variables.

In addition, information was obtained about the actions performed by both the speaker and the addressee. What people do when they talk about persons is usually not articulated at the moment of talk. In order to be able to describe such acts, a specific vocabulary was needed. Such a vocabulary has been developed out of the semantic field of language that is most apt for this goal, namely the domain of verbs (see De Raad, 1985). For each situation, the action performed by the speaker and the action performed by the addressee was accordingly described by a set of verbs. This resulted in two more sets of variables, namely action variables describing the speakers' moves in the interaction, and action variables describing the addressees' moves.

In sum, the speaker's move was characterized by four sets of variables, namely variables describing person-form, predicate, intention, and action. And the addressee's move was characterized by variables describing the reaction and the action.

In order to find patterns of person-talk sequences, the relationships are investigated between the speaker-variables and the addressee-variables. This was done by means of canonical correlation analysis.

Predicates, Intentions, and Reactions

Space limitations preclude a detailed account of the judgement procedures pertaining to predicate, intention, and reaction. This account can be found in De Raad (1984). The essential characteristics of the involved procedures and the pertaining results are briefly presented below.

The predicates: As was argued earlier, everyday person-talk can be said to constitute an important source for the emergence of conceptions about people (see also John et al., 1984). De Raad (1985) showed that utterances about persons differ in the amount of information they convey about the personalities of these persons. In order to investigate the extent to which such utterances are *descriptive* of (the differences between) the object-persons' personalities, it is necessary to use a system that provides the means to categorize the information in the utterances. A system of personality descriptive adjectives seems to be the most appropriate one to meet this requirement. In the present research, the so-called Standard Personality Adjective List (Hofstee, Brokken, & Land, 1981) was used, which represents the basic meaning dimensions of the (Dutch) language of personality. This list consists of seven dimensions such as (Un)culture, (In)stability, and Agreeableness (see Table 5). These dimensions comprise small groups of adjectives, for instance, dutiful, punctual, accurate.

For each of the 244 predicates, judges were asked to rate, with respect to the given groups of adjectives, what the speaker expressed of the object-person referred to in the propositional act, *given* the propositional act, and *given* the description of the context. In fact, the judges were provided with cards presenting all the information that preceded the reaction, and that was, in principle, accessible for the addressee. This procedure resulted in a 244 x 7 matrix, which was used as input in the canonical correlation analysis.

The intentions of the speakers: The intentions were internally structured on the basis of similarity judgements between the 244 intention-descriptions. The result of these similarity judgements was a matrix of associations between the 244 intentions. This matrix was reduced by means of factor-analysis, yielding 13 useful intention factors interpreted as, for example, *To utter own feelings, To make somebody conscious of something,* or *To speak unfavorably about a person.* The 13 factor labels are given in Table 5. The differences between the intentions are expresses by their loadings on each of the factors. This matrix of loadings (244 x 13) was used for the canonical correlations analysis.

The reactions by the addressees: For reactions exactly the same procedure was followed as in the case of intentions. The 244 reaction-descriptions were judged on their similarity. The resulting association matrix was factor-analyzed, yielding 11 useful factors such as *Assent to, Emotional rejection,* or *Trying to understand* (For reasons to be explained later, these 11 factor labels are not listed here (see also De Raad, 1984, 1985).

Actions

The acts performed by the speaker and by the addressee were described by means of an instrument for rating social acts. The major objective underlying the construction of this instrument was a pragmatic one. The instrument should provide a standard vocabulary by which the meanings of the activities performed in a social situation can be appropriately expressed. The instrument was constructed on the basis of about 1000 verbs, selected from a Dutch dictionary. This set of verbs may be conceived of as representing most of the meanings that can be attached to interpersonal activities (De Raad, 1985). The instrument consists of 37 scales. Each of these scales comprises two or three verbs (See Table 1).

The rating task was performed by 60 paid subjects, mainly from the departments of social sciences. The task consisted of two parts. In the first part the subjects were asked to describe the act performed by the *speaker, given* the context of the propositional act. This rating task was attended with the instruction to indicate, for each of the 37 verb-scales, whether the pertaining groups of two or three verbs did apply, according to their *common meaning,* to what the speaker was doing in performing the propositional act. The scales had four points anchored by *Does not apply* (1) and *Does apply* (4). In the second part the same subjects were asked, *given* both the context description and the propositional act performed by the speaker, to describe the act (reaction) performed by the *addressee,* using the same groups of verbs.

This prodecure resulted into two matrices of 244 by 37 (verb-scales), the first representing the speakers' acts and the second representing the addressees' acts.

TABLE 1: *Rating scales for social actions**

1 whine, sulk, complain	18 pass over, ignore, exclude
2 confide, confess, have a good cry	19 judge, name, attribute
	20 give way, control o.s., acquiesce
3 impose, summon, demand	21 offer, provide, give
4 associate with a p., contract, consort with a p.	22 bring to reason, awake, disenchant
	23 cajole, coax, flirt
5 repair, indemnify, redeem	24 disapprove, criticize, deny
6 pretend (act), fib, joke	25 scold, insult, blame
7 plot, contrive, scheme	26 play a p. a nasty trick, victimize, betray
8 incite, rouse. stimulate	
9 meet, welcome, make acquaintance	27 take under protection, defend, support
10 giggle, snigger, chatter	28 argue, propagate, give opinion
11 keep aloof, take distance withdraw	29 hurt, attack, torture
	30 challenge, tempt a p.
12 excuse, approve, smooth over	31 teach, explain, point out
13 keep watch, look after, observe	32 fondle, coddle, tickle
	33 bear the brunt, attempt, drudge
14 compete, stand up to a p.	34 trumpet forth, pose, boast
15 extol, praise, applaud	35 obscure, distort, conceal
16 tolerate, accept, permit	36 chatter, twaddle, have a chat
17 influence, persuade, insist	37 inquire after, consult, sound a p.

*) Translation by the author
"p." is the abbreviation of "person"

Speaker's Actions: Factor-analysis

The matrix comprising the speaker's actions was factor-analyzed by means of Principal Components Analysis. This yielded 10 factors with eigenvalues > 1. These factors, explaining 65 percent of the variance, were rotated according to Varimax. The factors are shown in Table 2. Each factor is represented by the two or three highest loading variables, and headed by a summary label.

Adressee's Actions: Factor analysis

For the addressee's actions a different procedure was followed. There were two sets of variables that both describe the addressee's moves in the interaction, namely the 11 reaction variables discussed earlier and the 37 verb variables. Both the similarity judgements in the earlier task on which the 11 reaction variables were based and the ratings of the acts by means of the verbs, were performed on the basis of the same objects, namely the 244 reaction descriptions. The reaction-variables and the act-ratings were therefore put together, and were in combination subjected to factor analysis. Principal Components Analysis performed on the correlations between the pertaining 48 variables yielded 13 factors with eigenvalues > 1. These factors explained 69 percent of the variance. The varimax-rotated factors in

TABLE 2: *Factors of speakers' actions in terms of verbs*

I "Aggressiveness" (12.5)		VI "Control" (5.3)	
24 disapprove, criticize, deny	89	13 keep watch, look after,	
25 scold, insult, blame	88	observe	59
29 hurt, attack, torture	83	19 judge, name, attribute	59
		15 extol, praise, applaud	54
II "Incitement" (9.9)			
17 influence, persuade, insist	87	VII "Edification" (4.9)	
8 incite, rouse, stimulate	86	31 teach, explain, point out	79
3 impose, summon, demand	77	28 argue, propagate, give	
		opinion	79
III "Aloofness" (7.3)		2 confide, confess, have	
11 keep aloof, take distance,		a good cry	41
withdraw	75		
20 give way, control o.s.,		VIII "Conspiracy" (4.7)	
acquiesce	73	7 plot, contrive, scheme	76
35 obscure, distort, conceal	66	4 associate with a p.,	
		contract, consort with a p.	54
IV "Cajolery" (6.8)			
32 fondle, coddle, tickle	77	IX "Account" (4.0)	
23 cajole, coax, flirt	75	5 repair, indemnify, redeem	61
9 meet, welcome, make		33 bear the brunt, attempt,	
acquaintance	72	drudge	55
		12 excuse, approve, smooth over	48
V "Entertainment" (6.2)			
10 giggle, snigger, chatter	86	X "Gregariousness" (3.6)	
6 pretend (act), fib, joke	86	34 trumpet forth, pose, boast	85
30 challenge, tempt a.p.	48	36 chatter, twaddle, have	
		a chat	44

The numbers behind the factor-labels indicate the amounts of variance.
The numbers before the verb-groups refer to the codings in Table 1.
The numbers behind the variables are the loadings; decimal points are
omitted.

Table 3 are represented by the highest loading variables, and are
headed by a proper label.

To many of the reaction-forms presented in Table 3 special
importance has been attached in the literature. Sarason, Levine,
Basham, & Sarason (1983), for instance, discussed the meaning of
"Social Support", and defined it as "the existence or availability of
people on whom we can rely, people who let us know that they care
about, value, and love us". These authors maintain that social support
contributes to positive adjustment, and that it provides a buffer
against the effects of stress. The Factors V (Love), VI (Empathy), IX
(Support) and, maybe, II (Incitement), might also perform this
function (see also Davis, 1983).

Fink and Walker (1977) discussed the function of humorous

TABLE 3: *Factors of addressees' actions in terms of reactions and verbs*

I "Rejection" (11.1)			
25 scold, insult, blame	87	19 judge, name, attribute	70
29 hurt, attack, torture	84	28 argue, propagate, give	
(emotional rejection)	80	opinion	57

II "Incitement" (6.1)		VIII "Agreement" (4.8)	
17 influence, persuade, insist	82	7 plot, contrive, scheme	76
3 impose, summon, demand	80	4 associate with a p.,	
8 incite, rouse, stimulate	77	contract, consort with a p.	70
		(assent to)	68

III "Entertainment" (5.8)			
10 giggle, snigger, chatter	87	IX "Restoration" (4.7)	
6 pretend (act), fib, joke	85	5 repair, indemnify, redeem	71
(reaction of relief)	76	12 excuse, approve, smooth over	66
		33 bear the brunt, attempt,	
		drudge	54

IV "Aloofness" (5.7.)			
11 keep aloof, take distance,		X "Self-justification" (4.4.)	
withdraw	78		
35 obscure, distort, conceal	74	2 confide, confess, have	
(avoidance or denial,		a good cry	79
hardly any reaction)	68	(explaining, excusing, jus-	
		tifying personal feelings,	
V "Love" (5.6)		attitude, or behavior)	78
32 fondle, coddle, tickle	77		
15 extol, praise, applaud	66	XI "Support" (4.7)	
(more or less enthousiastic		(closing a conversation with	
approval)	62	a conclusion or an	
		incitement)	65
VI "Empathy" (5.4)		21 offer, provide, give	62
37 inquire after, consult,		27 take under protection,	
sound a p.	87	defend, support	45
(asking for information			
sympathetically)	85	XII "Gregariousness" (3.5.)	
13 keep watch, look after,		34 trumpet forth, pose, boast	66
observe	42	9 meet, welcome, make	
		acquaintance	64
VII "Agreement and		36 chatter, twaddle, have	
Extension (4.9)		a chat	58
(assent to, and giving or			
adding an opinion)	76	XIII "Surprise" (2.8)	
		(expression of surprise)	83

The expressions between brackets are reaction variables.

responses such as irony, banter, joking, and laughter, in the maintenance of interpersonal communication systems in the face of a break of such systems. In the present context, Factor III (Entertainment) might perform such a function.

Abelson and Miller (1967) mentioned the effect of insulting an addressee. The reaction of an addressee will be negative, not only in terms of his or her feelings towards the speaker but also in terms of attitude change. Factor I (Rejection) might also imply such an incidental attitude change.

Hewitt and Stokes (1975) and Scott and Lyman (1968) have discussed the intricacies involved in interrogating people for their undue acts. Particularly the Factors IX (Restoration) and X (Self-justification) seem good representatives of what these authors called forms of "account".

Action-Reaction Contiguities: Canonical Correlation Analysis

In order to investigate the contiguities between the speakers' moves on the one hand, and the addressees' moves on the other, a canonical correlation analysis was performed.

In canonical correlation analysis a process of maximizing the correlation between linear functions from two sets of variables takes place. The linear functions that yield the maximum correlations are the canonical variates. Variates formed from successive roots are orthogonal to the previous variates. The canonical correlations (Rc) are Pearson Product-Moment correlations between pairs of canonical variates.

In the present application of this analysis the three person-forms, the predicates, the intentions, and the speakers' actions comprised the first set of variables (Set 1). The 13 factors for the addressees' actions comprised the second set of variables (Set 2). For the intentions the factor-loading matrix was used. For the predicates the pertaining matrix of scale-scores was used. For both the speakers' actions and the addressees' actions the factor-scores matrix was used. The result of the analysis was 13 pairs of canonical variates. Bartlett's (1941) Chi-square was used to test the significance of the canonical correlations. The first six pairs of canonical variates had significant correlations and were therefore considered for further investigation (Table 4).

TABLE 4: *Canonical correlation analysis and redundancy analysis on person-form, predicate, intention, speakers' actions, and addressees' actions*

Roots	Rc	Chi-square	df.	p	Redundancy Set 1	Set 2
1	.81	1123.00	416	.000	.048	.050
2	.77	891.02	372	.000	.038	.046
3	.75	690.83	330	.000	.031	.043
4	.71	505.91	290	.000	.023	.039
5	.55	354.08	252	.000	.013	.024
6	.54	273.91	216	.004	.011	.022
				Total	.164	.224

Rc = Canonical Correlation

The square of the Rc indicates the amount of variance shared by a pair of *variates*. The interpretation of this Rc depends on the importance of the respective variates as regards the extent to which they summarize amounts of information in the two sets of variables. Stewart and Love (1968) developed the index of *redundancy* which combines the measure of the explained variance shared by the variates with a measure of importance of the respective variates within their sets. The index indicates the amount of variance in the Set 1 variables explained by a canonical variate in the Set 2 variables, and vice versa; the index is asymmetric. In Table 4 these redundancies are presented. For instance, the redundancy for the first root of the Set 1 variables is .048. This means that the first variate of the Set 1 variables accounts for 4.8 percent of the total variance of the Set 2 variables. The total redundancy for Set 1, given Set 2, is 16 percent. The total redundancy for Set 2, given Set 1, is 22 percent.

For the interpretation of the canonical variates, canonical component loadings were computed (Meredith, 1964). To that end, the correlations were computed between the canonical variates per set and the individual variables within that set (Timm, 1975). These correlations indicate the contribution of each variable to the *compiled* canonical variate. The combined matrix of loadings for person-form, predicate, intention, speaker's action, and addressee's action was rotated according to Varimax (Table 5).

Each of the canonical variates may describe a variant of person-talk scenarios. The *first* variate is characterized by second-person utterances that refer to the addressee as being aggressive and uncultural, by intentions that are addressee-directed, by actions described as aggressiveness and incitement, and by reactions involving rejection and restoration. The pattern may be typified by *negative persuasion*.

The *second* variate is characterized by third-person utterances, referring to someone being uncultural and conservative, by intentions that involve an exchange of negative information about this third person, by actions described by conspiracy, and by reactions that involve assent on the part of the addressee. This variate may be typified as *gossip*.

The *third* variate is characterized by first-person-utterances in which speakers consider themselves as being aggressive or irritated, conscientious, and unstable, by intentions that involve the speakers' expressions of feelings, by actions that indicate a lack of control, and by reactions that involve support and incitement. This variate may be typified by the *submission-dominance* relationship.

The *fourth* variate is characterized by predicates referring to people as uncultural and agreeable, by intentions that involve smoothing over one's own behaviour, by actions that are described as entertainment, and by reactions that are also described as entertainment. This variate is, accordingly, typified as *entertainment*.

The *fifth* variate is characterized by first-person utterances in which speakers consider themselves as unstable, by intentions that involve the speakers' views of self, by actions that are described by edification and account, and by reactions that involve empathy. Prototypical for these qualities is the "therapy-situation".

The *sixth* variate involves utterances in which persons are described as agreeable, actions that indicate cajolery and

B. De Raad

TABLE 5: *Canonical structure for person-form, predicate, intention, speakers' actions, and addressees' actions (varimax solution)*

	Variates					
SET 1	1	2	3	4	5	6
Person-form						
first person	-30	-09	68	03	25	01
second person	36	-65	-26	12	-31	16
third person*	-08	74	-42	-15	06	-16
Predicates (Adjective Scales)						
1 (Un)culture	38	30	-10	22	-14	-12
2 (In)stability	04	00	20	-10	26	-12
3 Agreeableness	-50	-27	-22	22	03	35
4 Aggression (Irritation)	56	15	24	-02	-08	-15
5 Conscientiousness	-16	-07	22	-33	-02	00
6 Introversion	-09	-08	10	-26	14	-10
7 Conservatism	12	26	-04	17	-15	-03
Intentions						
1 to utter own feelings	-28	-10	27	-13	38	-17
2 speaker has no specific intention	-23	17	-12	12	-07	17
3 to make somebody conscious	41	-37	-23	05	-02	-02
4 to encourage or to ease a person	-05	-39	04	-09	-15	17
5 to get somebody do something	37	-01	-02	-07	-12	-12
6 to make clear how one sees oneself	-23	-06	15	02	33	03
7 to speak unfavorably about a person	13	35	07	17	-23	-06
8 to inform somebody about the state somebody else is in	-17	30	-37	-17	11	13
9 to smooth over own behavior	-02	00	15	27	04	-11
10 to express opinion about something	04	21	-20	09	-26	02
11 to talk about the relationschip with the other	-10	-25	17	-15	03	20
12 to get to know something about the why of somebody's behavior	09	06	-07	-23	-04	09
13 to utter irritation about somebody else	08	10	17	07	-05	-24
Speaker's Action						
1 Aggressiveness	65	21	-05	07	01	-10
2 Incitement	58	-30	-09	-11	-07	10
3 Aloofness	17	21	17	01	37	25
4 Cajolery	-09	-23	05	-09	-02	78
5 Entertainment	02	02	-05	89	-02	05
6 Control	08	11	-72	-02	02	11
7 Edification	08	14	00	-06	51	09
8 Conspiracy	-01	56	04	-07	-06	06
9 Account	20	-14	16	09	42	-02
10 Gregariousness	-07	31	-06	19	02	38

TABLE 5 Continued

SET 2	1	2	3	4	5	6
Addressee's Action						
1 Rejection	58	04	11	17	-01	04
2 Incitement	10	18	56	-13	10	-03
3 Entertainment	-02	05	02	90	-04	11
4 Aloofness	38	03	-19	00	20	14
5 Love	-21	-09	25	-14	26	37
6 Empathy	-13	03	-09	01	71	03
7 Agreement and Extension	-14	59	-31	-02	35	-10
8 Agreement	27	67	03	-16	-18	14
9 Restoration	53	-21	-19	05	34	-08
10 Self-justification	22	-31	00	-26	07	25
11 Support	05	08	65	13	21	03
12 Gregariousness	-12	04	-13	09	01	79
13 Surprise	12	08	-05	-14	-28	31

*) the three person-forms were recoded into two variables; decimal points are omitted.

gregariousness, and reactions described by gregariousness and by love. This variate may be typified by *gregariousness.*

DISCUSSION

The general question throughout this text was how to extract from short strips of person-talk activity the meaning of that activity as an organized pattern of events. The more specific questions concerned the meaning of the utterances about persons both with respect to their role in the organization of the talk-situation (the pragmatic function) and with respect to their role in providing information that contributes to the object-persons' personalities (the descriptive function).

Patterns of Person-talk

In order to provide for a certain degree of organization and understanding of person-talk activities, two framing-perspectives were used. The "speech-act" perspective had the specific function of laying out some important aspects of taking about persons, viz., the propositional acts, the illocutionary acts, and the effects aimed at and/or achieved. These aspects are considered as the generic features of person-talk. The second perspective concerns the cooperative principle with respect to everyday life. The general consequence of the application of this perspective is its emphasis on the sedimentation of everyday knowledge into cognitive systems, i.e., scripts and scenarios. It was argued that this sediment of knowledge functions as a *cooperation-metascript*, to which people tacitly adhere.

Both these combined perspectives and the procedures followed in obtaining and analysing the data did a good job in providing insightful patterns of talk-activity. The canonical correlation analysis shows some significant variates, to be conceived as person-talk scenarios. Each of the scenarios involve enactments of scripts for both parties in the conversation, viz. *redressive* scripts and *terminating* scripts. The obtained scenarios are rather nuanced descriptions of forms of person-talk, witness the scenarios that are called *entertainment* and *gregariousness*, respectively. These two scenarios usually remain unarticulated social concourses of the same kind.

The prototypical descriptions used do not explain the scenarios, but are to be conceived as "representative anecdotes" (Burke, 1945), which may, metaphorically, give dramatic unity to what happens in person-talk situations (Kouwer, 1973). The significance of the scenarios may be further investigated, for instance, by providing subjects with descriptions of prototypical person-talk situations (constructed on the basis of the scenarios) with certain elements (person-form, intention, etc.) left out. The subjects can then be asked to fill these gaps (Abelson, 1980). The extent to which subjects are able to reconstruct the original scenarios may indicate their powerfulness.

The Pragmatics of Person-utterances

The utterances about persons within the conversational encounters are usually provided with reference to the social context in which they appear. On the one hand, the social context is more or less embodied, so to speak, in the conversational exchange. On the other, the social context is organized by reference to it in the communication. This is particularly noticeable when somebody's behaviour is inconsistent with the ratified definition of the situation (Garfinkel, 1967).

De Raad (1985) observed that utterances about persons are usually made if a breach of expectations is experienced by the speaker. In other words, person-utterances can be said to figure at the nexus of culture and experiences that depart from cultural expectations. The observation confirms the idea that conceptions about personality especially emerge in "problematic" situations (Jones & Davis, 1965). The experiences the speaker has thus form a potential basis for the ascription of particular personalities to the object-persons. This conclusion needs further investigation, especially with respect to the question which kinds of personality ascriptions are contingent upon which kinds of experiences.

A first differentiation among these problematic events takes place in connection with the persons who are the objects of the speakers' experiences, viz., self or other.

The major finding in the present research is that person-form affects person-talk predictably. The use of personal pronouns imply differences in behavioural orientation. This differentiation through the use of personal pronouns not only pertains to personality conceptions, but also to intentions, to acts, and to reactions. The three kinds of utterances connected with the personal pronouns reflect special types of situations that give rise to different conceptions of people. It is not only surprising that some scenarios found in this research are linked to such fundamental notions as the use of personal pronouns, it is also intriguing that the implied differences in behavioural orientation correspond to different fields of psychological practice and theory such as therapy (first-person talk), advise, consult, and persuasion (Abelson & Miller, 1967), etc. (second-person talk), and clinical case seminars and case conferences (Rosenberg & Medini, 1982) (third-person talk). For example, in first-person utterances people make themselves vulnerable and give power over themselves to the other. Such events are characteristic of self-disclosing communication (Cozby, 1973). The bulk of the research on self-disclosure has stemmed from an attempt to assess the factors facilitating successful psychotherapy, and a desire to understand the formation and function of interpersonal relationships such as friendship.

Descriptive function of Person-utterances

Part of the everyday problem-solving tactics is that words or labels are used to contribute to the restoration. For instance, if a person violates social order by yelling at a respectable old man, that person may be apt to earn the label "impertinent". This label may reintroduce order by discrediting the person who yells and justifying social reactions to him (Scott & Lyman, 1968). Usually, however, the meaning of the personality of the object-person within such everyday encounters remains rather unarticulated because it is imbued with proper organizational value. One cannot simply isolate the utterance or part of the utterance (e.g., adjective or noun) as a marker of the personality of the object-persons.

One of the recurrent findings is that personality descriptive adjectives are hardly used in spontaneous talk. This result may be ascribed to the fact that everyday talk is not so much characterized by descriptive purposes, but rather by a variety of other (pragmatic) motives, witness the different intention descriptions. This suggests a rudimentary or inchoate kind of knowledge of people.

In this respect it is interesting to turn to the reasons some of the subjects who refused to fill out the questionnaire spontaneously provided for their refusal. Three sorts of reasons can be distinguished, which, in sum, suggest that the kind of situations referred to, were found too insignificant to be paid due attention.

One sort of reason was that they were unable to give detailed accounts of the situation, let alone a literal report of the utterance, because they were usually not consciously involved in everyday activities such as referred to in the questionnaire. Therefore, they would have had to construct the situation from what had stuck. Although this does not imply that the people who actually did fill out the questionnaire, took a line of phantasy, it may query the objectivity of some reports. For instance, there may have been subjects who bolstered and augmented current pieces of memory for narrative purposes (Snyder & Uranowitz, 1978).

An approach to overcome the problem of construction is to unobtrusively record conversations on tape and select person-talk situations from transcriptions of such recordings. This method has the advantage of providing more relevant cues for the understanding of the pragmatic meanings. But it has the disadvantage that certain settings have to be selected beforehand. Moreover, not all kinds of settings are equally accessible for making recordings.

The second and third kinds of reasons were subsequently that the respondents had not been in a talk-situation such as requested, during the last few days, and that they considered the kind of information they had to provide trivial, silly, or unimportant.

The three kinds of reasons stress on the one hand the idea that person-talk situations have an inchoate character. On the other, they suggest that the reported person-talk situations may have been selected on the basis of their relative dramatic salience. It is possible that the retrievability of instances of person-talk situations is affected by their salience (Tversky & Kahneman, 1974). In this respect it can be argued that, although the selection of more salient situations may not be representative of true frequency, it is particularly the more dramatic event that provides for the necessary information about the pragmatic impact of utterances about persons.

Where descriptive information is contained in the utterance, the procedure followed in this study, in which other people than the speakers themselves rated the amount and the kind of personality descriptive information, may not have been the most appropriate one. For new research it may be considered to ask the subjects who make the utterances, to indicate themselves (in terms of adjective dimensions) to what extent their utterances are informative with respect to the personality of the object-person. This might be done, for instance, by asking such questions as, e.g., what is your impression of the object-person, and how does your utterance relate to this impression.

One way to find out what the role of personality in person-talk situations is, relative to the role of intentions, acts, and reactions, is to ask people which aspect of the talk situation made the most lasting impression.

In so far as descriptive motives are present in everyday talk about persons, they may usually be overshadowed by other motives. There seems to be no avowed intention in the talk situations to be articulate about the personality of the object-person. To the extent that personality is present, it remains implicit in the social process between the involved participants. In other words, personality in everyday life is an *inchoate* category.

CONCLUSION

The obtained scenarios describe the different ways in which participants in the conversational encounters orient their activities to each other. It is somewhat disappointing to observe that the utterances about persons contained in the scenarios suggest only rudimentary conceptions about personality. The utterances are part of a social context in which presumably pragmatic motives predominate. It is unclear to what extent the utterances are representative of the involved parties' conceptions. Maybe the utterances are only *pars pro toto* verbalizations of more articulate propositional structures (Herrmann, 1982).

If everyday language of personality is to be assigned utility for personality research (e.g., Wiggins, 1973), it is somewhat artificial to focus only on the information bearing aspects of the utterances with respect to the personality of the object-person. We should also take into account both the origin and the instrumental character of the pertaining communications. Suggestions for research in this respect have been provided.

REFERENCES

Abelson, R.P. (1980). Common sense knowledge representations. *De Psycholoog, 15*, 431–449.

Abelson, R.P., & Miller, J.C. (1967). Negative persuasion via personal insult. *Journal of Experimental Social Psychology, 3*, 321–333.

Austin, J.L. (1962). *How to do things with words.* Oxford: Oxford University Press.

Bartlett, M.S. (1941). The statistical significance of canonical correlations. *Biometrika, 32*, 29–38.

Berger, P.L., & Luckmann, T. (1966). *The social construction of reality.* New York, NY: Doubleday.

Burke, K. (1945). *A grammar of motives.* Englewood Cliffs, NJ: Prentice-Hall.

Buss, D.M., & Craik, K.H. (1983). The act frequency approach to personality. *Psychological Review, 90*, 105–126.

Cantor, N. (1981). Perceptions of situations: Situation prototypes and person-situation prototypes. In D. Magnusson (Ed.), *Toward a psychology of situations: An interactional perspective* (pp. 229–44). Hillsdale, NJ: Erlbaum.

Cicourel, A.V. (1978). Interpretation and summarization: Issues in the child's acquisition of social structure. In J. Glick & K.A. Clarke-Stewart (Eds.), *The development of social understanding* (pp. 251–82). New York, NY: Gardner.

Cozby, P.C. (1973). Self-disclosure: A literature review. *Psychological Bulletin, 79*, 73–91.

Davis, M.H. (1983). Measuring individual differences in empathy: Evidence for a multidimensional approach. *Journal of Personality and Social Psychology, 44*, 113–126.

De Raad, B. (1984). Person-talk in everyday situations. In H. Bonarius, G. Van Heck, & N. Smid (Eds.), *Personality psychology in Europe: Theoretical and empirical developments* (pp. 31–44). Lisse: Swets & Zeitlinger.

De Raad, B. (1985). *Person-talk in everyday life: Pragmatic aspects of personality.* Unpublished doctoral dissertation, University of Groningen, the Netherlands.

Douglas, J.D. (1971). Understanding everyday life. In J.D. Douglas (Ed.), *Understanding everyday life: Toward the reconstruction of sociological knowledge* (pp. 3–44). London: Routledge & Kegan Paul.

Elias, N., & Scotson, J.L. (1965). *The established and the outsiders.* London: Frank Cass.

Fine, G.A., & Rosnow, R.L. (1978). Gossip, gossipers, gossiping. *Personality and Social Psychology Bulletin, 4,* 161-168.

Fink, E.L., & Walker, B.A. (1977). Humorous responses to embarrassment. *Psychological Reports, 40,* 475-485.

Garfinkel, H. (1967). *Studies in ethnomethodology.* Englewood Cliffs, NJ: Prentice-Hall.

Goffman, E. (1959). *The presentation of self in everyday life.* New York: Anchor Books.

Goffman, E. (1976). Replies and responses. *Language in Society, 5,* 257-313.

Grice, H.P. (1975). Logic and conversation. In P. Cole & J.L. Morgan (Eds.), *Syntax and semantics. Vol. 3: Speech acts* (pp. 41-58). New York: Academic Press.

Grimshaw, A.D. (1982). Comprehensive discourse analysis: An instance of professional peer interaction. *Language in Society, 11,* 15-47.

Hampson, S.E. (1982). *The construction of personality: An introduction.* London: Routledge & Kegan Paul.

Hampson, S.E. (1984). The social construction of personality. In H. Bonarius, G. Van Heck, & N. Smid (Eds.), *Personality psychology in Europe: Theoretical and empirical developments* (pp. 3-14). Lisse: Swets & Zeitlinger.

Harré, R. (1972). The analysis of episodes. In J. Israel & H. Tajfel (Eds.), *The context of social psychology* (pp. 407-24). London: Academic Press.

Herrmann, T. (1982). Language and situation: The pars pro toto principle. In C. Fraser & K.R. Scherer (Eds.), *Advances in the social psychology of language* (pp. 123-58). Cambridge: Cambridge University Press.

Hewitt, J.P., & Stokes, R. (1975). Disclaimers. *American Sociological Review, 40,* 1-11.

Hofstee, W.K.B., Brokken, F.B., & Land, H. (1981). Constructie van een standaard-persoonlijkheids-eigenschappen-lijst (SPEL) [The construction of a standard list of personality traits]. *Nederlands Tijdschrift voor de Psychologie, 34,* 443-452.

John, O.P., Goldberg, L.R., & Angleitner, A. (1984). Better than the alphabet: Taxonomies of personality-descriptive terms in English, Dutch, and German. In H. Bonarius, G. Van Heck, & N. Smid (Eds.), *Personality psychology in Europe: Theoretical and empirical developments* (pp. 83-100). Lisse: Swets & Zeitlinger.

Jones, E.E., & Davis, K.E. (1965). From acts to dispositions: The attribution process in person perception. In L. Berkowitz (Ed.), *Advances in experimental social psychology* (Vol. 2, pp. 220-66). New York: Academic Press.

Kouwer, B.J. (1973). *Existentiele psychologie: Grondslagen van het psychologische gesprek* [Existential psychology: Foundations of the psychology of discourse]. Meppel: Boom.

Meredith, W. (1964). Canonical correlations with fallible data. *Psychometrika, 29,* 55-65.

Miller, G.R., & Steinberg, M. (1975). *Between people.* Palo Alto, CA: Science Research Associates.

Rosenberg, E.H., & Medini, G. (1982). Describing the third person: Some difficulties in therapeutic communication. *The Journal of Psychology, 112,* 245-250.

Sacks, H. (1973). *Lecture notes: Summer institute of Linguistics.* Michigan: Ann Arbor.

Sarason, I.G., Levine, H.M., Basham, R.B., & Sarason, B.R. (1983). Assessing social support: The social support questionnaire. *Journal of Personality and Social Psychology, 44,* 127-139.

Schank, R., & Abelson, R.P. (1977). *Scripts, plans, goals and understanding: An inquiry into human knowledge structures.* Hillsdale, NJ: Erlbaum.

Scott, M.B., & Lyman, S. (1968). Accounts. *American Sociological Review, 33,* 46-62.

Searle, J.R. (1969). *Speech acts: An essay in the philosophy of language.* Cambridge: Cambridge University Press.

Smid, N.G. (1984). A judgmental framework of personality data with some research applications. In H. Bonarius, G. Van Heck, & N. Smid (Eds.), *Personality psychology in Europe: Theoretical and empirical developments* (pp. 15-29). Lisse: Swets & Zeitlinger.

Snyder, M., & Uranowitz, S.W. (1978). Reconstructing the past: Some cognitive consequences of person perception. *Journal of Personality and Social Psychology, 36,* 941-950.

Stech, E.L. (1979). A Grammar of conversation with a quantitative empirical test. *Human Communication Research, 5,* 158-170.

Stewart, D.K. & Love, W.A. (1968). A general canonical correlation index. *Psychological Bulletin, 70,* 160-163.

Timm, N.H. (1975). *Multivariate analysis with applications in education and psychology.* Monterey, CA: Brooks/Cole.

Tversky, A., & Kahneman, D. (1974). Judgment under uncertainty: Heuristics and biases. *Science, 185,* 1124-1131.

Van Heck, G.L. (1984). The construction of a general taxonomy of situations. In H. Bonarius, G. Van Heck, & N. Smid (Eds.), *Personality psychology in Europe: Theoretical and empirical developments* (pp. 149-64). Lisse: Swets & Zeitlinger.

Watzlawick, P., Beavin, J.H., & Jackson, D.D. (1967). *Pragmatics of human communication.* New York, NY: Norton.

Wiggins, J.S. (1973). *Personality and prediction: Principles of personality assessment.* Reading, MA: Addison-Wesley.

THE ASSESSMENT OF SITUATIONAL POWER

Joop Hettema, Guus Van Heck, Marie-Thérèse Appels and Ine Van Zon

Tilburg University
The Netherlands

The interactional approach to personality rests on the assumption that an adequate description of individual behaviour can only be provided if the situational conditions in which behaviour manifests itself are taken into account. The interactionist position is that neither personality factors alone, nor situational factors alone, are sufficient in predicting behaviour. Therefore, both must be considered jointly (cf. Kenrick & Dantchik, 1983). A relatively simple way to elaborate this statement is to conceive of interactionism as a conditional version of trait theory as has, for instance, been suggested by Hofstee (1984). Such a point of view inevitably restricts the investigator of personality to the study of so-called mechanistic interactions between persons and situations. Mechanistic interactions are concerned with the structure of the interactions and not with the process. Although mechanistic interaction research may serve as the basis for formulating an interactional psychology of personality, the ultimate goal is an understanding of the dynamic interplay between behaviour and situational events (cf. Endler, 1982). Therefore, a number of interactionistic theorists have advocated a much more radical conceptualization in terms of dynamic interactions between persons and situations (e.g., Endler, 1975; Endler & Magnusson, 1976; Hettema, 1979).

Dynamic multidirectional process conceptualizations of interaction require the investigator to specify a number of additional conditions affecting behaviour, and, specifically, to conceptualize the person as well as the situation in such terms that dynamic interactions become possible. Personality should be seen as an open system allowing slight changes in situational conditions to exert their influence. The situation, on the other hand, should be conceptualized as a field having the *power* to influence individual behaviour.

The strong controlling influence that situations can exert, overriding almost completely the personal qualities of the individuals, has been vividly demonstrated in various studies. Milgram's (1963) research on the determinants of obedience to authority has made us aware of the deep consequences of psychological forces operative in a powerful conflict situation. The fact that most people continued to deliver painful electric shocks to strangers, showing an indiscriminate submission to authority, lead Milgram to conclude that dispositions a person brings to the situation are not always important causes of behaviour: "...often, it is not so much the kind of person a man is as the kind of situation in which he finds himself that determines how he will act." (Milgram, 1974, p. 205).

Another dramatic demonstration is the well-known study of prison life conducted by Hancey, Banks, and Zimbardo (1973), in which subjects assumed the roles of 'prisoner' or 'guard' for several days. It was found that the simulated prison environment was sufficiently forceful to elicit the same type of intense, almost pathological reactions from the majority of the participants.

The potency of situational effects has also been demonstrated in the interaction sequences studies of Raush and his colleagues (e.g., Raush, 1965; Raush, Farbman, & Llewellyn, 1960), which revealed strong relationships between situational elements, that is, antecedent affectional behaviour of one person, and subsequent acts of another.

Within the general milieu of a psychiatric inpatient ward Moos (1968, see also Moos et al., 1964) found that some settings tended to evoke a particular hierarchy of reactions regardless of whether patients or staff were responding in them. Other studies have highlighted the power of situational conditions in domains as diverse as, for instance, psychotherapy (Bandura, Blanchard, & Ritter, 1969), artificial laboratory tasks (Wachtel, 1973), leisure time activities (Bishop & Witt, 1970), and assertiveness (Furnham, 1979).

The history of psychology shows several attempts to *define* the situation as a source of power acting upon individuals operative in that situation. For instance, Murray (1938) has introduced the concept of *press* to indicate "the power of situations to affect the well-being of the subject in one way or another" (p. 121). Lewin (1936, 1951) has emphasized the psychological environment containing valences, forces, vectors and barriers determining individual behaviour next to internal needs and tensions. Allport (1961) has pointed to the *demand characteristics* of the situation and considered them to be influential with respect to the behaviour of individuals. Chein (1954) has stated that situations may be described in terms of the number of *degrees of freedom* available to the individual.

More recently, the rise of the interactional view of personality has revived interest in situational factors (Blass, 1984; Magnusson, 1984; Wakenhut, 1978). Current terms like *situational constraints* (Monson, Hesley, & Chernick, 1982; Price & Bouffard, 1974; Rommetveit, 1981; Secord, 1977), *salience* (Sarason & Sarason, 1981), *situational clarity* (Stokols, 1981), *ambiguity* (Block & Block, 1981; Mischel, 1979; Schank & Abelson, 1977), *situational norms and rules* (Argyle, 1977, 1981; Argyle, Graham, Campbell, & White, 1979), or *freedom of choice* (Proshansky, Ittelson, & Rivlin, 1970) provided cases in point.

Perhaps the most explicit emphasis on the power of situations to determine individual behaviour has been layed by Mischel (1973) in his *Psychological Review* article in which he attempted to reconceptualize personality in terms derived from cognitive social learning theory. In contrast with other theorists, Mischel's views on situational power provide us with the opportunity to come to grips with the impact of situations empirically as well as theoretically. Mischel (1973, p. 276) made the following statement: "to the degree that subjects are exposed to powerful treatments, the role of individual differences will be minimized. Conversely, when treatments are weak, ambiguous, or trivial, individual differences in person variables should exert significant effects." In elaborating this view, Mischel (1973, 1977a, 1977b) points out that a powerful situation leads all persons to construe the particular events the same way, induces uniform expectancies regarding the most appropriate response pattern, provides adequate incentives for the performance of that response pattern, and instills the skills necessary for its satisfactory construction and execution. A closely related view is expressed in Magnusson (1974).

These ideas offer a basis for the development of measuring procedures for the assessment of situational power. The present authors have used these notions to develop indices of situational power versus weakness that can be meaningfully applied to any situation as appearing in situational taxonomies.

Two additional questions asked in the context of the present study were: (a) to what extent can a power index be generalized over different criteria, and (b) what is the best index, that is, the most representative index for a number of different criteria.

METHOD

The experimental situations

As experimental situations we used 20 situations chosen from a taxonomy developed by Van Heck (1984). The situations were selected on intuitive grounds to represent powerful as well as weak situations. In order to achieve maximal differentiation two raters who were familiar with the literature on situational power rated all 248 situations in the taxonomy. On eight situations they agreed that these situations would be strong. Eight other situations would be weak, whereas on the other four the raters disagreed. The 20 situations are presented in Table 1.

The general way of approaching the power of situations in this study was to look whether aspects or elements of the situation are constructed the same way by different subjects. If so, the situation would be considered powerful; if not, it would be weak. In the present study, we distinguished between *cognitive* situational aspects on the one hand, and *behavioural* situational aspects on the other (see Table 2).

Eight different criteria were developed and tested:
1. *Situational cues and features.* One hundred one different features were randomly selected from the situation taxonomy developed by Van Heck (1984). They refer to the major components of situations: place, people, action, and time (cf. Pervin, 1977). The complete list of cues is presented in Table 3.

TABLE 1: *The 20 Situations selected from Van Heck's (1984) Taxonomy*

Conflict	Interview
Conversation	Judgement
Cooperation	Lesson
Declaration of love	Official inquiry
Discussion	Phone call
Elections	Quarrel
Examination	Quiz
Exchange of thoughts	Religious ceremony
Feast	Tea-table gossip
Funeral	Visit

TABLE 2: *Criteria used to determine Situational Power*

CRITERIA	SITUATIONAL ELEMENTS
A. Cognitive	1. Situational cues and features 2. Antecedent situations 3. Consequent situations 4. Connotative meaning
B. Behavioural	5. Expected goals 6. Own behaviour 7. Behavioural consequences 8. Behavioural norms

TABLE 3: *The List of Situational Cues used as Stimuli*

War, adventure, problems within the family, commemoration, politics, apartment-buildings, shop, garage, theater, bedroom, highway, abroad, in the air, at the door, farm, dike, canteen, sex club, snow and ice, exposed place, rack, fence, grave, fog, mirror, colleague, sportsman, friend, foreigner, clergyman, board-member, driver, youth, cook, fugitive, adversary, evening wear, being dismissed, being disabled, losing one's temper, being rich, hunger, many persons, being disguised, being a volunteer, travel, awake, loan, expose for sale, smoke, remove, sail, offer, prey, drink, read, climb, guard, take a bath, warn, call names, clean up, take prisoner, pursue, pick up, extinguish a fire, trow a bomb, beat, have a look at, discover, inform, shoot, dig, bring, push, declaration of love, request, build, encourage, curse, plane, tool, monument, form, motion-picture, liquor, animal, corpse, cloth, paper, lavatory, sweets, cash-desk, ground, regularly, summer, suddenly, duration of a few hours, every year, with a one year duration.

TABLE 4: *The List of Situation Concepts used for Criteria 2 and 3*

1. arrival	18. outrage	34. reception
2. thrashing	19. rejoining	35. dispute
3. farewell	20. house arrest	36. conspiracy
4. appointment	21. assistance	37. job application
5. motor tour	22. autospy	38. strike
6. deceit	23. meal	39. punishment
7. deliberation	24. failure	40. obstruction
8. accusation	25. turning night into day	41. therapy
9. meeting	26. bribery	42. advances
10. rivalry	27. intermission	43. speech
11. confrontation	28. negotiation	44. holiday
12. dinner	29. small intimate party	45. interrogation
13. drinking-bout	30. discharge	46. house-moving
14. duel	31. procession	47. traffic accident
15. divorce	32. adultery	48. match
16. flirt	33. protest	49. work
17. fight		

    Subjects were asked to indicate on seven-point Likert-type scales
how essential and typical each cue is for each of the 20 experimental
situations.

2. *Antecedent situations.* It may be that a situation can only be
understood in relation to the sequence or pattern of which it is a part
(cf. Pervin, 1978). Consequently, the construction of situations is
partly a function of the situation preceding it. Therefore, subjects
were asked to indicate on seven-point scales, ranging from *Never* to
Always, how typical each of 49 other situations is as a predecessor of
the experimental situations. The 49 situations to be judged, were
derived from the taxonomic study mentioned above (Van Heck, 1984).
These 49 situations are listed in Table 4.

3. *Consequent situations.* The argument to include this criterion was
much the same as in 2. With respect to the same set of 49 situations
(see Table 4) it was asked to indicate how often these situations
followed the experimental situations.

4. *Connotative meaning of the situation.* The subjects were asked to
indicate the position of each experimental situation on 41 Semantic
Differential scales. The bipolar adjectival scales selected, were derived
from Osgood, Suci, and Tannenbaum (1957), Mehrabian and Russell
(1974), Flade (1978), and studies by Forgas (1976, 1978) on the
perception of social episodes. All scales are presented in Table 5.

TABLE 5: *Semantic Differential Scales*

1. good-bad	22. severe-lenient
2. beautiful-ugly	23. sociable-solitary
3. big-small	24. witty-dull
4. strong-weak	25. contented-melancholic
5. sophisticated-naive	26. excitable-calm
6. active-passive	27. moving-still
7. fast-slow	28. noisy-quiet
8. occasional-regular	29. predictable-unpredictable
9. hard-soft	30. dominant-submissive
10. happy-sad	31. healthy-sick
11. lucid-obscure	32. interesting-uninteresting
12. generous-thrifty	33. complex-simple
13. serious-humorous	34. pleasant-unpleasant
14. free-constrained	35. intimate-nonintimate
15. altruistic-egotistic	36. emotional-unemotional
16. impulsive-deliberate	37. familiar-unfamiliar
17. hearty-cool	38. friendly-unfriendly
18. talkative-silent	39. conventional-eccentric
19. aggressive-peaceful	40. cooperative-competitive
20. organized-disorganized	41. formal-informal
21. realistic-dreamy	

5. *Goals to be attained within the situation*. Each situation may be characterized with respect to the goals that can be realized within their context. To develop a power index on this consideration goal categories were derived from Schank and Abelson's (1977) work on the goal aspects of human actions. The following 13 goals were selected: 1. *satisfy bodily needs*, e.g., hunger, thirst, sleep, or sex; 2. *enjoy yourself; 3. seek entertainment*; 4. *try to learn something*; 5. *obtain possession of something*; 6. *get a power position*; 7. *start social relationships*; 8. *achieve something*; 9. *exert oneself*; 10. *receive social approval*; 11. *preserve possession*; 12. *seek sensation*; and 13. *preserve social relations*. The subjects were asked to indicate on seven-point scales *(Not at all - Very much)* the degree to which each particular goal could be realized in each of the 20 experimental situations.

6. *Probability of own behaviour within the situation*. For each experimental situation the subjects were confronted with 100 different activities occurring in our situation taxonomy (see Van Heck, 1984). Again, seven categories were available for indicating the probability of each behaviour in each of the 20 experimental situations. The list of 100 activities fairly well covered the whole gamut of social and nonsocial reactions available to persons when confronted with situations like examination, feast, quarrel, etc. The activities are given in Table 6.

7. *Behavioural consequences*. For the same set of 100 activities (see Table 6) subjects were asked to rate how positive or negative their consequences would be in the 20 experimental situations. Seven-point category scales were used.

8. *Behavioural norms*. Subjects had to indicate how appropriate each of 100 activities (see under 6 and 7) would be in each of the 20 experimental situations. Again, the subjects used seven-point category scales.

TABLE 6: *The List of Actions used for the Criteria 6, 7, and 8*

Surrender, wake a person, close, ignore, loan, save, prepare, approve, assert, push, use drugs, instigate, honour, escape, apologize, leave, take care of, protest, offer, give, cry, prey, enter, investigate, collect, compliment a person, ridicule, reward, accuse, address, liberate, dance, distribute, take a bath, eat, serve, touch, bury, comply, call names, ride, control, clean up, lock, answer, applaud, clear away, threaten, drink, sacrifice, separate, hire, deceive, snatch away something from a person, extinguish (a fire), agree upon, summon, make a mistake, study, beat, stand (e.g., a drink), hunt, meet, search, hide, discover, step out, phone, rope, criticize, overpower, shoot, write, joke, pursue, demolish, come home, reside, marry, carry, persuade, forbid, go to sleep, seize, sail, creep, open, declaration of love, rest, be silent, reconcile, plead, record, dig, kick, save up (e.g., money), stay at home, awake, manufacture, predict.

Design of the study

Each criterion was applied to each of the 20 experimental situations by a new group of 20 subjects.

Subjects

One hundred sixty subjects participated in this study. Ages ranged from 18-30 years. One hundred one subjects were non-students recruited via a subject panel; the other 56 were students of Tilburg University. Half of the sample were males, the other half females. Care was taken to include 10 male and 10 female subjects for each of the eight criteria.

Analysis

The data were analysed per situation per criterion to yield information on the question: How far can the profile of element scores for any experimental situation be generalized over subjects. The analysis consisted of the following steps: First, an analysis of variance with elements and subjects as facets was carried out. Second, estimated variance components were calculated for elements, subjects, and the interaction of the two, including error. Computation of these components was conducted according to an all-random model. Finally, the coefficient of generalizability for profiles across subjects (cf. Cronbach, Gleser, Nanda, & Rajaratnam, 1972) was computed. The formula used, was:

$$\hat{\rho}^2 = \frac{\sigma_i^2}{\sigma_i^2 + \sigma_{pi,\varepsilon}^2}$$

In which: $\hat{\rho}^2$ = the coefficient of generalizability for a particular situation; σ_i^2 = the variance component for situational elements; and $\sigma_{pi,\varepsilon}^2$ = the variance component for the residual.

RESULTS

Hundred and sixty coefficients of generalizability were obtained to indicate the power of the 20 situations according to eight criteria. These coefficients ranged from .15 to .68 with a mean of .35. This average value may seem rather modest at first sight. However, it is quite high, if one realizes that it has been derived from unit sample analyses (cf. Golding, 1975). The mean values for each of the eight criteria were of comparable magnitude.

To answer the question whether the power indices generalize over the eight criteria rank order correlations were computed between the indices for the criteria. These rank order correlations are presented in Table 7.

TABLE 7: *Spearman Rank Order Correlations among the eight Power Indices*

criterion	1	2	3	4	5	6	7	8
Cues (1)	–	21	57	49	17	16	22	05
Antecedent situations (2)		–	42	18	07	-35	07	38
Consequent situations (3)			–	50	30	19	37	53
Connotative meaning (4)				–	37	31	48	49
Expected goals (5)					–	68	31	36
Own behaviour (6)						–	70	38
Behavioural consequences (7)							–	71
Norms (8)								–

Note: Decimal points omitted.

TABLE 8: *Power Indices for 20 Situations*

Situations	General index	Cognitive index	Behavioural index
conflict	34	36	32
conversation	39	38	37
cooperation	40	31	35
declaration of love	53	42	30
discussion	25	35	36
elections	28	40	24
examination	28	40	54
exchange of thoughts	41	31	31
feast	60	43	50
funeral	37	45	30
interview	16	28	31
judgment	19	24	32
lesson	27	36	47
official inquiry	25	32	28
phone call	24	39	36
quarrel	44	35	35
quiz	17	30	22
religious ceremony	18	34	22
tea-table gossip	38	34	46
visit	57	41	46
Mean	33	36	35

Note: Decimal points omitted.

As can be seen from Table 7, the power indices form two distinct groups: The *cognitive* indices and the *behavioural* indices. The mean correlation was .40 for the criteria 1, 2, 3, and 4, and .52 for the criteria 5, 6, 7, and 8. The mean correlation between the criteria 1, 2, 3, and 4, on the one hand, and the other four criteria, on the other hand, was .24. Furthermore, Table 7 reveals that one criterion, namely, Osgood's Semantic Differential, is more general than the others in that it shows significant correlations with cognitive as well as behavioural criteria.

Thus, the conclusion can be drawn from these findings that situations that are cognitively powerful are not always powerful in the behavioural sense and vice versa. So, it seems appropriate to continue research in the area of situational power with *different criteria for both power aspects*. For the moment, we have construed three different power indices, attending to the obtained pattern of correlations: (a) a *general* power index, that is, criterion 4, the connotative meaning, (b) a *cognitive* power index, that is, the mean of the criteria 1 and 3, namely, cues and consequent situations, and (c) a *behavioural* power index, i.e., the criteria 5 and 6 (expected goals and probability of own activities). These power indices are shown in Table 8.

According to Mischel (1973), variance for individual differences will be smallest when situations are highly *structured*. Such situations can be found in settings which impose relatively narrow limits on the range of possible behaviours. Mischel (1973) gives the following examples: church, school, theatre, and conferences. Some of our experimental situations, namely, examination, funeral, lesson, and religious ceremony, belong to those social settings of life. Are they, according to our subjects, all powerful? Let us look at the general connotative meaning index. The first column of Table 8 reveals relatively low generalizability coefficients for lesson, examination and religious ceremony. As a matter of fact, the latter situation was among the weakest situations: only interview and quiz were characterized by lower generalizability across subjects. Using a median split, only the funeral situation belonged to the group of more powerful situations. Who is wrong? The connotative meaning index? Our subjects? Mischel?

An inspection of the two other columns of Table 8 reveals that two situations, namely, examination and lesson, were relatively strong. Both school situations had generalizability coefficients above the median for the cognitive as well as the behavioural index. Religious ceremony appeared to be a relatively weak situation in terms of both indexes. This is rather surprising. Guided by Mischel's (1973) and Barker's (1966) statements regarding the limits on the range of possible constructions and reorganizations of stimulus conditions, religious ceremony can be conceived of as one of the prototypes of a highly structured, powerful situation that minimizes the role of individual differences. However, our subjects informed us that *in church not everybody behaves 'church'*. The most striking effect was found with respect to the funeral situation. In terms of our cognitive power index, featuring cues and consequent situations, funeral was the most powerful situation in the whole set of 20 experimental situations. However, in terms of goals and own activities, that is, the behavioural power index, funeral was relatively weak.

Finally, Table 8 reveals that only eight situations were *strong* or *weak* irrespective of type of criterion. Only visit, feast, and conversation were unequivocally strong, whereas official inquiry, interview, judgement, quiz, and religious ceremony were weak according to all indexes.

DISCUSSION

The environmental context in which persons operate, plays an important role in their life. Studies of life events show that, for instance, certain health-related events, or family conflicts have a significant impact on social or psychological functioning. Traumatic occurrences, such as the death of a family member, or the loss of a job or business, can change someone's life completely. Such situations are powerful in the sense that they affect much behaviour and can transform behaviour over long periods of time. In naive as well as professional psychology situations are often construed as powerful when the range of behaviours involved and/or the duration of the effects are taken into account.

In the present study the powerfulness of situations is conceptualized differently. Degree of strength refers to the extent to which a situation allows for individual variation, particularly in regard to the encoding of events, the expectancies about outcomes, and patterns of actions. Strong situations minimize variability between individuals. Weak situations, on the other hand, permit the expression of individual differences.

A psychology of personality which has no models or methods of research for incorporating situations is doomed to be predictively inadequate (Cattell, 1979). Therefore, personality psychologists should bring properties of situations and types of situations into their equations predicting behaviour. It should be clear, that information about these properties becomes more essential when situations are stronger. Until now, however, current models and research methods do not try systematically to account for the position of particular situations on the *strong-weak* continuum.

A possible exception forms Cattell's (1979) econetic model, in which role patterns are added to the general specification equation. This new development in Cattell's theoretical framework, especially the separation of personality and role traits provides the opportunity to distinguish between situations with high behavioural indices for ability, temperament and dynamic traits, on the one hand, and situations which allow for effects of differences of personality traits to a lesser degree, on the other hand. In the latter situations, when the predicted behaviours are largely role actions, the weigth on role factors will be much greater than those of the personality traits. Thus, the econetic model seems to be capable of expressing strength of situations, be it in a somewhat restricted sense, focussing primarily on role concepts.

In general, however, Mischel's (1973) question "When do individual differences make a difference?" has unjustly received too little attention. For instance, in the construction of S-R inventories (cf. Endler, Hunt, & Rosenstein, 1962) it is not tried to balance these inventories with respect to the degree of strength of the included hypothetical situations. For instance, Endler and Hunt (1969) have reported that individual differences in the intensity of the trait of hostility were genuinely more prominent than individual differences in the intensity of the trait of anxiousness. It was concluded that hostility and anxiousness operate differently in human functioning. Perhaps that is precisely what is happening. But maybe it is only the reflection of stronger situations in the anxiety questionnaire.

To give another example, we strongly believe that information concerning the degrees of freedom persons have at their disposal in situations they are confronted with, can be used fruitfully in modern conceptions of personality traits, like, for instance, the act frequency approach (Buss & Craik, 1983; see also this volume). In its most general form this approach focusses on the relative frequencies with which individuals display acts counting as members of a particular dispositional category over a period of observation. Situational considerations only play a role as qualifications in the description of prototypical acts. Beyond that, the acts once specified in this manner are credited to the individual's account without any further effort to control for situational factors. In our opinion, power indices of situations provide a more thorough and systematic method for matching and controlling for situational factors compared to situational qualifiers of prototypical acts reported in act nomination studies.

The amount of degrees of freedom that a situation offers for coping with or changing it should be a main topic of the analysis of situations (cf. Hacker, 1981). The present study is a first attempt to provide a more rigorous definition of situational power as referred to in the literature. Obviously much more research is needed to establish procedures to be used in Person x Situation interaction studies in which power is deemed to be an important variable. As a directive for further efforts in this area it seems worthwhile to stress the distinction into cognitive versus behavioural indexes of situational power. Mischel's (1973) pioneering efforts seem to have been formed by the tacit assumption that situational power should be conceived of as an unequivocal aspect of situations. The same construction of situations leads to the same expectancies, which in turn leads to the same incentives, and, finally, to the same skills. Our results have cast doubt on this notion. Rather than opening the door for one unequivocal index of situational power, they point into the direction of a more differential approach of the problem. That approach is primarily characterized by a basic distinction into *cognitive situational power* and *behavioural situational power*.

This distinction is not a completely new one. Throughout the history of psychology investigators have emphasized the distinction between afferent and efferent behaviour. For instance, Tolman and Brunswik (1935) have made a distinction between *discriminanda* and *manipulanda* in human ecology. *Discriminanda* are situational elements which are the relatively direct causes of immediate sensory cues. They are the properties whereby the situation is differentiated from other situations. *Manipulanda* have a different relevancy for the organism. They form the essential behavioural core of situations. They are the properties, for instance, the discuss-ableness, the run-away-ableness, the intensify-ableness, which make possible and support actual behavioural manipulations.

If personality psychologists are willing to incorporate this basic feature of situations in their thinking, they should deepen their insights in the dynamics of situations. An important notion in this respect, frequently used by interactional theorists, is the notion of transactions between persons and situations, or reciprocal causality. This notion implies that "...not only do events affect the behavior of organisms but the organism is also an active agent influencing environmental events" (Endler & Magnusson, 1976, p. 969). It seems only logical in this context, to use two different conceptions of situational power: one referring to the cognition and recognition of situations, the other to the manipulation and transformation of the situation. The senior author (Hettema, 1979) has made a distinction into two dimensions in the personality system, that is, *equilibrium* and *transformation*. The first dimension refers to afferent cognitive aspects, the second dimension to efferent behavioural aspects. Both dimensions are to some extent autonomous, and it seems to us now that in the realm of situations they have their counterparts in two different types of situational power. Our findings would imply that situations enhancing or withstanding recognition, proper identification, useful labelling, etc., are not necessarily the ones enhancing or withstanding actual behavioural manipulations and transformations. More research is obviously needed to demonstrate the fruitfulness of this conception.

REFERENCES

Allport, G.W. (1961). *Pattern and growth in personality*. New York: Holt, Rinehart & Winston.

Argyle, M. (1977). Predictive and generative rules models of P x S interaction. In D. Magnusson & N.S. Endler (Eds.), *Personality at the crossroads: Current issues in interactional psychology* (pp. 353-370). Hillsdale, NJ: Erlbaum.

Argyle, M. (1981). The experimental study of the basic features of situations. In D. Magnusson (Ed.), *Toward a psychology of situations: An interactional perspective* (pp. 63-83). Hillsdale, NJ: Erlbaum.

Argyle, M., Graham, J., Campbell, A., & White, P. (1979). The rules of different situations. *New Zealand Psychologist, 8,* 13-27.

Bandura, A., Blanchard, E.B., & Ritter, B. (1969). Relative efficacy of desensitization and modeling approaches for inducing behavioral, affective, and attitudinal changes. *Journal of Personality and Social Psychology, 13,* 173-199.

Barker, R. (1966). *The stream of behavior*. New York: Appleton-Century-Crofts.

Bishop, D.W., & Witt, P.A. (1970). Sources of behavioral variance during leisure time. *Journal of Personality and Social Psychology, 16,* 352-360.

Blass, T. (1984). Social psychology and personality: Toward a convergence. *Journal of Personality and Social Psychology, 47,* 1013-1027.

Block, J., & Block, J.H. (1981). Studying situational dimensions: A grand perspective and some limited empiricism. In D. Magnusson

(Ed.), *Toward a psychology of situations: An interactional perspective* (pp. 85-102). Hillsdale, NJ: Erlbaum.

Buss, D.M., & Craik, K.H. (1983). The act frequency approach to personality. *Psychological Review, 90*, 105-126.

Cattell, R.B. (1979). *Personality and learning theory. Vol. 1. The structure of personality in its environment.* New York: Springer Publishing Company.

Chein, I. (1954). The environment as a determinant of behavior. *Journal of Social Psychology, 39*, 115-127.

Cronbach, L.J., Gleser, G.C., Nanda, H., & Rajaratnam, N. (1972). *The dependability of behavioral measurements: Theory of generalizability for scores and profiles.* New York: Wiley.

Endler, N.S. (1975). The case for person-situation interactions. *Canadian Psychological Review, 16*, 12-21.

Endler, N.S. (1982). Interactionism comes of age. In M.P. Zanna, E.T. Higgins, & C.P. Herman (Eds.), *Consistency in social behavior. The Ontario Symposium* (Vol. 2, pp. 209-249). Hillsdale, NJ: Erlbaum.

Endler, N.S., & Hunt, J.McV. (1969). S-R inventories of hostility and comparisons of the proportions of variance from persons, responses, and situations for hostility and anxiousness. *Journal of Personality and Social Psychology, 37*, 1-24.

Endler, N.S., & Magnusson, D. (1976). Toward an interactional psychology of personality. *Psychological Bulletin, 83*, 956-974.

Endler, N.S., Hunt, J.McV., & Rosenstein, A.J. (1962). An S-R Inventory of Anxiousness. *Psychological Monographs, 76*, No. 17.

Flade, A. (1978). Die Beurteilung umweltpsychologische Konzepte mit einem konzeptspezifischen und einem universellen Semantischen Differential [The judgement of environmental concepts with a concept-specific and a universal Semantic Differential]. *Zeitschrift für experimentelle und angewandte Psychologie, 25*, 367-378.

Forgas, J.P. (1976). The perception of social episodes: Categorical and dimensional representations in two different cultural milieus. *Journal of Personality and Social Psychology, 34*, 199-209.

Forgas, J.P. (1978). Social episodes and social structure in an academic setting: The social environment of an intact group. *Journal of Experimental Social Psychology, 14*, 434-448.

Furnham, A. (1979). Assertiveness in three cultures: Multidimensional and cultural differences. *Journal of Clinical Psychology, 35*, 522-527.

Golding, S.L. (1975). Flies in the ointment: Methodological problems in the analysis of the percentage of variance due to persons and situations. *Psychological Bulletin, 82*, 278-288.

Hacker, W. (1981). Perceptions of and reactions to work situations: Some implications of an action control approach. In D. Magnusson (Ed.), *Toward a psychology of situations: An interactional perspective* (pp. 113-134). Hillsdale, NJ: Erlbaum.

Hancey, C., Banks, C., & Zimbardo, P. (1973). Interpersonal dynamics in a simulated prison. *International Journal of Criminology and Penology, 1*, 69-97.

Hettema, P.J. (1979). *Personality and adaptation.* Amsterdam: North-Holland.

Hofstee, W.K.B. (1984). What's in a trait: Reflections about the inevitability of traits, their measurement, and taxonomy. In H. Bonarius, G. Van Heck, & N. Smid (Eds.), *Personality psychology in Europe: Theoretical and empirical developments* (pp. 75-81). Lisse: Swets & Zeitlinger.

Kenrick, D.T., & Dantchik, A. (1983). Interactionism, idiographics, and the social psychological invasion of personality. *Journal of Personality, 51*, 286-307.

Lewin, K. (1936). *Principles of topological psychology*. New York: McGraw-Hill.

Lewin, K. (1951). *Field theory in social science: Selected theoretical papers*. New York: Harper.

Magnusson, D. (1974). The individual in the situation: Some studies on individuals' perception of situations. *Studia Psychologica, 16*, 124-132.

Magnusson, D. (1984). The situation in an interaction paradigm of personality research. In V. Sarris & A. Parducci (Eds.), *Perspectives in psychological experimentation: Toward the year 2000* (pp. 211-233). Hillsdale, NJ: Erlbaum.

Mehrabian, A., & Russell, J.A. (1974). *An approach to environmental psychology*. Cambridge, MA: MIT Press.

Milgram, S. (1963). Behavioral study of obedience. *Journal of Abnormal and Social Psychology, 67*, 371-378.

Milgram, S. (1974). *Obedience to authority: An experimental view*. New York: Harper & Row.

Mischel, W. (1973). Toward a cognitive social learning reconceptualization of personality. *Psychological Review, 80*, 252-283.

Mischel, W. (1977a). The interaction of person and situation. In D. Magnusson & N.S. Endler (Eds.), *Personality at the crossroads: Current issues in interactional psychology* (pp. 333-352). Hillsdale, NJ: Erlbaum.

Mischel, W. (1977b). On the future of personality measurement. *American Psychologist, 32*, 246-254.

Mischel, W. (1979). On the interface of cognition and personality. Beyond the person-situation debate. *American Psychologist, 34*, 740-754.

Monson, T., Hesley, J., & Chernick, L. (1982). Specifying when personality traits can and cannot predict behavior: An alternative to abandoning the attempt to predict single act criteria. *Journal of Personality and Social Psychology, 43*, 385-399.

Moos, R.H. (1968). Situational analysis of a therapeutic community milieu. *Journal of Abnormal Psychology, 73*, 49-61.

Moos, R.H., Daniels, D.N., Zukowsky, E., Sassano, M., Hatton, J., Dueltgen, A., Beilin, L., & Moos, B.S. (1964). The ecological assessment of behavior in a therapeutic community. *International Journal of Social Psychiatry*, Special Congress Ed., No. 1, 87-96.

Murray, H. (1938). *Explorations in personality*. New York: Oxford University Press.

Osgood, C.E., Suci, G.J., & Tannenbaum, P.H. (1957). *The measuring of meaning*. Urbana, IL: University of Illinois Press.

Pervin, L.A. (1977). The representative design of person-situation research. In D. Magnusson & N.S. Endler (Eds.), *Personality at the crossroads: Current issues in interactional psychology* (pp. 371-384). Hillsdale, NJ: Erlbaum.

Pervin, L.A. (1978). Theoretical approaches to the analysis of individual-environment interaction. In L.A. Pervin & M. Lewis

(Eds.), *Perspectives in interactional psychology* (pp. 67-85). New York/London: Plenum Press.

Price, R.H., & Bouffard, D.L. (1974). Behavioral appropriateness and situational constraint as dimensions of social behavior. *Journal of Personality and Social Psychology, 30,* 579-586.

Proshansky, H.M., Ittelson, W.H., & Rivlin, L.G. (1970). Freedom of choice and behavior in a physical setting. In H.M. Proshansky, W.H. Ittelson, & L.G. Rivlin (Eds.), *Environmental psychology:Man and his physical setting* (pp. 173-183). New York: Holt, Rinehart & Winston.

Raush, H.L. (1965). Interaction sequences. *Journal of Personality and Social Psychology, 2,* 487-499.

Raush, H.L., Farbman, I., & Llewellyn, L.G. (1960). Person, setting and change in social interaction: II. A normal-control study. *Human Relations, 13,* 305-333.

Rommetveit, R. (1981). On meaning of situations and social control of such meaning in human communication. In D. Magnusson (Ed.), *Toward a psychology of situations:An interactional perspective* (pp. 151-167). Hillsdale: NJ: Erlbaum.

Sarason, I.G., & Sarason, R.R. (1981). The importance of cognition and moderate variables in stress. In D. Magnusson (Ed.), *Toward a psychology of situations:An interactional perspective* (pp. 195-210). Hillsdale, NJ: Erlbaum.

Schank, R.C., & Abelson, R.P. (1977). *Scripts, plans, goals and understanding. An inquiry into human knowledge structures.* Hillsdale, NJ: Erlbaum.

Secord, P.F. (1977). Social psychology in search for a paradigm. *Personality and Social Psychology Bulletin, 3,* 41-50.

Stokols, D. (1981). Group x place transactions. Some neglected issues in psychological research on settings. In D. Magnusson (Ed.), *Toward a psychology of situations:An interactional perspective* (pp. 393-415). Hillsdale, NJ: Erlbaum.

Tolman, E.C., & Brunswik, E. (1935). The organism and the causal texture of the environment. *Psychological Review, 42,* 43-77.

Van Heck, G.L. (1984). The construction of a general taxonomy of situations. In H. Bonarius, G. Van Heck, & N. Smid (Eds.), *Personality psychology in Europe: Theoretical and empirical developments* (pp. 149-164). Lisse: Swets & Zeitlinger.

Wachtel, P.L. (1973). Psychodynamics, behavior therapy, and the implicable experimenter: An inquiry into the consistency of personality. *Journal of Abnormal Psychology, 82,* 324-334.

Wakenhut, R. (1978). Über die Einbeziehung von Situationen in psychologische Messungen. Ein Beitrag zur interactionistischen Persönlichkeitsforschung [On the incorporation of situations in psychological measurements. A contribution to interactional personality research]. Europäische Hochschulschriften: Reihe 6, Psychologie; Vol. 33. Frankfurt am Main: Peter Lang Verlag.

PART III

THE MEANING OF TRAITS:
COGNITIVE AND BEHAVIOURAL APPROACHES

PERSONALITY TRAITS AS COGNITIVE CATEGORIES

Sarah E. Hampson

Birkbeck College
University of London
England

For the past 30 years or so, the trait approach has been the predominant theoretical perspective in personality psychology. Despite the specific differences between various theoretical positions (Guilford, 1975), personality traits have been widely assumed to be inferred, hypothetical constructs within the individual giving rise to stable and consistent individual differences in behaviour.

Indeed, it is precisely this conceptualization of personality which has been the subject of a lengthy debate initiated by Mischel's (1968) critique of personality psychology and extended to lay or implicit personality theories by Shweder (1975, 1977, 1982) and Shweder and D'Andrade (1980). Mischel (1968) argued powerfully against the trait concept by marshalling evidence apparently refuting the behavioural consistency that traits were designed to both explain and predict. In response, loyalists to the trait cause challenged Mischel's arguments (Craik, 1969), and thus personality psychology was headed off course onto a seemingly endless detour of debate.

At the same time that the trait in the psyche of the actor has been under fire, there has been another and equally damaging assault underway on the trait in the eye of the beholder. According to Shweder (1977), traits are misleading generalizations based on erroneous beliefs about behavioural consistency. The lay personality theorist is no different from any other social cognizer with respect to her susceptibility to illusory correlations (Kahneman & Tversky, 1973). Hence, she supposedly overestimates the extent to which traits similar in meaning may be said to actually co-occur in the same individuals. The lay personality theorist projects her beliefs about personality onto the targets of her observations instead of being a truly objective observer (for further discussion of this issue, see Borkenau's chapter in this volume).

The two-pronged attack on the trait has left its victim seriously enfeebled but, as the interminable nature of the hostilities attests, the wounds are not mortal. The behavioural consistency debate has demonstrated that individuals do not behave in as predictable and stable ways as has been generally assumed, and the implicit personality theory debate has demonstrated that top-down processing in personality perception can be misleading. Neither set of arguments has totally invalidated the traditional view of the trait as a hypothetical construct located within the individual. Nevertheless, they have succeeded in talking all the fun out of it. Although the traditional trait concept may linger for another thirty years, its problems are serious enough to prevent it from being the focus of creative and powerful developments in personality psychology. Such developments must come from new conceptualizations of the trait concept.

THE SOCIAL CONSTRUCTION OF PERSONALITY

The transformation of the trait being proposed here draws on the lessons learned from the failures of the traditional view primarily by regarding the role of constructive processes in personality perception as the focus of interest rather than the source of embarrassment. A major consequence of this re-focussing is a shift in the metaphorical location of traits from *within* individuals to *between* individuals. Personality construction is a process which involves observers as much as actors. The building blocks of personality are (a) the behaviours the actor performs within a social context, (b) the constructive understanding and interpretation of these behaviours by the observer, and (c) the constructive understanding and interpretation of these behaviours by the actor her or himself (Hampson, 1982a, 1984). Traits are shorthands for behaviours-plus-ascribed-social-significance. They are the means by which we represent and communicate the product of this constructive process. Hence, traits may be regarded as cognitive categories of the same form as those we use for other domains of knowledge (Buss & Craik, 1983 and this volume; Hampson, 1982b). These views were inspired by the work of Eleanor Rosch and her associates on the categorization of the object world (e.g., Rosch, 1978; Rosch & Mervis, 1975; Rosch, Mervis, Gray, Johnson, & Boyes-Braem, 1976).

We use personality traits both for describing behaviour and for describing people. The cognitive-category model of traits is concerned with the use of traits for describing behaviour. It is assumed that the instances of trait categories are *acts,* and not the people performing the acts. Reconceptualizing the trait concept as it applies to behaviour prompts a reconsideration of how the trait concept applies to people. The process of trait attribution ('from act to disposition') has been regarded as a one-step transition from the observation of an act to the attribution of a disposition to the actor (Jones & Davis, 1965). In the light of the cognitive-category model of traits, this view of trait attribution appears too simple. The process of personality construction may be seen as requiring three relatively distinct phases: The comprehension of an act, the categorization of an act with trait categories, and the attribution of dispositions to people. Personality construction takes us from acts through traits to dispositions. These phases of the construction process put together the elements of socially constructed personality: The actor's behaviour and the social meaning of that behaviour ascribed by the observer and the self-observer.

THE INVESTIGATION OF TRAIT CATEGORIES

The research to be described in this paper focuses on the use of traits for categorizing behaviour. This work is being done in collaboration with Lewis R. Goldberg and Oliver P. John of the

University of Oregon and is still in its early stages: hence it will only be possible to give a flavour of the kind of findings emerging from our research program.

Category Breadth

Categories for the object world vary on a dimension of category breadth. For example, the same object can be categorized at the broad level as a "musical instrument," at the middle level as a "piano," or at the narrow level as a "grand piano." The first hypothesis to be tested in the systematic investigation of traits as categories (and acts as instances of these categories) is that traits vary in category breadth. For example, the act "Handing in an assignment on time" could be categorized at the broad level as "responsible," at the middle level as "reliable," and at the narrow level as "punctual." Although it is intuitively reasonable to suppose that traits vary on a breadth dimension, the assignment of trait categories to different levels is less obvious than the assignment of object categories to different levels. Therefore, we have asked judges to rate traits on category breadth, and we have assessed the degree of their agreement.

Guided by Goldberg's previous taxonomic work (e.g., Goldberg, 1982), 456 traits were selected for the category-breadth rating study. They were chosen because they were familiar to college students, they were reasonably representative of the five major domains of personality description (Norman, 1963) – the Big Five – and they included approximately equal numbers of socially desirable and undesirable characteristics. Judges have rated these traits for category breadth, which was defined for them, in one part of the instructions, as follows:

> We want you to rate each of the following words on category breadth. Very broad words are those that include in their definitions a wide range of behaviours; very narrow words are those that include a much more limited range of behaviours. For each word you are to decide how broad (abstract, general, global) is its range of behavioural referents, relative to the other words in the list.

A category-breadth scale-value for each trait was then derived from the factor scores on the first unrotated principal component of the intercorrelations among the judges' ratings. The interjudge reliability of the ratings from only three subjects, as assessed by coefficient alpha, is already .69.

On the basis of these preliminary ratings, the two broadest traits in our list are *active* and *extroverted,* and the narrowest traits are *faultfinding, fidgety, jittery, miserly, overstudious, punctual, musical,* and *wordy.* Table 1 gives some more examples. The traits are presented in groups of three, and each of these triads describes the same domain of personality at different levels of breadth. The category-breadth ratings are given in standard scores (with a mean of zero and a standard deviation of 1, the decimal point omitted); positive numbers indicate broader categories and negative numbers indicate narrower categories. The traits are divided into desirable and

TABLE 1: *Preliminary Category Breadth (CB) (N = 3) and Social Desirability (SDy) (N = 100) Ratings for Desirable and Undesirable Traits Organized in Triads*

Desirable Traits	CB	SDy	Undesirable Traits	CB	SDy
EXTROVERTED	+238	6.6	INTROVERTED	+173	3.7
Sociable	+111	7.5	*Reserved*	-21	5.3
talkative	-171	5.3	silent	-199	4.2
CONFIDENT	+177	8.1	DOMINEERING	+46	3.2
Assertive	+123	6.2	*Nagging*	-171	1.7
outspoken	-155	5.3	pushy	-166	?
CONSIDERATE	+83	8.4	INCONSIDERATE	+29	1.8
Polite	-68	8.0	*Impolite*	-51	2.0
tactful	-140	8.0	tactless	-140	2.4
KIND	+177	8.5	UNKIND	+112	1.7
Generous	+66	7.8	*Rude*	-138	1.9
helpful	+83	8.0	greedy	-49	1.7
RELIABLE	+76	8.4	UNRELIABLE	+44	1.8
Dutiful	-78	6.7	*Careless*	+66	2.5
punctual	-227	7.3	unpunctual	-195	3.2
COMPETENT	+210	?	IRRESPONSIBLE	+177	1.9
Methodical	-17	5.8	*Negligent*	+11	2.1
systematic	-78	6.9	forgetful	-11	3.0
STABLE	+145	7.6	UNSTABLE	+84	2.8
Secure	+50	7.7	*Insecure*	+72	3.2
calm	+17	7.4	jumpy	-166	?
HAPPY	+111	8.3	UNHAPPY	+111	2.4
Optimistic	+72	7.3	*Sad*	+50	2.4
cheerful	+10	8.2	pessimistic	+07	3.2
TALENTED	+65	?	UNTALENTED	+76	?
Artistic	-134	7.2	*Unartistic*	-134	3.7
musical	-195	6.6	unmusical	-227	?
CULTURED	+05	7.4	UNCULTURED	?	2.7
Sophisticated	-45	6.5	*Unsophisticated*	+87	3.9
polished	-122	7.0	unpolished	-90	3.4

undesirable triads and the social desirability ratings, where available from Norman (1967), are also shown. As identified by the category-breadth ratings, BROAD Traits are printed in upper case, *Middle* level traits are in italics, and narrow traits are in lower case.

These preliminary rating data are encouraging. They suggest both that judges find the category breadth dimension a meaningful one and that judges demonstrate acceptable levels of agreement in their ratings. However, we do not regard these ratings as our final criterion for category breadth. For this purpose, we have devised a category-breadth judgement task, to be described below.

The Hierarchical Organization of Trait Categories

The second hypothesis currently under investigation is concerned with the hierarchical organization of trait categories. In the object world categories frequently demonstrate some degree of class inclusion (e.g., a "grand piano," is a kind of "piano," and a "piano" is a kind of "musical instrument"). A broad category subsumes a middle level category which in turn subsumes a narrow category. An object that has been categorized as a "grand piano" must also belong to the higher level categories "piano" and "musical instrument". This is an example of a hierarchical taxonomy with strict class inclusion. Recent work by Hampton (1982) suggests that there are hierarchies in the object domain which do not demonstrate strict class inclusion. In his investigation of three-level hierarchies of natural-object categories, he found evidence for intransitive relations within some of these hierarchies. For example, whereas subjects agreed that a *Chair* was a kind of FURNITURE and that a ski-lift was a kind of a *Chair*, they did not agree that a ski-lift was a kind of FURNITURE. If the hierarchy was a strictly inclusive one (FURNITURE, *Chair*, ski-lift), then no such intransitivities would have been observed.

In our model, the instances of trait categories are behavioural acts, and therefore a strictly hierarchical organization of traits implies that all of the acts subsumed by a narrow trait (e.g., *punctual*) are also included in the set of acts categorized by a broader trait describing the same aspect of personality (e.g., *reliable*). The principle of class inclusion, which characterizes a hierarchical organization of classes, applies to the acts. Given the findings of Hampton (1982), we do not expect to find a strictly inclusive hierarchical organization throughout the personality domain; however, some degree of class inclusion is predicted. We are currently developing techniques for exploring the degree of hierarchicality to be found in traits which describe the same aspect of personality but differ in category breadth.

One such technique is based on the asymmetrical relations that characterize a hierarchical organization of categories: Whereas it makes sense to say that a narrow category is included in a broad category, a broad category cannot be included in a narrow category. For example, the sentence "A piano is a kind of musical instrument" makes sense, whereas the sentence "A musical instrument is a kind of piano" does not. The categories are related asymmetrically to one another. We are studying trait asymmetries by inserting trait pairs differing in category breadth into sentences of the following form: "To be X is a way of being Y" and "To be Y is a way of being X". Subjects are presented with these sentence pairs and asked to choose "which sentence is more meaningful - in other words which makes the most sense to you." For example, which is more meaningful: (a) "To be talkative is a way of being extroverted" or (b) "To be extroverted is a way of being talkative"? If the behaviours referred to by the narrower trait are regarded as a subset of those referred to by the broader trait, then the sentence in which the narrower trait precedes the broad trait should be chosen as more meaningful (in this example, "To be talkative is a way of being extroverted").

In our first study, we used the traits shown in Table 1. For each triad, three sentence pairs were generated, each contrasting two traits. Forty-eight introductory psychology students took part in this

TABLE 2: *Interjudge Agreement on Concept Asymmetries (N = 48).*

Desirable Concepts	Undesirable Concepts
I. Nouns	
100%: ANIMAL / *Bird* / eagle (100%) (100%)	100%: REPTILE / *Snake* / rattlesnake (98%) (100%)
100%: MUSICAL INSTRUMENT/*Piano*/grand piano (100%) (96%)	98%: INSECT / *Spider* / tarantula (96%) (100%)
II. Verbs	
100%: CLEAN / *Wash* / shampoo (88%) (98%)	100%: OFFEND / *Snub* / ignore (94%) (77%)
96%: SOCIALIZE / *Party* / barbeque (96%) (100%)	96%: ARGUE / *Disagree* / squabble (65%) (63%)
III. Adjectives	
96%: COLORED / *Green* / emerald (98%) (89%)	83%: ROTTEN / *Rancid* / sour (75%) (53%)
77%: CURVED / *Spherical* / circular (79%) (54%)	75%: ANGULAR / *Rectangular* / square (86%) (81%)
IV. Personality Traits	
92%: EXTROVERTED / *Sociable* / talkative (95%) (98%)	81%: INTROVERTED / *Reserved* / silent (66%) (60%)
92%: CONFIDENT / *Assertive* / out-spoken (66%) (75%)	89%: DOMINEERING / *Nagging* / pushy (84%) (52%)
71%: CONSIDERATE / *Polite* / tactful (52%) (73%)	75%: INCONSIDERATE / *Impolite* / tactless (60%) (73%)
75%: KIND / *Generous* / helpful (88%) (50%)	96%: UNKIND / *Rude* / greedy (75%) (89%)
94%: RELIABLE / *Dutiful* / punctual (73%) (81%)	89%: UNRELIABLE / *Careless* / unpunctual (89%) (75%)
83%: COMPETENT / *Methodical* / systematic (80%) (63%)	94%: IRRESPONSIBLE / *Negligent* / forgetful (64%) (77%)
84%: STABLE / *Secure* / calm (58%) (83%)	92%: UNSTABLE / *Insecure* / jumpy (69%) (92%)
89%: HAPPY / *Optimistic* /cheerful (48%) (66%)	71%: UNHAPPY / *Pessimistic* / sad (54%) (59%)
92%: TALENTED / *Artistic* / musical (75%) (94%)	87%: UNTALENTED / *Unartistic* / unmusical (66%) (85%)
79%: CULTURED / *Sophisticated* / polished (64%) (79%)	79%: UNCULTURED/*Unsophisticated*/unpolished (54%) (75%)

How to read this table: Each hierarchy is listed in BROAD / *Middle* / narrow order, as determined by the responses from this sample. In front of each hierarchy are the values for the comparison of the BROAD with the narrow concepts. Under each slash are the values for the comparison of the BROAD with the *Middle*, and the *Middle* with the narrow concepts. Each of these values is the proportion of subjects ordering the concepts in this direction.

study. As a way of familiarizing the subjects with this task, they began with sentences containing pairs of nouns, verbs, and adjectives ranging in category breadth before moving on to the trait sentences. A further 54 subjects, drawn from the same population, completed the category-breadth judgement task in which the same trait pairs used in the asymmetry task were presented and the subjects were asked to judge which of the traits in each pair was broader. Here is a portion of the instructions from the task (labelled "Deciding which of two categories is the broader: A test of verbal knowledge"):

> Broad traits are those that refer to a wide range of different types of behaviours, whereas narrow traits are those that refer to a much more limited range of types of behaviours. For example, consider the two traits "punctual" and "dependable." There are many types of behaviours referred to by the trait "dependable," whereas there are only a few types of behaviours (all of which involve arriving on time) that are referred to by the trait "punctual." So, clearly "dependable" is broader than "punctual."

The results of the asymmetry task are shown in Table 2.

The triads are ordered from left to right: BROAD, *middle,* and narrow. The values refer to the percentage of subjects who preferred the sentence in which the narrower concept preceded the broader one.

Table 2 shows the decline in interjudge agreement between the nouns, verbs, adjectives, and traits, here deliberately confounded with their order of presentation to the subjects. Nevertheless, the majority of the trait triads produced marked asymmetries, and in all except one case (HAPPY/*Optimistic*) the asymmetry was in the direction predicted by the category-breadth ratings. However, the strength of these asymmetries (as indexed by the size of the interjudge percentages) showed considerable variation (50% to 94%). What are the reasons for this variation? We have tried to answer this question both statistically and empirically.

Inspection of the percentages in Table 2 suggests that the largest asymmetry effects occurred where the category-breadth difference between the traits in the pair was greatest (i.e., in the BROAD versus narrow comparisons). The correlations between the intra-pair differences on initial category breadth ratings and the asymmetry proportions are shown in Table 3.

Whether based on the 30 desirable pairs, the 30 undesirable pairs, or all 60 pairs, the initial category breadth ratings were highly predictive of the direction and strength of the asymmetry effect (.88, .80, and .84, respectively). These correlations are indicative of the validity of the initial category-breadth ratings. The category-breadth judgement task yielded category-breadth agreement proportions (i.e., the proportion of the sample agreeing on which of the two traits was broader). When these proportions were correlated with the asymmetry proportions, they proved to be highly predictive of the asymmetry effect across the desirable, the undesirable, and all trait pairs combined (.81, .72, and .76, respectively). It should also be noted that the two measures of breadth are highly correlated. So, we may conclude that the greater was the difference in independently assessed category breadth, the higher was the proportion of subjects selecting the sentence where the narrow trait preceded the broad trait.

S.E. Hampson

TABLE 3: *Intercorrelations across All of the Trait Pairs Included in Study 1*

Variable	Type of Pairs	Category Breadth Proportions	Intra-pair Differences	
			Initial Category Breadth Ratings	Social Desirability Ratings
Asymmetry Proportions	30 Desirable	.81	.88	.51
	30 Undesirable	.72	.80	-.38
	All 60	.76	.84	.17
Category-Breadth Proportions	30 Desirable		.81	.62
	30 Undesirable		.72	-.20
	All 60		.77	.28
Initial Category-Breadth Ratings	30 Desirable			.65
	30 Undesirable			-.34
	All 60			.27

Note: All correlations are r_c coefficients (Cohen, 1969) computed across the 2 x k pairs (where k equals the number of pairs) constructed by including each pair twice, once in each term-order (e.g., *Reliable – Punctual* and *Punctual – Reliable*). This coefficient is invariant to the order of these paired values.

Unfortunately, however, within this set of traits there was some confounding between intra-pair differences in category breadth and in social desirability. For the desirable pairs, these two variables were highly positively related, whereas for the undesirable pairs the relation was weaker and negative in sign. As a consequence, across all 60 trait pairs, there was a low positive relation between desirability and breadth. To test whether the predicted relation between category breadth and asymmetry proportions could be explained away by differences in social desirability between the two traits in each pair, we computed the partial correlations between the asymmetry and category-breadth proportions, with the effect of social desirability statistically controlled. Happily, these analyses showed that the size of the asymmetry vs. breadth relationships were not substantially attenuated when social desirability was partialled out.

Finally, in order to determine whether the social desirability findings were an artifact of the particular traits selected for this study, the correlation between social desirability and the initial category-breadth ratings was calculated across all traits for which both measures were available. This correlation was positive and statistically significant for the 231 desirable traits (r = .19), and essentially zero for the 212 undesirable traits (r = .015). Thus, the finding appears to be a general one.

In subsequent experiments, the stimulus materials were changed to unconfound social desirability and category-breadth differences. The selection of the traits for the triads was constrained by equalizing as far as possible the social desirability of the traits within each triad. In addition, 39 of the same subjects who performed the asymmetry judgements also supplied category-breadth preferences, judging which was the broader of the two words in each trait pair that had been used in constructing the asymmetry sentences.

Two groups of 53 and 58 subjects respectively have been tested with these new materials and the asymmetry percentages obtained from each group correlated .77, thus demonstrating the reliability of the asymmetry task. The experimental control for social desirability had the effect of lowering the strength of the asymmetry judgements for the desirable traits but not substantially altering the asymmetries for undesirable traits. This pattern of results was expected since, in the first experiment, social desirability and category breadth were correlated only in the desirable traits. Experimental control of social desirability served to eliminate some reliable category breadth variance for the desirable but not the undesirable traits.

The category-breadth preferences were used to test the hypothesis that although the subjects *were* using differences in category breadth when making their asymmetry judgements, the category-breadth differences *they* perceived were not the same as the category-breadth differences derived from the judges' category-breadth ratings from our earlier study. This hypothesis was partially supported. The percentage of subjects choosing the broader trait (as defined by our rating data) in the category-breadth preference task correlated .50 with these same subjects' asymmetry percentages. However, computing the same correlation for each subject individually revealed tremendous between-subject variation. For the majority of subjects, their category-breadth preferences mirrored their asymmetry judgements, whereas for a minority there was no relationship between the judgements made on one task and the judgements made on the other.

Thus it may be assumed that, for most subjects, both the asymmetry and the category-breadth judgements engaged the same understanding of the concept of category breadth. The instructions for the category-breadth judgement task emphasized that category breadth referred to the variety of behavioural manifestations of the trait, with broad words referring to a wide range of behaviours and narrow words referring to a much more limited range of behaviours. There is no evidence to suggest that subjects were using some other definition of category breadth (e.g., in terms of the number of acquaintances who manifest this trait). Note that the definition of category breadth supplied in the instructions allows for the greater situational range of broad as opposed to narrow traits.

Buss and Craik (in this volume) draw attention to the role of individual differences, such as sex and cognitive styles, in the perception of trait categories. We have not observed the sex difference to which they refer, but it may be that an examination of a cognitive style variable such as need for cognition (Caccioppo & Petty, 1982) would prove helpful in understanding why some subjects appeared to have interpreted the two tasks differently. So far, we have not collected a systematic corpus of behavioural instances of these trait categories upon which to test our ideas concerning category breadth and hierarchicality. However, Buss and Craik (in this volume) report obtaining asymmetries in their multiple sorting task which suggest that this would prove a useful line of research. Although they do not offer a theoretical explanation for their asymmetries, these effects are predicted by the present theorising. The one example they give is for quarrelsome and dominant: behaviours generated as manifestations of quarrelsome were frequently miscategorized as dominant, whereas behaviours generated for dominant were only infrequently miscategorized as quarrelsome. This finding can be readily explained by the concepts of category breadth and class inclusion (dominant is the broader trait and hence inclusive of acts also categorizable as quarrelsome, but dominant acts need not necessarily be categorized as quarrelsome).

    Although we still have a long way to go in fully understanding how subjects arrive at asymmetry judgements, we can conclude that category breadth does play a part in the process. These studies have isolated some sets of traits which demonstrate strong asymmetries suggestive of strict class inclusion (e.g., UNINTELLIGENT/*Imperceptive*/ short-sighted), as well as others with virtually no hierarchical structure (e.g., AGREEABLE/*Diplomatic*/tactful). In our current attempts to understand these asymmetry data, we have been led to think more carefully about the features of trait categories, and it is to some of our ideas about features that I will now turn.

The Features of Trait Categories

The category-breadth and asymmetry judgements are ways of exploring the vertical organization of trait categories. Another part of our research program is concerned with investigating the horizontal organization of trait categories - the instances of trait categories and the issues concerning category membership. The starting point for these studies is the development of a theory of the features of trait categories. We believe that an understanding of trait categories at the feature level is essential. Just as the same idea can be expressed in language in many different ways, the behavioural manifestations of a particular trait can take on many different forms. It is therefore vital to understand how these different acts come to be categorized by the same trait. We must look for similarity between the acts at the feature level. In our research group, it is Oliver John who has been making the major contribution to the theory of trait features (see his chapter in this volume). We expect features to vary in abstractness, with more concrete features consisting of the motor movements out of which the behavioural acts are composed, and more abstract features referring to the intentional and motivational inferences that may be drawn from behaviours. It will be these abstract features, we suspect, that will prove most important in discriminating among trait categories.

    Although every category has a potentially huge number of features, we only focus on a small subset when we use a category. Context seems to be an important factor in determining which feature or subset of features becomes the focus of attention, or becomes most 'salient' (Miller, 1978; Ortony, 1979; Tversky, 1977). For example, in talking about picnics, a 'treestump' can become a 'table' (Miller, 1978). To return to the asymmetry task, the presentation of two traits in the same sentence means that the second trait can provide a context for the understanding of the first. Many traits have several shades of meaning (e.g., 'rough' can mean aggressive or coarse), and the proximity of another trait will increase the likelihood of focussing on the meaning prompted by the features common to the two traits. For example, in the context of 'inelegant', 'rough' is more likely to be interpreted as 'coarse'. In our category breadth ratings, *Rough* was rated as broader than inelegant, and yet subjects in the asymmetry task showed a marked preference (76%) for the sentence in which *Rough* preceded inelegant. The presence of inelegant may have increased the salience of the 'coarse' feature of *Rough,* causing *Rough* to appear in this context as a relatively narrow word referring to a specific set of behaviours.

Analyzing the asymmetry task in terms of features is just one example of the potential power of working with trait categories at the feature level. More generally, we believe that a full understanding of category membership depends on specifying the features associated with their categories and on being able to analyze acts in terms of their features. We assume that the acts belonging to a trait category share a family resemblance and not an identical set of defining features (Rosch & Mervis, 1975). Since category membership is not all or none, some acts are more prototypical for a particular category than others (Buss & Craik, 1980). To understand prototypicality it is necessary to have a theory of features, since the prototypicality of an act should be a function of the proportion of features associated with the category to features not associated with the category.

The Use of Trait Categories at Different Levels

The investigation of category breadth, hierarchicality, and features provides the essential groundwork for the study of people's use of trait categories for describing behaviour. Rosch proposed that there is a middle or basic level of categorization which is preferred in most contexts (Rosch et al., 1976), but we suspect that in the personality domain the preferred level will be particularly susceptible to context effects such as the degree of the perceiver's expertise or the purpose for which the trait categorization is being made. By studying these context effects we hope to discover what level of trait categorization represents the best trade-off between informativeness and cognitive economy for various different kinds of naturally-occurring personality descriptions (e.g., casual conversation, assessing job candidates, letters of recommendation, case reports).

The Wider Relevance of the Cognitive-Category Model of Personality Traits

This chapter began by sketching the debate over the validity of the trait concept in both personality psychology and lay theories of personality. With no satisfactory resolution of this debate in sight, it was argued that a major reconceptualization of the trait concept was called for. The reconceptualization of traits as cognitive categories is seen as just such a development, and therefore it has important implications both for personality psychology and the study of lay personality theories.

The cognitive-category model of personality traits reflects a constructivist view of personality by encompassing both the correlated features of real-world behaviours and the cognitive constructions we put upon them. The essence of the constructivist approach to personality is that the traditional distinction between personality as studied by personality psychologists, and the beliefs about personality studied by social psychologists, should no longer be made. Much of personality psychology has been concerned with personality assessment in which personality traits are assumed to be identified exclusively with the individual being assessed. The constructivist view of personality and the associated cognitive-category model of traits proposes that personality cannot be seen as having an existence independent of the cognitive constructions of the observer of the behavioural event being used to infer personality.

To determine whether a particular trait is appropriate for categorizing a person's behaviour, it is necessary to assess the degree to which that person performs the behaviours perceived as prototypical for that trait. In this regard, the present view of traits is similar to the act-frequency approach (see Buss & Craik, this volume), except for one important modification. Buss and Craik argue that the acts which make up a trait category have a causal potency independent of cognitive constructions. By insisting on this extreme realist position, Buss and Craik have rejected a constructivist view of personality traits and embraced the traditional view of traits along with all its accompanying weaknesses. In contrast, the present cognitive-category view of traits sees the act-frequency approach to personality assessment as a powerful new development so long as the constructive aspect is recognised by, for example, using individualized act lists to insure that the assessor and the assessee agree on the construction of the trait, and by considering both self-assessed act frequencies and peer assessments.

The present reconceptualization of personality traits also has implications for the study of beliefs about personality, in other words, for lay theories of personality assessment. Our research program is primarily concerned with knowledge about personality as it is represented in the form of trait categories. However, investigating the structure of personality knowledge still leaves many unanswered questions surrounding the process of personality construction. At the beginning of this chapter a distinction was made between act categorization and trait attribution, the former referring to the categorization of acts with traits, the latter referring to the attribution of traits or dispositions to people. Our present research is concerned with the categorization of acts with traits and we have yet to explore how traits are used in describing the people performing the acts. However, the reconceptualization of traits as cognitive categories requires a reconceptualization of the trait attribution process.

The study of socially constructed personality involves both an understanding of the constructive processes involved in comprehending personality-relevant behaviour (act categorization) and an understanding of the constructive processes involved in explaining behaviour in personality terms (trait attribution). Emphasizing the distinction between the use of traits to describe behaviours (act categorization) and the use of traits to describe people (trait attribution) leads to three sets of empirical questions for future research. First, it should be possible to specify the conditions which will result in act categorization and how they differ from the conditions which will result in trait attributions. Second, the information used in each process ought to be different, at least in some respects. Third, the benefits to the personality cognizer ought to be different in each case.

Trait attribution is not usually regarded as an appropriate topic for personality psychologists, since it is concerned with people's beliefs about personality, rather than the study of actual individual differences. The constructivist view of personality eschews this distinction. Individual differences have to be perceived and comprehended by the actor or the observer, or both, in order that they be recognized as such, and this is a constructive process. Therefore, trait attribution becomes a vital step in the construction of personality, and this is the next target for a constructivist reconceptualization.

ACKNOWLEDGMENTS

Some of the material in this chapter was presented at the 56th Annual Meeting of the Midwestern Psychological Association, Chicago, May 3-5, 1984. The research described here is supported by Grant MH-39077 from the National Institute of Mental Health. Several of these studies were conducted while I was a visiting professor at the University of Illinois (1983/84), and I am most grateful to members of the Department of Psychology for their assistance. I would like to thank Lewis R. Goldberg and Oliver P. John for their advice and help during the preparation of this manuscript.

REFERENCES

Buss, D.M., & Craik, K.H. (1980). The frequency concept of disposition: Dominance and prototypically dominant acts. *Journal of Personality, 48*, 379-392.

Buss, D.M., & Craik, K.H. (1983). The act frequency approach to personality. *Psychological Review, 90*, 105-126.

Caccioppo, J.T., & Petty, R.E. (1982). The need for cognition. *Journal of Personality and Social Psychology, 42*, 116-131.

Cohen, J. (1969). r_c: A profile similarity coefficient invariant over variable reflection. *Psychological Bulletin, 71*, 281-284.

Craik, K. (1969). Personality unvanquished. (Review of *Personality and assessment* by W. Mischel). *Contemporary Psychology, 14*, 147-148.

Goldberg, L.R. (1982). From Ace to Zombie: Some explorations in the language of personality. In C.D. Spielberger & J.N. Butcher (Eds.), *Advances in personality assessment* (Vol. 1, pp. 203-234). Hillsdale, NJ: Erlbaum.

Guilford, J.P. (1975). Factors and factors of personality. *Psychological Bulletin, 82,* 802–814.

Hampson, S.E. (1982a). *The construction of personality: An introduction.* London: Routledge & Kegan Paul.

Hampson, S.E. (1982b). Person memory: A semantic category model of personality traits. *British Journal of Psychology, 73,* 1–11.

Hampson, S.E. (1984). The social construction of personality. In H. Bonarius, G. van Heck, & N. Smid (Eds.), *Personality psychology in Europe* (pp. 3–14). Lisse: Swets & Zeitlinger.

Hampton, J.A. (1982). A demonstration of intransitivity in natural categories. *Cognition, 12,* 151–164.

Jones, E.E., & Davis, K.E. (1965). From acts to dispositions: The attribution process in person perception. In L. Berkowitz (Ed.), *Advances in experimental social psychology* (Vol. 2, pp. 219–266). New York: Academic Press.

Kahneman, D., & Tversky, A. (1973). On the psychology of prediction. *Psychological Review, 80,* 237–251.

Miller, G.A. (1978). Practical and lexical knowledge. In E. Rosch & B.B. Lloyd (Eds.), *Cognition and categorization* (pp. 305–319). Hillsdale, NJ: Erlbaum.

Mischel, W. (1968). *Personality and assessment.* New York: Wiley.

Norman. W.T. (1963). Toward an adequate taxonomy of personality attributes: Replicated factor structure in peer nomination personality ratings. *Journal of Abnormal and Social Psychology, 66,* 564–583.

Norman, W.T. (1967). *2800 personality trait descriptors: Normative operating characteristics for a university population.* Department of Psychology, University of Michigan.

Ortony, A. (1979). Beyond literal similarity. *Psychological Review, 86,* 161–180.

Rosch, E. (1978). Principles of categorization. In E. Rosch & B.B. Lloyd (Eds.), *Cognition and categorization* (pp. 27–48). Hillsdale, NJ: Erlbaum.

Rosch, E., & Mervis, C.B. (1975). Family resemblances: Studies in the internal structure of categories. *Cognitive Psychology, 7,* 573–605.

Rosch, E., Mervis, C.B., Gray, W.D., Johnson, D., & Boyes-Braem, P. (1976). Basic objects in natural categories. *Cognitive Psychology, 8,* 382–439.

Shweder, R.A. (1975). How relevant is an individual differences theory of personality? *Journal of Personality, 43,* 455–484.

Shweder, R.A. (1977). Likeness and likelihood in everyday thought: Magical thinking in judgements about personality. *Current Anthropology, 18,* 637–658.

Shweder, R.A. (1982). Fact and artifact in trait perception: The systematic distortion hypothesis. In B.A. Maher & W.S. Maher (Eds.), *Progress in experimental personality research* (Vol. 2, pp. 65–100). New York: Academic Press.

Shweder, R.A., & D'Andrade, R.G. (1980). The systematic distortion hypothesis. *New Directions for Methodology of Social and Behavioral Science, 4,* 37–58.

Tversky, A. (1977). Features of similarity. *Psychological Review, 84,* 327–352.

HOW SHALL A TRAIT BE CALLED:
A FEATURE ANALYSIS OF ALTRUISM

by

Oliver P. John

University of Oregon
and
Oregon Research Institute
United States

The various and highly diverse approaches to the study of individual differences share one important concern: How shall a trait construct be defined? Whether one favors a biological (Gray, 1981; Strelau, 1983), social-learning (Mischel, 1973), social-construction (Hampson, 1982), summary-label (Wiggins, 1974), or psychometric (Goldberg, 1972; Hofstee, 1984) view of traits, a conceptual analysis of the trait construct is a prerequisite to subsequent empirical work. Explicit theoretical definitions, the first step in a research program of construct validation, are essential to the development of good measuring instruments, and good measurement is at the very heart of empirically founded progress in personality psychology.

Currently, however, personality psychology is a field characterized by a motley collection of theories and a plethora of diverse measures of partially overlapping constructs. Operational definitions of traits vary from study to study and from test to test, partly because test authors have different conceptions of the construct and partly because researchers do not define their constructs in sufficient detail. The lack of explicit construct definitions has particularly impeded progress in personality questionnaire construction (Angleitner, John, & Löhr, 1986). Loevinger's (1957, p. 658) characterization of the practice of writing (or selecting) items and labeling a scale as a highly idiosyncratic, arbitrary, and therefore largely nonreproducible process is as valid today as it was 25 years ago.

As recently as 1983, Furnham and Henderson (1983) noted that the concept and definition of assertiveness is by no means clear, and they conducted a content analysis of five self-report inventories commonly used to assess this trait. Whereas these scales all purport to measure the global concept of assertiveness, Furnham and Henderson's analysis showed substantial differences in the "types" of assertiveness measured and, consequently, low intercorrelations among subjects' scores on these scales. Thus, as the Furnham and Henderson analysis suggests, theory and assessment of assertiveness might benefit from a careful analysis of the features of assertive behaviors and a construct-oriented approach to measurement. Eventually, one would hope, the conceptual analysis of the trait should precede, not follow, the construction of a scale to measure it.

It is time that we personality psychologists become more theoretically minded. We should start doing what we have left in the past to philosophers and linguists - and what they, being caught up in their own endeavours and controversies, have, of course, *not* done for us. We must provide descriptions of the meaning of those personality trait terms that are so commonly used by psychologists and lay people alike. Currently, we employ these words and pretend that everybody knows what they mean. At the same time, however, we witness within our own field heated disputes about the meanings of such terms as Assertiveness, Altruism, and Extraversion (e.g., Eysenck, 1977; Gray, 1981; Guilford, 1977; Wilson, 1978). Not only do we need to define our constructs more precisely, we also need to understand how our subjects, their peers, and their teachers use those trait terms in construct-validation studies.

Indeed, personality questionnaires often contain items that require subjects to make trait attributions to themselves; responses to such items are taken as evidence for the trait, without much theoretical reflection about the processes by which people arrive at such attributions. Even Bem and Allen's (1974) Cross-Situational Behavior Survey, supposedly assessing only specific behaviors in specific situations, contains statements such as "How *conscientious* are you about your homework?" (emphasis added). Moreover, personality psychologists employ trait concepts in both ordinary and scientific language contexts without making a clear distinction between the two. Cattell, in fact, did make an effort "to avoid the pollution of meaning in scientific discussion" (1973, p. 54) by inventing a "host of neologic gobbledegook" (Goldberg, 1980) for his structural dimensions. The problem with his approach is that it did not work. Personality psychologists, like everybode else, communicate via the natural language, and must, in order to understand what Cattell means by Harria, Premsia, or Zeppia translate those terms back into their natural equivalents. Moreover, *if* Cattell's new terms described some important individual difference in a new and unique way, they would soon be popularized and become part of everyday language, just as has happened with the term *extraversion* (Goldberg, 1980).

If we employ ordinary-language concepts in our research, we need an in-depth understanding of everyday-language usage, including an appreciation of its fuzzy nature, context dependency, and powerfulness in communication. What is urgently needed, then, are analyses of the *meaning* of common trait terms. Such analyses must specify the relationship between each trait concept and its observable referents (i.e., events in the "real world") as well as the similarities and differences among related traits.

TRAIT TERMS AND THE CLASSIFICATION OF SOCIAL BEHAVIOR

British empiricist philosophy (e.g., Locke, 1690) viewed concepts as consisting of an intension (meaning) and an extension (the objects or events designated by the concept). The intension is a specification of those qualities that a thing or event must possess to be a member of the class; the extension consists of things that have those qualities. Thus, qualities (nowadays called features or attributes) serve to relate concepts to the real world, thus connecting the meaning of a concept with the objects or events that fit that meaning.

In research on the categorization of objects (e.g., Rosch, 1978; Mervis & Rosch, 1981), the features or attributes that specify the meaning of a category are generally of four types, specifically parts, physical characteristics such as color or shape, relational concepts such as *taller*, and functional concepts. What features might connect the meaning of personality trait concepts with the real-world, that is, their extension? How can the extension of a trait concept be described? How can we conceptualize the relations among trait concepts? These issues can be studied within a framework that conceptualizes traits as categories of behavioral acts or events.

Some Background on Categorization Research

Recent cognitively oriented approaches to personality psychology consider traits as concepts or categories applied to observations of people and their behaviors (Buss & Craik, 1980, 1983; Cantor & Mischel, 1979; Hampson, 1982; Mischel & Peake, 1982). The common source of inspiration for these views has been Rosch's work on semantic categories (e.g., Rosch, Mervis, Gray, Johnson, & Boyes-Braem, 1976).

In the domain of objects, some categories can be organized hierarchically, such that one category includes a set of less inclusive ones (Rosch, 1978). For example, the category *furniture* is broader and more inclusive than *chair*, which in turn is more inclusive than *armchair*. This is illustrated in the lower half of Figure 1. Members of a category at any level of a hierarchy are referred to as instances. For example, one particular instance of the category *chair* is the one on which you are currently sitting. Instances, in turn, can be viewed as being composed of features (Smith & Medin, 1981; Tversky & Hemenway, 1984). Finally, category membership can be defined in terms of shared features (Tversky, 1977), although not in an all-or-none fashion; rather, instances may be more or less "prototypical" members of the category, depending on the proportion

Category	Chair	Helpful
Instance	The one on which you are sitting	Giving the beggar five dollars
Features		
Perceptual:	Legs, Seat	??
Functional:	Sit-on-ableness, Human-made	??

HIERARCHICAL STRUCTURE

Superordinate	FURNITURE	ALTRUISTIC
Middle (Basic)	Chair	Helpful
Subordinate	armchair	charitable

Figure 1: *Categories in the World of Objects and of Social Episodes.*

of features they share with the category prototype. That is, although penguins and ostriches may belong to the category *birds,* they are not as good (or prototypical) bird exemplars as are bluejays and robins.

Similarly, trait concepts have been viewed as categories, with similar general properties as such other conceptual categories as *red, chair,* or *lie.* This is shown in the right-hand side of Figure 1. In Buss and Craik's (1983) as well as Hampson's (1982) model, instances of trait categories are behavioral acts, such as "Demanding a back rub" or "Talking on the phone to a friend for two hours." Empirical research on a small set of traits has already led to a substantial amount of knowledge about the characteristics of these categories. At the category level, we know that traits vary on a dimension of breadth and that some sets of traits that describe the same behavioral domain seem to be organized hierarchically (see Hampson, this volume). At the instance level, we know that acts generated for a trait vary in their prototypicality (Buss & Craik, 1980, 1983; Mischel & Peake, 1982) and that more prototypical acts are more likely to be correctly matched to their categories than are less prototypical acts (Hampson, 1982). At the feature level, however, we know very little about trait categories, both theoretically and empirically. Thus, the next stage in the analysis of traits as categories is the specification of their features. This paper reports a first step towards that goal.

Behavioral Acts as Parts of Social Events

Most of the empirical research on trait categories has focused on acts as the fundamental unit of analysis, thus studying the extension, the particular real-world referents, of traits. Nevertheless, it is the intension, the meaning, of a trait that specifies how diverse behavioral acts come to be recognized as instances of a particular trait category; an understanding of the meaning of a trait thus requires an understanding of the features that form the basis for this categorization. Although acts may be the atoms that constitute the concept that is called personality, acts can be further broken down into their component parts. Features are as important to a trait as is grammar to a language. The number of particular sentences that can be generated from any given language is infinite; so is the number of acts that exemplify any given trait. A grammar specifies the rules underlying the construction of all sentences possible in a language; in the same way, features specify rules (or criteria) for the categorization of behaviors.

The recent work on act categorization (Buss & Craik, 1983; Hampson, 1982) raises some new questions about the definition of behavioral acts. What exactly is a behavioral act and how should it be described? How much social context needs to be included in the description of an act? Compare the following two descriptions:
(1) Mary gave the cashier a $5 bill;
(2) Fred gave the beggar a $5 bill.
Why would we call Fred's, but not Mary's, behavior *charitable?* Both descriptions involve essentially the same set of overt behaviors, namely the transfer of a five dollar bill from one person to another. Thus, the criterion for deciding whether to call a behavior *charitable* does not seem to reside in the observable behavior *per se* but rather in its

situational context (i.e., transfer to cashier vs. beggar). In recent years, psychology has gradually come to recognize that context is of overwhelming importance (e.g., Labov, 1973; Miller, 1978). The agent who performs an act is, to some extent, aware of this social context, and so is the observer. Thus, the context will be reflected in both the agent's behaviors and the observer's interpretations. The vast amount of available contextual information usually includes the conditions preceding the behavior as well as their direct or anticipated consequences. This information is essential to the meaning of the behavior; thus, in our search for features we need to analyze the context in which the individual acts. In order to do so successfully, we must choose an appropriate unit of analysis that encompasses both the overt behavior and the relevant context. To emphasize the importance of the context, this unit of analysis might be called a behavioral episode or behavioral scene.

It is, of course, impossible to include *all* the available contextual information in the description of a behavioral episode. Fortunately, it is also unnecessary. Many missing contextual details can be reconstructed, since we rely on extensive generalized knowledge about similar kinds of events when interpreting a particular behavioral episode. The relevant knowledge is incorporated in event schemata, often termed frames (Minsky, 1975) or scripts (Schank & Abelson, 1977). I will here adopt the term *script* because it best captures the procedural and dynamic character of these knowledge structures. A script specifies the elements of an event and the relations among these elements, including the time course of the event. Scripts can be viewed as an abstract representation of the event; they can be described verbally (Schank & Abelson, 1977), by flow charts and diagrams (Fillmore, 1977), or even by a comic strip like the one presented in Figure 2. In summary, I am proposing that the intension of a trait term be described by features that form an event script, whereas the extension of the trait consists of an infinite number of behavioral episodes that match these features.

What are the elements of a behavioral-episode script? Besides including the relevant contextual information, we must find a way to represent the act itself within the script. Natural language points the

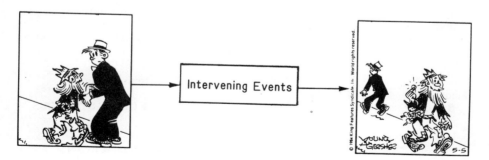

Figure 2: *An Example of Script-Guided Processing of a Comic Strip (The comic strip is reprinted with special permission of King Feature Syndicate, Inc.).*

way; as nouns constitute the language of objects, verbs make up the language of people's acts and experiences. Thus, at the heart of the script must be a verb describing the behavior. In Table 1, I have sketched out the beginnings of a script-based taxonomy of traits, illustrating that each of the "Big Five" personality dimensions (Norman, 1963) can be viewed as corresponding to a broad class of verbs. Extraversion traits, for example, seem to involve self-expression of the individual, as implied by activities such as entertain, affiliate, talk, etc. The second dimension, Agreeableness or Warmth, groups together interpersonal traits involving acts of giving, helping, or agreeing. It might be interesting to empirically study the relations between particular trait categories and specific verbs; the trait category *dishonest* might then be found to involve acts captured by verbs such as lie, cheat, trick, etc.

Fillmore's (1977) "commercial-exchange" script nicely illustrates how a verb (representing a class of actions in a rather abstract form) and a situational context work together. The verb *give* implies the roles of agent (who performs the act of giving), recipient, and some

TABLE 1: *The "Big Five" Personality Dimensions (Norman, 1963) and Associated Verb Classes*

Personality Domain	Global Verb	Specific Verbs	General Script Underlying These Events
Extraversion	EXPRESS	Entertain Affiliate Talk Dominate Etc.	Interpersonal AGENT – PATIENT Relation
Agreeableness	EXCHANGE	Agree Lie to Give Help Etc.	Interpersonal AGENT – PATIENT Relation
Conscienti-ousness	PERFORM	Attempt Organize Forget Produce Etc.	Impersonal: AGENT- GOAL/TASK Relation
Emotional Stability	FEEL	Envy Fear Worry Relax Etc.	Internal/Covert: EXPERIENCER – STIMULUS
Intellect/ Culture	PERCEIVE	Introspect Analyze Invent Notice Etc.	Internal/Covert: EXPERIENCER – GOAL/TASK

commodity, the ownership of which is transferred from the agent to the recipient (Dixon, 1982). This rather abstract conceptual scheme can be adapted to various situational contexts. In a commercial setting, acts of giving (such as paying or selling) can be represented by a script that specifies slots for buyer, seller, goods, and price, as well as the relations among them. In addition, the commercial-exchange script contains information about the actors' motives (e.g., the buyer was interested in the goods), their relationship (e.g., a contractual agreement), and the consequences (e.g., no further social or material obligations).

FEATURE ANALYSIS OF TRAITS:
A SCRIPT FOR NON-RECIPROCAL GIVING

To illustrate how this approach might be applied to personality traits, I have chosen to analyze the features of just one slice of the general taxonomy outlined in Table 1. In particular, I elucidate the features of those traits from the Agreeableness dimension that refer to non-reciprocal giving, such as *altruistic, helpful,* and *charitable.* These trait concepts have almost universal import for human interactions. The notion of sacrifice, of giving without receiving, is a human characteristic that can be traced through history and cultures. The ancient Greeks, for example, tried to appease the anger of the Gods; the Hindu believe that donating in this life will produce a reward in the next life; buying a letter of indulgence was considered mandatory to be assured of a place in heaven during a period in Christianity; and helping the "lame, blind, and crippled" is the aim of many humanitarian individuals and organizations today. All these practices exemplify the same phenomenon. Similarly, research on altruism and helping behavior has been one of the central concerns of personality, social, developmental, and clinical psychology (Rushton, 1980).

Deriving the Initial Script from Behavioral Episodes

Non-reciprocal giving is particularly informative about personality because such behaviors run counter to the general "give-and-take" or equity norm (Adams, 1965) governing most human interactions. Compare again the two behavioral scenes:
   (1) Mary gave the cashier a $5 bill;
   (2) Fred gave the beggar a $5 bill.
Whereas the act of giving in scene (1) can be easily understood in terms of the commercial-event script (Fillmore, 1977), that script does not fit scene (2). The role title "beggar," or the pictorial representation in Figure 2, focuses our attention on an implicit difference in wealth between Fred and the other person, who seems to be needy. Thus, whereas in (1) "gives" is interpreted as "pays in exchange for goods" within the commercial event script, the same act implies a non-reciprocal exchange in (2). That is, we are likely to infer that Fred neither expected nor actually received anything in

return for his \$5 and that his intent was altruistic (or more specifically *charitable*). That the social meaning of *give* is a non-reciprocal one in this context becomes obvious when the verb *donate* is substituted for *give* in scenes (4) and (5):

    (4) Fred donated \$100 to the hospital;

    (5) Fred donated \$100 to the hospital *for* removing his appendix.

To most of us, (5) does not make much sense. Thus, one criterion for deciding whether an act is charitable is that the agent does not gain something in the episode.

    Similarly, it would be strange to interpret *give* as *lend,* within the context provided in (2). The incompatibility of this scene with the commercial-exchange script is illustrated in Figure 3. Our knowledge about beggars tells us it is unwise to lend them money since they are unlikely to pay it back; thus, it is more reasonable to assume Fred's intent was to benefit the beggar, as implied in:

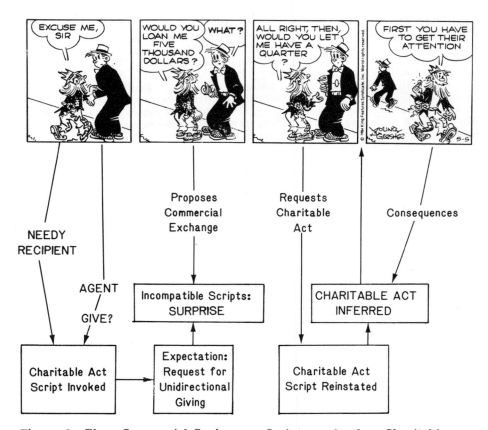

Figure 3: *The Commercial-Exchange Script and the Charitableness Script: A Clever Ruse.*
(The comic strip is reprinted with special permission of King Feature Syndicate, Inc.).

(6) Fred gave $5 to the beggar *for* a good dinner.

Note that in the charitable episode described in (6) the other person benefits from the agent's act of giving, whereas in (5) Fred's purpose (or behavioral intent) was to pay for an operation that benefitted himself. Thus, another feature of charitableness is that another person benefits from the act.

Finally, we would tend to believe that Fred performed this act *voluntarily*, because in the episodes discussed thus far Fred's behavior was not caused by strong external factors of the kind present in the following scene:

(7) Threatened with a knife, Fred gave the beggar all his cash.

The Features of Charitable Acts

Figure 4 summarizes these conclusions. Charitable episodes, such as "Fred gave the beggar a $5 bill," are those that fit the script characterized by the following features: (a) a physical event caused by a human agent and represented by some specific instance of the general verb *give* (e.g., donate, contribute, sacrifice); (b) some effort made by the agent (e.g., a commodity or service, such as

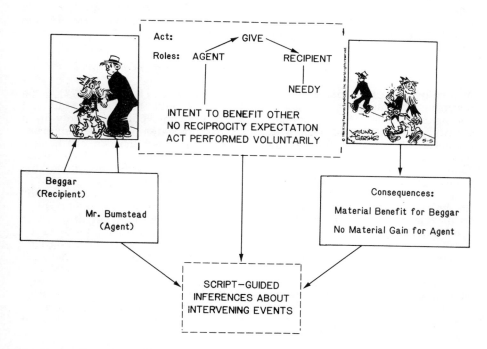

Figure 4: *Summary of the Charitableness Script.*
(The comic strip is reprinted with special permission of King Feature Syndicate, Inc.).

money, goods, or time); (c) a needy recipient (e.g., an individual or institution); and three additional features specifying the psychological conditions under which the act occurred, namely, (d) the agent's intention to benefit the recipient, (e) no expectation of gain for self or "reciprocity," and (f) volition, that is, the freedom to decide whether to perform the act.

This script, consisting of the six interrelated features summarized above, specifies the intension of charitableness and also connects this concept with events in the real world: Any particular episode that fits this script would be called *charitable*. However, in contrast to classically defined "Aristotelian" concepts, this definition of charitableness does not assume an either-or type of category membership; any given episode is *charitable* to the degree to which its features fit this script.

One advantage of such an explicit definition is that it can be stated in a procedural form. The current interest in modeling categories by means of explicit procedures that can be implemented as a computer program (Mervis & Rosch, 1981) suggests an alternative representation of the charitableness script. In Figure 5, the categorization of acts of giving is shown as a sequence of decision or production rules (E. Smith, 1984). If, upon empirical test, the features proposed here turn out to characterize the meaning of charitableness, it should be possible to write a computer program representing the algorithm in Figure 5. Such a program would, when given the feature values of an episode as the input, compute the estimated prototypicality value of that episode.

Boundaries of the Charitable-Act Category: Testing the Features

According to the principles of categorization (Rosch, 1978), the features of the trait category *charitable* should be typical but not necessarily true of the category, and any one episode involving a charitable act may possess a feature to a greater or lesser degree. Nevertheless, it is important to show that episodes that do *not* have a particular feature are less prototypical instances of charitableness. Thus, I will now discuss some "boundary" cases of charitable behaviors, which lack some of the features elaborated above.

For example, episodes may differ in the commodity that is "given" to the recipient. One can donate money (which seems most prototypical to American students), or goods (e.g., blood, clothes, furniture), or even one's time and services. Less prototypical efforts tend to be those to which no corresponding material value can be assigned. Moreover, the agent's effort, whatever form it takes, must have at least some value; that is, the agent must have incurred some cost. Consider again the summary of the script in Figure 4. As is shown there, information about the *size* of the effort is necessary to infer whether the agent had intended to benefit the recipient by performing the act. This inference is not an "either-or" decision but a question of

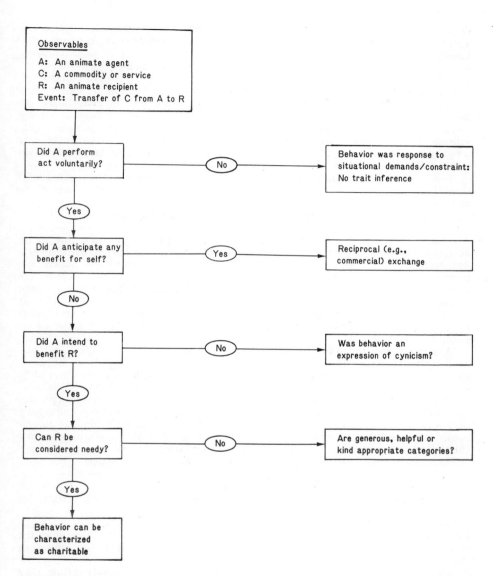

Figure 5: *The Categorization of Acts of Giving as a Sequence of Decision Rules.*

degree. For example, if money is involved, the higher the monetary value relative to the agent's wealth, the more prototypical the episode. Compare:

(8) When asked for spare change, Fred gave the beggar a penny;
(9) When asked for spare change, Fred gave the beggar 10 cents;
(10) When asked for spare change, Fred gave the beggar 50 cents.

In this context, giving one penny is rarely labeled as charitable; 10 cents maybe; 50 cents certainly is. Since a penny won't buy anything anymore, it would be of little immediate benefit to a poor person. Our standards of what size of effort is charitable change with inflation; what was an act of charity 30 years ago is today no more than an expression of cynicism.

Similarly, the concept of "white elephants" suggests that gifts and donations are sometimes only *seemingly* motivated by the intent to benefit the recipient. Consider the following episode:

(11) Fred emptied his attic of truly useless junk and gave it to
     the Salvation Army.

Although in some cases one person's worthless junk may turn out to be someone else's treasure, in this scene Fred seems to know the Salvation Army could not possibly sell his donation to anybody; consequently, we might infer that his intent was primarily to clean his attic and look good at the same time, rather than to benefit the cause of the Salvation Army.

Another feature listed in Figure 4 suggests that a needy recipient is a necessary feature of charitable acts. However, boundary cases such as:

(12) Fred donated $500 to the Man-Boy Love Society,

make one realize that there is no clear-cut dividing line between worthy and unworthy causes; worthiness (and, similarly, neediness) is a question of degree, and of course personal opinion. Nevertheless, most people agree that the act described in (12) is not prototypically charitable. Other behavioral episodes of questionable category membership are those which, in addition to benefitting a needy recipient, can be expected to also lead to desirable consequences for the agent. If the agent clearly anticipated a material gain, as in:

(13) Years ago Fred bought a painting for $10,000; it is now
     worth $150,000. Fred donated this painting to the museum
     and deducted $150,000 from his income taxes;

or if the agent was trying to achieve some desirable social effect, as in:

(14) To impress his girl friend, Fred gave the beggar $5;

we tend to infer a selfish motivation. This violation of the "no gain for self" feature renders these episodes less prototypical instances of charitableness.

Finally, episodes whose situational context is so constraining that the agent has little freedom in deciding how to behave lack one of the typical features of charitableness. Constraints on the agent's volition can vary from very subtle social expectations to strictly enforced societal norms.

(15) When asked by his boss whether he had "forgotten" to
     contribute to the United Way, Fred gave $20.
(16) Fred donated $20 to the United Way.

In episode (15), Fred apparently submitted to his boss' pressure; consequently, we infer that his primary motive was probably to avoid negative sanctions by his boss, rather than to help needy others. Therefore, this act seems less charitable than (16). This pair of episodes also illustrates how strongly we rely on the prototype scene specified by the script; in (16), where neither presence nor absence of situational pressures are specified, we just assume that there was freedom of choice, which apparently is the default value of the script for this feature.

In summary, these features do not define the trait category in an all-or-none fashion. However, episodes that possess fewer relevant features seem to be less prototypical instances of the trait.

THE HIERARCHICAL MODEL APPLIED TO ALTRUISM

A conceptual definition of a trait should not only specify the meaning of the trait and its behavioral referents but also discriminate it from other traits (Loevinger, 1957). How can the feature approach be used to differentiate among related traits within the same behavioral domain?

A model of the conceptual relationship among different traits is a prerequisite to the development of discriminable measures for each of these traits. Personality questionnaire scales that attempt to assess *altruism* tend to contain items describing charitable acts. For example, on the Self-Report Altruism Scale devised by Rushton et al. (1981) subjects indicate how frequently they have performed particular acts, such as "I have donated food or clothes to a charity," "I have donated blood," or "I have bought charity Christmas cards deliberately because I knew it was a good cause." By now, it is probably apparent to the reader that these items, used to assess altruism, possess all the features specified by the script for charitableness. They all involve some voluntary effort intended to benefit a needy or worthy recipient without expecting reciprocity.

Relations Among Traits: Category Breadth

Nevertheless, altruism and charitableness are not synonymous; altruism is generally used to refer to a *broader* domain of behaviors (Rushton, 1980). The hierarchical model of trait categories presented in Figure 1 can easily represent this fact because it assumes that (1) some traits are broader and more inclusive than others, and (2) in the same behavioral domain, the behaviors associated with a subordinate category are also included in the superordinate category. How does this model apply to altruism? Specifically, how can we describe the relations between altruism and the many other traits in the personality lexicons of Dutch (Brokken, 1978), English (Goldberg, 1982), and German (John & Angleitner, in preparation) that also refer to acts of non-reciprocal giving?

One important variable seems to be the *category breadth* or inclusiveness of the trait. In a recent study (see Hampson, this volume), we obtained ratings of category breadth for 456 trait terms. Category breadth was defined for the raters as follows:

Very broad words are those that include in their definitions a wide range of behaviors; very narrow words are those that include a much more limited range of behaviors. For each word you are to decide how broad (abstract, general, global) is its range of behavioral referents, relative to the other words in the list.

The ratings showed an acceptable level of interjudge agreement. As it turns out, *charitable* was rated as quite specific, referring only to a narrowly defined set of behaviors; *generous* and *helpful* were rated in the middle, denoting somewhat broader ranges of behaviors; and, finally, *altruistic* and *kind* were judged to be extremely broad traits.

These findings suggest that altruistic behaviors follow a hierarchical model such that prototypically *charitable* acts are subsumed by middle-level categories such as *generous* and *helpful* which, in turn, are included within the broadest categories in this domain, namely *kind* and *altruistic* (the latter being a less common term in everyday discourse). In order to test this proposition, we included these traits in some of our studies of category asymmetries (described by Hampson, this volume). In the concept-asymmetry task, subjects are asked to judge which of two statements makes more sense. For example, the statement "A piano is a kind of musical instrument" makes more sense than the statement "A musical instrument is a kind of piano." In general, if the two categories in the statement are hierarchically related, the statement in which the narrower category precedes the broader one should be chosen. And, indeed, in several studies we found that a majority of subjects agreed with the predicted subset-superset relations in the domain of altruism traits: The subjects stated that to be *charitable* is a way of being *generous* (or *helpful*, or *kind*), whereas the reverse is not true; moreover, they stated that to be *generous* (or *helpful*) is a way of being *kind*. Thus, Rushton et al.'s (1981) decision to include six charitableness items in their Altruism scale seems theoretically justified: Charitable acts also tend to be altruistic ones.

Features of Traits at Different Hierarchical Levels

What is the basis for people's intuitions about the breadth and hierarchical level of trait categories? To answer these questions, one must examine the features that are characteristic of categories at different levels of the hierarchy.

In the domain of object categories, Rosch et al (1976) have argued that broad categories, such as *furniture* or *food*, have very few features that are shared by all instances of the category, whereas the instances of very specific categories, such as *kitchen chair* or *acorn squash*, have a large number of features in common. Moreover, Rosch reported that in some hierarchies subordinate categories (e.g., *apple*) possessed all the features of their superordinate (e.g., *fruit*), plus some additional features. These additional features impose more constraints on the number of instances that qualify as members of the category, and thus they serve to make the category more specific. To investigate whether these principles apply as well to trait categories, I analyzed the characteristic features of some of the traits included in the hierarchical model of altruism.

Tabel 2 presents an overview of my analysis of five traits. They are, in ascending order of category breadth, *charitable*, *generous*, *helpful*, *kind*, and *altruistic*. The category-breadth values of these traits are given in the first column. To keep the table as simple as possible, two of the features discussed above are not included there, namely the slots for the agent and the specific behavioral event (i.e., some instance of giving).

On the basis of Rosch's findings, I expected that *charitable*, the most specific category in this set, would possess all the features of the other traits in this domain, plus a few more, Therefore, the already-identified features of the charitableness script served as a starting point for this analysis.

As shown in the second column of Table 2, there is a trend to more abstract behavioral modes (i.e., symbolic communication) with increasing category breadth. That is, the agent's efforts become less

TABLE 2: *Traits of Non-Reciprocal Giving: A Matrix of Feature Values*

Traits	Features				
(Category Breadth)	Nature of Effort	State of Recipient	Consequences Benefit Recipient	Gain for Agent	Volition
Charitable (-.50)	material: money, goods or time	*needy* or *worthy*	intended	not expected	yes
Generous (+.66)	mostly material	animate	intended; *greater than expected*	not expected	yes
Helpful (+.83)	material, intellectual (emotional)	animate (involved in task)	must be *realized by other*	not explicit	yes
Kind (+1.77)	symbolic (*emotional* or intellectual) or material	(animate)	intended	completely absent	yes
Altruistic	symbolic (emotional or intellectual) or material	human	intended	completely *absent*	yes

Note: Especially salient features of a trait are italicized. The category breadth values (in parentheses) are standard scores with a mean of zero and a standard deviation of one. Low values indicate that the trait category was judged to have a narrow and highly specified set of behavioral referents, whereas large values indicate broad and global traits. *Altruistic* is not commonly used as a trait descriptor in everyday language and was therefore not included in the category breadth study.

"materialistic" in nature, as category breadth increases; for example, some *altruistic* or *kind* episodes may not contain any observable behavior at all but involve "giving" in a symbolic (intellectual or emotional) sense, as evident in the expression of concern, consideration, or sympathy. In contrast, the behavioral referents of *charitable*, the most narrow trait, are most constrained on this feature; *generous* and *helpful* are located somewhere between these extremes. That is, one can be *generous* or *helpful* in both tangible (e.g., lend a friend $500) and intangible ways (e.g., give a depressed co-worker emotional support); however, intangible acts of giving (e.g., give a beggar helpful advice or sympathy) are unlikely to be viewed as *charitable*.

In the third column of Table 2, the constraints specified for the role of the recipient are listed. As discussed previously, in order to apply the term *charitable*, the recipient must be needy, or represent a worthy cause. In contrast, the other traits do not specify any particular characteristics of the recipient. For example, it is perfectly acceptable to feed your cat *generously*, or to be *kind* to your pets, to animals in general, or maybe even to your teddy bear and plants. Thus, since needy people are a subset of people-in-general, there are fewer occasions to be *charitable* than to be *helpful, generous*, or *kind* (to anybody).

Intentions, I have argued, are inferred from the consequences of the act. *Charitable*, for example, classifies episodes from the *agent*'s point of view; if someone makes an effort that under normal circumstances can be expected to benefit a needy individual, we are likely to infer unselfish intentions. The meaning of *generous*, however, attaches a more specific constraint to this feature: The agent's effort must be special, or greater than what is normally expected. Thus, whereas most *charitable* episodes (at least the prototypical ones) can be called *generous* as well, a few acts are marginally *charitable* but not at all *generous*, as shown in (17):

(17) Fred finally contributed something, but it wasn't what one
        would call a generous donation.

On this one particular feature then, *generous* has a narrower behavioral meaning than does *charitable*. On the other hand, the script associated with *helpful* does not seem to focus on the intent of the agent but on the perspective of the recipient. That is, the trait *helpful* is applied to an episode only if the recipient actually benefitted from the act. Examples come easily to mind; consider the context of doing the dishes after dinner, as in the following scene:

(18) Fred really tried to help, but he was only in my way.

Fred's good intent is irrelevant; it is the recipient's perspective that counts. Similarly, behaviors *not* intended to be *helpful* may nevertheless be categorized as such:

(19) Fred still tries to scare me with his nasty criticism, but that
        has actually helped me learn to stand up for myself.

In contrast, *altruistic, kind*, and *generous* refer to the agent's intentions rather than to the actual consequences for the recipient. Consequently, a gift that is not regarded as *helpful* by the recipient may still be categorized as *generous*:

(20) Fred's gift was really generous, but I just couldn't find any
        use for it, and so I gave it to my brother.

Finally, each of the five traits implies that there is no gain for the agent, although the recipient who has been helped may feel some degree of social or "moral" obligation to reciprocate in the future. Similarly, the last feature listed in Table 2, volition, seems to be uniformly associated with all five traits; all of them are less likely to be applied to episodes characterized by highly constrained behavioral choices. This obversation is in line with theories of causal attribution (e.g., Jones & Davis, 1965; Kelley, 1973), which hold that people do not attribute causality to agents when behavior can be sufficiently explained by situational factors.

Features and Category Breadth: A Summary

Although the five traits differed from each other in their category breadth, their features could be subsumed under the same general script of non-reciprocal giving. That is, the essential difference between these traits was not their number of features but rather the specificity with which these features are described. In other words, the feature values of subordinate traits seem to specify the extension (i.e., behavioral episodes) of the trait in much more detail. Consequently, ratings of the breadth of trait categories seem to be predictable from the amount of contextual detail specified by their features. Specifically, *charitable* has more detailed (and constraining) values on two of the features (i.e., nature of the agent's effort and characteristics of the recipient) than do *generous* and *helpful,* which in turn are more constrained than *altruistic* and *kind.* The category-breadth ratings listed in Table 2 mirror this rank order, suggesting that category-breadth differences between these traits may depend primarily on two variables: The greater the number of possible beneficial efforts (i.e., relevant acts) and the greater the number of potential recipients of the act (i.e., relevant situations), the broader the trait. The first variable comes as no surprise, since our category-breadth rating instructions stressed that "very broad traits are those that include in their definitions a wide range of behaviors." The hypothesis that the number of *occasions* on which relevant behaviors can be observed (Rothbart & Park, in press) is an additional determinant of category breadth should be further investigated.

    To summarize, altruism is, as both the psychological literature and our data show, an extremely broad trait. The analyses presented in this section suggest that altruistic behaviors can be defined as those voluntary efforts that are intended to benefit someone else without expecting reciprocity. Morever, different facets of altruism (i.e., subordinate traits) were conceptually differentiated and shown to differ from each other in the specificity of their features. Although all of these concepts refer to the same global behavioral domain – altruism – each of them seems to focus differentially on some particularly salient aspects of these behaviors.

    As Brown (1958, p. 20) pointed out in his classic paper on naming, "though we often think of each thing as having a name – a single name – in fact, each thing has many equally correct names." Thus, if we want to emphasize the recipient and his need, we call the act *charitable*; if we want to emphasize how much was given, we use *generous*; if we stress the good effects or consequences for the other person, *helpful* is the category of choice; and if the effort was mostly immaterial, we might use *kind*. These examples underscore the immense conceptual richness of the language available to categorize behaviors and to describe personality.

CONCLUSIONS AND IMPLICATIONS

The explication of the intension and extension of altruism traits began with an analysis of behavioral episodes that varied in their prototypicality for the most specific trait in this domain, namely *charitable*. These detailed analyses suggested that the intension of this concept can be described by a script consisting of six features. These features were then shown to be applicable to related but distinct traits in the domain of altruism. The next step is to collect empirical data to test these theoretical deductions.

In interpreting the present analyses, it is important to consider whether the features suggested here are specific to this particular trait domain, or whether they have more general importance. Overall, the most general features appear to be those that specify the consequences of the act and the agent's volition. These features are central to inferences about the intent "behind the act." Even for those traits that refer to behaviors not subject to one's conscious control, the intentionality feature seems to be important; that is, the inference that the behavior was *un*intentional is part of their meaning. For example, behaviors that are referred to as *shy, anxious,* or *dumb* have undesirable effects both on others *and* on the agent, implying that the agent would usually not perform such behaviors intentionally. In regard to the volition feature, research on causal attribution has shown that people are less likely to infer intent when situational conditions limit the agent's freedom of choice (Jones & Davis, 1965; Kelley, 1973). Similarly, Mischel (1977) has emphasized that "powerful" situations constrain people's behavioral options and thus attenuate the effect of individual differences on behavior. Thus, the observed or expected consequences of an act and the related inferences about the agent's intent and freedom of choice seem to be central features of personality trait concepts in general.

How do the more specifically interpersonal features of altruism traits relate to theoretical conceptions of social behavior? Foa and Foa (1974) have argued that interpersonal behavior can be understood as the exchange of six kinds of resources, specifically, love, status, information, goods, money, and services. These resources are reflected in one of the features of altruism, namely the nature of the effort made by the agent (see Table 2). Unfortunately, the efforts associated with each trait do not correspond directly to Foa and Foa's resource classes; rather, they involve combinations. For example, *charitable* was here characterized by efforts that involve giving money, goods, or one's time. Indeed, these three resources, although regarded as distinct by Foa and Foa, may be psychologically equivalent and form a class of "material resources" (Adamopoulos, 1984). However, the other traits of altruism involve less coherent combinations of resources; for example, I have argued that *kind* refers to emotional and intellectual as well as to material efforts, and thus involves all but one of the six resource classes postulated by Foa and Foa.

Stimulated by Foa and Foa's theory, Wiggins (1979) distinguished material traits (those involving money, goods, and services) from interpersonal traits (those involving love and status); he then constructed a general taxonomy of interpersonal traits, based on three dichotomous features, namely direction (accept vs. reject), object (self vs. other), and resource (love vs. status). Obviously, Wiggins' model and the present analyses differ in the degree of detail with which the meaning of each particular trait is described, as well as in the mapping of Foa and Foa's resource classes onto trait categories. In particular, the taxonomy developed by Wiggins covers a much broader range of trait concepts (more than 700) than the few traits I have considered here. The theoretical restriction of Wiggins' taxonomy to two resources, however, leads to the exclusion of some important interpersonal traits, such as honesty which involves the exchange of information rather than that of love and status. Traits related to honesty, in fact, share many features with the altruism traits, in particular, volition, consequences, and the notions of agent and recipient. That is, dishonest behaviors (i.e., conveying misleading information) lead to desirable consequences for the agent and undesirable ones for the recipient.

Status is the only resource mentioned by Foa and Foa and Wiggins that did not emerge in the feature analyses of the altruism traits, presumably because status is not particularly relevant for that behavioral domain. In other trait domains, however, status plays a crucial role (Wiggins, 1979). Acts of dominance, assertiveness, boldness, etc. generally lead to consequences that in some way improve the agent's status relative to that of others, be it in terms of power, self-actualization, or the admiration and respect one gets from others. Whereas Foa and Foa (1974) have conceptualized status as a "resource" in interpersonal exchanges, status as a characteristic of the other person may also be an important *feature* of many personality traits. That is, whereas *charitable* specifies neediness as a characteristic of the recipient, traits such as *lax* or *lenient* imply that the other person has lower status than the agent. Moreover, status differences between agent and recipient can be reflected in the "volition" feature; one of the important differences between the concepts *polite* and *respectful* is that the former implies an agent freely choosing to consider the other's feelings, whereas the latter implies that this behavior was dictated, in part, by the status of the other.

Finally, Foa and Foa have arranged their six resources on a concreteness-abstractness dimension; some resources exchanged during interactions are symbolic in character (i.e., status and information), whereas others are more concrete (i.e., good and services). Using Foa and Foa's terminology, category breadth differences between traits might then be interpreted as follows: Broader traits refer to "exchanges" that involve one of many different types of resources, some of which are quite abstract or symbolic, whereas narrow traits refer to exchanges of fewer types of resources, all of which are relatively concrete.

In conclusion, I hope that the feature analysis of trait concepts will complement earlier efforts to describe traits in terms of their interrelations (Goldberg, 1982; Norman, 1963; Wiggins, 1979) and behavioral referents (Buss & Craik, 1980, 1983; Mischel & Peake, 1982). Together, these efforts should help us be more explicit about the meaning and the behavioral referents of trait terms, an important task because "the careful specification of the behavioral exemplars of a trait domain and their interrelationships is an essential precondition for the construct validity of a measure and for evidence of behavioral consistency" (Jackson & Paunonen, 1985, pp. 554). Similarly, Mischel (1984; Mischel & Peake, 1982) has emphasized that the search for behavioral consistency must be guided by a theoretical conception of how behavior may be classified. That is, even an explicitly behavioral orientation does not relieve us from the burden of defining trait terms; when deciding which behaviors to sample as exemplars of a trait, investigators make choices that depend on their (often implicit) understanding of that trait. Thus, definitions are central to the construction of *any* measures of constructs, whether they are behavioral observations, physiological recordings, ratings, or questionnaire items.

Indeed, featural definitions of traits provide explicit theoretical rationales for the generation and selection of questionnaire items.[1] The present model conceptualizes global traits as superordinate categories composed of more subordinate ones; thus, to assess a global trait, separate scales should be constructed for each of its subordinates. Similarly, facet-oriented approaches to personality scale construction (Butt & Fiske, 1968, 1969; Foa, 1961, 1965) require the trait to be conceptually delineated and subdivided into its component parts of "facets" *before* scales are developed to measure it. The elucidation of the features of each facet (i.e., subordinate trait) will provide the precise definitions necessary to specify an item universe and to systematically generate items for each facet. The sound theoretical foundation of the resulting scales is an advantage that should eventually help improve personality measurement in the service of psychological theory.

In sum, detailed analyses of traits at both the instance (i.e., behavioral episodes) *and* the feature level should aid (a) the elaboration of the theoretical network surrounding any personality trait, (b) the search for behavioral consistency, and (c) the process of item generation and personality questionnaire construction.

---

[1] For example, Rushton et al.'s (1981) Altruism Scale contains, in addition to the six charitableness items, ten helpfulness items (e.g., "I have given directions to a stranger"), three items that seem to measure something akin to kindness and/or generosity (e.g., "I have offered my seat on a bus or train to a stranger who was standing"), and one honesty item (i.e., "I have pointed out a clerk's error (in a bank, at the supermarket), in undercharging me for an item"). How were these items generated? What was the theoretical rationale for this particular composition of items? Unfortunately, Rushton et al. (1981) do not present any information about how they generated their initial item pools or how they selected the final items.

ACKNOWLEDGMENTS

The author would like to thank David Buss, Robyn Dawes, Scott DeLancey, Morton Gernsbacher, Lewis Goldberg, Sarah Hampson, Dean Peabody, Mary Rothbart, and Myron Rothbart for providing suggestions and encouragement, and all those others who provided the author with episodes of altruistic behaviors. The work described here is supported by grant MH-39077 from the U.S. National Institute of Mental Health.

REFERENCES

Adamopoulos, J. (1984). The differentiation of social behavior. *Journal of Cross-Cultural Psychology, 15,* 487-508.

Adams, J.S. (1965). Inequity in social exchange. In L. Berkowitz (Ed.), *Advances in experimental social psychology* (Vol. 2, pp. 276-299). New York: Academic Press.

Angleitner, A., John, O.P., & Löhr, F.J. (1986). It's *what* you say and *how* you say it: An itemmetric analysis of personality questionnaires. In A. Angleitner & J.S. Wiggins (Eds.), *Personality assessment via questionnaires: Current issues in theory and measurement.* Berlin: Springer.

Bem, D.J., & Allen, A. (1974). On predicting some of the people some of the time: The search for cross-situational consistencies in behavior. *Psychological Review, 81,* 506-520.

Brokken, F.B. (1978). *The language of personality.* Meppel, The Netherlands: Krips.

Brown, R. (1958). How shall a thing be called? *Psychological Review, 65,* 14-21.

Buss, D.M., & Craik, K.H. (1980). The frequency concept of disposition: Dominance and prototypically dominant acts. *Journal of Personality, 48,* 379-392.

Buss, D.M., & Craik, K.H. (1983). The act frequency approach to personality. *Psychological Review, 90,* 105-126.

Butt, D.S., & Fiske, D.W. (1968). Comparison of strategies in developing scales for dominance. *Psychological Bulletin, 70,* 505-519.

Butt, D.S., & Fiske, D.W. (1969). Differential correlates of dominance scales. *Journal of Personality, 37,* 415-428.

Cantor, N., & Mischel, W. (1979). Prototypes in person perception. In L. Berkowitz (Ed.), *Advances in experimental social psychology* (pp. 3-52). New York: Academic Press.

Cattell, R.B. (1973). *Personality and mood by questionnaire.* San Francisco, CA: Jossey-Bass.

Dixon, R.M. (1982). *Where have all the adjectives gone? And other essays in semantics and syntax.* Berlin, Germany: Mouton Publishers.

Eysenck, H.J. (1977). Personality and factor analysis: A reply to Guilford. *Psychological Bulletin, 84,* 405-411.

Fillmore, C.J. (1977). Topics in lexical semantics. In R. Cole (Ed.), *Current issues in linguistic theory* (pp. 76-138). Bloomington, IN: Indiana University Press.

Foa, U.G. (1961). Convergences in the analysis of the structure of interpersonal behavior. *Psychological Review, 68,* 341-353.

Foa, U.G. (1965). New developments in facet design and analysis. *Psychological Review, 72,* 262-274.

Foa, U.G., & Foa, E.B. (1974). *Societal structures of the mind.* Springfield, IL: Charles C. Thomas.

Furnham, A., & Henderson, M. (1983). Assessing assertiveness: A content and correlational analysis of five assertiveness inventories. *Behavioral Assessment, 6,* 79-88.

Goldberg, L.R. (1972). Some recent trends in personality assessment. *Journal of Personality Assessment, 36,* 547-560.

Goldberg, L.R. (1980, May). Some ruminations about the structure of individual differences: Developing a common lexicon for the major characteristics of human personality. Paper presented at WPA, Honolulu, Hawaii.

Goldberg, L.R. (1982). From Ace to Zombie: Some explorations in the language of personality. In C.D. Spielberger & J.N. Butcher (Eds.), *Advances in personality assessment* (pp. 203-234). Hillsdale, NJ: Erlbaum.

Gray, J.A. (1981). A critique of Eysenck's theory of personality. In H.J. Eysenck (Ed.), *A model for personality* (pp. 246-276). Berlin: Springer.

Guilford, J.P. (1977). Will the real factor of extraversion-introversion please stand up? A reply to Eysenck. *Psychological Bulletin, 84,* 412-416.

Hampson, S.E. (1982). Person memory: A semantic category model of personality traits. *British Journal of Psychology, 73,* 1-11.

Hofstee, W.K.B. (1984). What's in a trait: Reflections about the inevitability of traits, their measurement, and taxonomy. In H. Bonarius, G. Van Heck, & N. Smid, *Personality psychology in Europe: Theoretical and empirical developments* (pp. 75-81). Lisse: Swets & Zeitlinger.

Jackson, D.N., & Paunonen, S.V. (1985). Construct validity and the predictability of behavior. *Journal of Personality and Social Psychology, 49,* 554-570.

John, O.P., & Angleitner, A. (in prep.). The German taxonomy project: Stage 1, the comprehensive personality dictionary. Research Reports from the Trait Taxonomy Project. Department of Psychology, University of Bielefeld, Germany.

Jones, E.E., & Davis, K.E. (1965). From acts to dispositions: The attribution process in person perception. In L. Berkowitz (Ed.), *Advances in experimental social psychology* (Vol. 2, pp. 219-266). New York: Academic Press.

Kelley, H.H. (1973). The process of causal attribution. *American Psychologist, 28,* 107-128.

Labov, W. (1973). The boundaries of words and their meanings. In C.J. Bailey & R.S. Shuy (Eds.), *New ways of analyzing variations in English* (pp. 340-373). Washington, DC: Georgetown University Press.

Locke, J. (1690). *An essay concerning human understanding.* (Annotated by A.C. Fraser, 1959). New York: Dover.

Loevinger, J. (1957). Objective tests as instruments of psychological theory. *Psychological Reports, 3,* 635-694.

Mervis, C.B., & Rosch, E. (1981). Categorization of natural objects. *Annual Review of Psychology, 32,* 89-115.

Miller, G.A. (1978). Practical and lexical knowledge. In E. Rosch & B.B. Lloyd (Eds.), *Cognition and categorization* (pp. 305-319). Hillsdale, NJ: Erlbaum.

Minsky, M. (1975). A framework for representing knowledge. In P.H. Winston (Ed.), *The psychology of computer vision* (pp. 211-277). New York: McGraw-Hill.

Mischel, W. (1973). Toward a cognitive social learning reconceptualization of personality. *Psychological Review, 80,* 252-283.

Mischel, W. (1977). On the future of personality measurement. *American Psychologist, 32,* 246-254.

Mischel, W. (1984). Convergences and challenges in the search for consistency. *American Psychologist, 39,* 351-364.

Mischel, W., & Peake, P.K. (1982). Beyond déjà vu in the search for cross-situational consistency. *Psychological Review, 89,* 730-755.

Norman, W.T. (1963). Toward an adequate taxonomy of personality attributes: Replicated factor structure in peer nomination personality ratings. *Journal of Abnormal and Social Psychology, 66,* 564-583.

Rosch, E. (1978). Principles of categorization. In E. Rosch & B. Lloyd (Eds.), *Cognition and categorization* (pp. 27-48). Hillsdale, NJ: Erlbaum.

Rosch, E., Mervis, C.B., Gray, W.D., Johnson, D., Boyes-Braem, P. (1976). Basic objects in natural categories. *Cognitive Psychology, 8,* 382-439.

Rothbart, M., & Park, B. (in press). On the confirmability and disconfirmability of trait concepts. *Journal of Personality and Social Psychology.*

Rushton, J.P. (1980). *Altruism, socialization, and society.* Englewood Cliffs, NJ: Prentice-Hall.

Rushton, J.P., Chrisjohn, R.D., & Fekken, G.C. (1981). The altruistic personality and the self-report altruism scale. *Personality and Individual Differences, 2,* 293-302.

Schank, R., & Abelson, R. (1977). *Scripts, plans, goals, and understanding.* Hillsdale, NJ: Erlbaum.

Smith, E.E., & Medin, D.L. (1981). *Categories and concepts.* Cambridge, MA: Harvard University Press.

Smith, E.R. (1984). Model of social inference processes. *Psychological Review, 91,* 392-413.

Strelau, J. (1983). *Temperament, personality, activity.* London: Academic Press.

Tversky, A. (1977). Features of similarity. *Psychological Review, 84,* 327-352.

Tversky, B., & Hemenway, K. (1984). Objects, parts, and categories. *Journal of Experimental Psychology: General, 113,* 169-193.

Wiggins, J.S. (1974, Feb.). *In defense of traits.* Invited address to the Ninth Annual Symposium on Recent Developments in the use of the MMPI, held in Los Angeles, CA.

Wiggins, J.S. (1979). A psychological taxonomy of trait-descriptive
    terms: The interpersonal domain. *Journal of Personality and Social
    Psychology, 37,* 395-412.
Wilson, G. (1978). Introversion/extroversion. In H. London & J.E.
    Exner, Jr. (Eds.), *Dimensions of personality* (pp. 217-261). New
    York: Wiley.

THE ACT FREQUENCY APPROACH
AND THE CONSTRUCTION OF PERSONALITY

David M. Buss
Harvard University
Cambridge, MA
United States

Kenneth H. Craik
University of California
Berkeley, CA
Unites States

It is an exciting time to be working in the field of personality psychology. After a decade of conceptual quiescence and existential self-scrutiny, the field is now re-emerging as a vigorous psychological discipline, with fresh approaches and innovative methods. The concept of disposition, long central to personality, is being reformulated with direct links to cognitive psychology at one end, and to observed conduct at the other (Buss & Craik, 1980, 1983a, 1983b, 1983c; Hampson, 1982a). New units of analysis such as scripts (Abelson, 1981) and personal projects (Little, 1983) promise to broaden the boundaries of the discipline. Simultaneously, more traditional units such as goals (Pervin, 1983) and motives (McClelland, 1980) reinstate conceptual concerns present since the field's inception.

As new approaches are more fully articulated, it becomes increasingly important to identify the connections among them. This chapter attempts to outline the major links between the act frequency approach (Buss & Craik, 1980, 1981, 1983a, 1983b, 1983c, 1984, 1985) and the constructivist approach to the analysis of personality (Berger & Luckmann, 1967; Hampson, 1982b, 1984). First, the basic framework of the act frequency analysis of personality will be outlined. Second, the central features of the constructivist position, particularly in the form of its application by Hampson (1982a, 1984), are identified. The third section points to the areas of agreement and disagreement between the two approaches. The fourth and fifth sections illustrate the different constructivist questions that are raised when moving from acts to constructs and when moving from constructs to acts. The final section draws some broader implications concerning the goals of personality psychology.

THE ACT FREQUENCY APPROACH TO PERSONALITY

The act frequency approach begins with the premise that the fundamental goal of all personality theories is to describe and account for regularities in individuals' actions, broadly conceived, occurring throughout the natural stream of everyday conduct. Dispositions are taken as central units that summarize general trends, or act frequencies, in conduct. To say that *Alois is altruistic,* from the act frequency perspective, means that he has displayed a high frequency of altruistic acts over a designated period of obversation. Dispositional concepts such as altruistic capture descriptive regularities in everyday

D.M.Buss/K.H.Craik

conduct. Saying that Alois is altruistic. however, does not *explain* why he made personal sacrifices, offered to make hotel arrangements, or bought his friend a beer. In this sense, dispositions serve descriptive, rather than explanatory, functions in the analysis of personality.

As objects are the basic elements of the inanimate world, acts are the basic elements of the world of human conduct. The network of dispositional constructs provides a fundamental system for categorizing acts by partitioning and granting conceptual order to the everyday stream of conduct. An intriguing feature of dispositional constructs is that they subsume individual acts that are often widely dispersed in time. In contrast, scriptal units (e.g., the restaurant script) subsume temporally contiguous act sequences. In this sense, dispositional constructs are highly selective, chunking acts that are extracted from temporally different points along the behavioral stream. Dispositions summarize the relative frequency of these temporally dispersed acts.

Although dispositions, from the act frequency perspective, serve this basic descriptive function, and therefore do not explain the act trends they summarize, act trends subsumed by dispositional constructs are far from powerless of inconsequential. Indeed, dispositional act trends can be expected to affect causally how individuals describe themselves (self-concept), how they are described by others (reputation), and the significant life outcomes that emerge over time in the person's fate in society.

The act frequency approach shares with lexical approaches (e.g., Allport & Odbert, 1936; Cattell, 1946; Goldberg, 1982; Norman, 1963; Wiggins, 1979) the notion that many dispositional constructs are socio-cultural products that have evolved to capture important performance phenomena. As linguistic products, dispositional constructs can be analyzed by their cognitive features. Two cognitive features are particularly relevant. First, dispositional categories are treated as "fuzzy sets" (Zadeh, Fu, Tanaka, & Shimura, 1975). That is, category boundaries are not sharply demarcated and different categories blend into one another just as the color red blends into orange and purple. Second, not all act members within a given dispositional category possess equal status within it. Some are more central and others are more peripheral, just as some red objects are "redder" than others and some birds (e.g., robins) are more "birdlike" than others (e.g., turkeys).

Rosch and her colleagues (Rosch, 1975; Rosch & Mervis, 1975; Rosch, Simpson, & Miller, 1976) have conceptualized the differing cognitive status of category members in terms of the notion of *prototypicality*. Highly prototypical members are the clearest cases, the best examples, the instances par excellence of the category. Thus, dispositional categories are composed of topographically dissimilar acts that differ in their within-category status from highly central or prototypical to progressively more peripheral until the fuzzy borders are reached and adjoining categories are entered.

In sum, the act frequency approach treats dispositional constructs as socio-cultural emergents that capture important descriptive regularities in everyday conduct. These regularities are the relative frequencies with which acts within the category are performed by persons during a specified period of observation. Dispositions in this sense are not viewed as causal or explanatory, although the act trends subsumed by them carry considerable potency in affecting self-concept, reputation, and significant life outcomes. Analysis of the cognitive features of category fuzziness and the prototypicality status of category members facilitates the precision with which dispositions, and the acts subsumed by them, can be analyzed and understood as socio-cultural emergents.

ACT FREQUENCIES AND THE
SOCIAL CONSTRUCTION OF PERSONALITY

It is undoubtedly more accurate to speak of constructivist positions in the plural since a number of alternatives are possible. The broad position, as put forth by Berger and Luckman (1967) has had a stronger impact on European psychologists (e.g., Hampson, 1982a, 1982b; Harré, 1979) than on American psychologists. The most explicit application of the constructivist position to personality psychology has been that of Hampson (1982, 1984), and her work will serve as the primary basis for comparison with the act frequency approach.

As articulated by Berger and Luckmann (1967), all reality is socially constructed. The world is presumed to originate in the thoughts and actions of persons in everyday conduct. The central task, therefore, is to clarify the foundations of knowledge of everyday life by objectifying what are essentially subjective processes and meanings by which the intersubjective (i.e., shared) common sense world is constructed. The central method for exploring social constructions, according to Berger and Luckman, is phenomenological analysis. As such, this approach refrains from causal analysis and does not make assertions about the ontological status of the phenomena under analysis. Language is crucial because it provides the necessary objectifications that afford order and meaning in everyday life. From their sociological perspective, Berger and Luckman stress *shared (intersubjective)* constructions rather than those unique to some individuals.

Hampson's (1984) application of the constructivist position to personality stresses that personality does not reside *within* individuals. Instead, it is a product created *between* them. As in the act frequency approach, dispositions are treated as categorizing concepts. But these semantic categories "do not refer directly to entities in the real world" (Hampson, 1984, p. 4). They serve instead as *labels* that group together aspects of the real world that share common attributes. As such, dispositional concepts provide a convenient shorthand for communication among lay persons in that they possess generally recognized social significance. Both actors and observers share common understandings as they are conveyed in trait terms. In general, personality is said to be constructed by lay persons from the actor's behavior combined with the meanings attributed to that behavior by observers and actors.

Further assumptions of Hampson's constructivist position entail links between actors and observers. Specifically, it is assumed that the actor is generally able to assess with some accuracy the views that observers have of the actor's personality; that social knowledge will

influence the actor's self-view, and that social interaction shapes the
behavior of the actor. These assumptions can be viewed as extensions
of Berger and Luckmann's emphasis on *shared* meanings, in this case
between actor and observer, but they appear to go beyond their
position in assigning more important consequences to lay persons'
constructions.

The constructivist position of Hampson (1982a, 1984) and the act
frequency approach (Buss & Craik, 1980, 1983a, 1983b, 1984) share
several points of convergence. Both approaches view dispositional
constructs as linguistic categories. Both emphasize the summarizing
function that dispositional terms carry. And both stress the
communicative functions that dispositions serve in everyday life (Buss
& Craik, 1983b). In addition, the approaches converge in not viewing
personality as *an entity within individuals* in the traditional sense
(e.g., Allport, 1937; Murray, 1938). From the act frequency
perspective, the causal bases for observed regularities in conduct
(e.g., in biological processes within persons; in existing environmental
contingencies) are not prejudged.

Several important lines of divergence exist between the act
frequency approach and constructivist approaches to personality.
First, the act frequency approach provides a set of operations for
systematically moving from representatively monitored acts in an
individual's course of conduct to dispositional assessments via
summated act trend indices. Constructivist approaches appear to focus
primarily on spontaneous attributions by observers about an
individual, made at the dispositional level. Second, act trends in
conduct carry consequences and impacts quite apart from the
constructs used to subsume them. Neither scientist nor social
construction is a necessary part of this causal potency. Thus,
performance of a high frequency of sensation seeking acts (e.g.,
parachute jumping, mountain climbing, downhill skiing) or ambitious
acts (e.g., staying up late to complete the team's progress report)
separately and in the aggregate affect life outcomes such as probability
of accidents (in the case of sensation seeking acts) and organizational
effectiveness and productivity (in the case of ambitious acts).

At the root of these differences is a crucial separation within the
act frequency approach between the use of dispositions as
socio-cultural categories for the scientific analysis of personality and
the use of dispositional terms by actors and observers in day-to-day
social discourse. For the scientific analysis of personality, dispositional
constructs are examined by identifying their cognitive properties,
uncovering the specific acts subsumed by them, and systematically
charting the frequencies with which individuals perform them over
time. This systematic analysis is *distinct from* the processes engaged
in by actors and observers in their immediate, direct, and presumably
less systematic constructions and usage. These two distinct uses of
dispositional constructs may be partially mapped on to each other, but
they carry different implications and generate different programs of
empirical research.

DISPOSITIONAL CONSTRUCTS IN THE
SCIENTIFIC ANALYSIS OF PERSONALITY

The use of dispositional constructs as socio-cultural emergents generates a program of research based on their analysis. There are three basic components to this research agenda: 1) identifying the internal cognitive structure of dispositions by exploring the acts subsumed by them and the status of specific acts with respect to dispositional categories; 2) using the information acquired from the cognitive mapping as a basis for charting manifested frequencies of acts as they occur in the everyday lives of persons, and 3) examining the impact of act trends upon the person's socio-physical environment and the consequences for the individual.

A. Procedures for Exploring Socio-Cultural Constructions

1. Act nominations. The first step in this research program entails identifying specific acts that are subsumed by each dispositional category. Act nominations can occur "on-line" (i.e., from direct observation) or retrospectively. The act frequency program has employed both methods of act nominations. Retrospective act nominations have used this instructional set: "Think of the three most dominant [sociable, aloof, calculating] individuals you know. With these individuals in mind, write down five specific acts or behaviors that they have performed that reflect or exemplify their dominance [sociability, aloofness, and so on]." These nomination procedures were designed to retrieve a large number of specific acts (100 or more) within each dispositional category. Examples of dominant acts yielded by this process are: She monopolized the conversation, He organized the group gathering, and She demanded a back rub.

Several on-line nomination procedures have been tested in a preliminary fashion. One entails observing interactions in cafes, writing down all acts that occur, and designating the category (e.g., dominance, aloofness) in which the act is consensually judged to belong. A second procedure entails observing interactions and writing down only those acts that are instances of specified dispositions such as dominance. These on-line procedures have yielded the following dominant acts: He decided at which table they would sit, She asked the waiter to make her order special, and He dominated the conversation. Clearly, one important research task involves systematic comparisons between recalled and on-line act nominations. A third approach that warrents exploration is the unobtrusive study of the stream of behavior of persons consensually reputed to be, for example, highly dominant (Craik, 1976). Presumably, these detailed behavior specimen records (Barker & Wright, 1951) would offer a relatively higher likelihood of containing acts prototypical of a given dispositional category.

2. Prototypicality ratings. For each list of acts generated through the nomination procedures, panels of judges rated the prototypicality of each act. Instructions for this task were adapted from the procedures used by Rosch and Mervis (1975) in the domain of colours: "Close

your eyes and imagine a true red. Now imagine an orangish
red. . .imagine a purple red. Although you might still name the
orange-red or the purple-red with the term *red*, they are not as good
examples of red (as clear cases of what red refers to) as the clear
"true" red. In short, some reds are redder than others." The purpose
of this procedure is to identify the shared cultural meaning or
prototypicality status of each act for the disposition in which it was
initially nominated. Panels of judges show reasonable agreement as
indexed by alpha reliability coefficients. Examples of submissive acts
differing in prototypicality are shown in Table 1.

TABLE 1: *Submissive Acts Differing in Prototypicality Status*

HE		SHE		
Mean	SD	Mean	SD	*Highly Prototypical Submissive Acts*
5.40	1.97	5.25	1.72	I accepted verbal abuse without defending myself.
5.29	1.94	5.75	1.61	I did not complain when I was overcharged at the store.
5.08	1.84	5.08	1.74	When I stood up to speak and the others continued talking, I simply sat down.
4.96	1.88	5.67	1.55	I made love with my partner when I didn't want to.
4.83	1.74	4.92	1.75	I did not talk back when my friend scolded me.
				Medium Prototypical Submissive Acts
4.54	1.75	4.53	1.58	I went to a concert with my date even though I didn't want to.
4.10	1.64	4.08	1.50	I let the others decide where to eat.
3.98	1.63	4.02	1.73	At the meeting, I let the others monopolize the conversation.
3.79	1.97	3.42	1.78	I let my partner chose the movie we would see.
3.71	1.83	3.71	1.58	I entered the conversation only when someone asked me a question.
				Low Prototypical Submissive Acts
3.40	1.87	2.96	1.58	I avoided direct eye contact when the shop clerk spoke to me.
3.29	1.89	3.25	1.82	I moved quietly aside when a passerby brushed against me in the corridor.
3.27	1.85	3.29	1.82	I said "thank-you" enthusiastically and repeatedly when someone did me an insignificant favor.
2.85	1.75	3.06	1.69	When the three of us set out on the journey, I took the back seat of the car.
2.52	1.61	2.48	1.41	I spoke softly when asked a personal question.

Note: Means and standard deviations refer to the prototypicality
ratings provided by a sample of 37 judges, using a scale of 1
(*low prototypically submissive*) to 7 (*highly prototypically
submissive*).

3. *Multiple dispositional act sorting.* Although prototypicality ratings yield simple and direct indices of the differential status of acts, they undoubtedly underestimate the complexity of the multiple constructs that may be used to interpret each act. In particular, some acts may be subsumed by more than one dispositional construct, especially if they fall toward the periphery of categories. To explore this complexity, a multiple-dispositional sorting and rating procedure was devised. Eight hundred acts, previously nominated within eight dispositional categories, were typed onto 3 x 5 index cards, one act per card. Panels of judges were asked to sort and rate each act with respect to each of the eight dispositional categories (Buss & Craik, Note 1). The 800 acts were shuffled randomly for each subject to disperse order effects. Each act was first sorted into the category or categories within which it was perceived to belong. Multiple category placement was permitted, and subjects were encouraged to nominate alternative categories to the eight provided if the act was judged to belong in a category other than those provided. Following the multiple sorting, each act was rated on its prototypicality for each of the categories within which it was placed.

This multiple sorting procedure yielded fascinating findings that were not uncovered by the more direct prototypicality ratings. In addition to frequent multiple placement of acts into two or more dispositional categories, certain differences emerged from a comparative analysis of the eight dispositions. In spite of the fact that each disposition started on an equal footing with 100 acts each, categories such as extraverted "pulled" acts from other categories when free sorting was permitted. Thus, the eight categories differed in the number of acts they ultimately drew. Even more interesting was the finding of asymmetries between dispositional categories. Acts that were initially nominated as quarrelsome were frequently placed into the dominant category, in addition to receiving the expected frequent sorting into the quarrelsome category. Dominant acts, in contrast, were only rarely placed in the quarrelsome category. Thus, quarrelsome acts are frequently seen as dominant, but dominant acts are only rarely seen as quarrelsome. Some illustrations of these asymmetries are shown in Table 2. Uncovering the shared cultural meaning of acts vis-a-vis dispositions may entail categorical asymmetries (and other differences) that are revealed by a comparative analysis of these constructs.

B. Assessing Manifested Act Trends

Within the act frequency approach, the assessment of the dispositions of specific individuals is based on monitored act trends over a period of observation. Analysis of the internal structure of dispositional constructs follows from the theoretical assumption that dispositions function as natural cognitive categories of acts (Buss & Craik, 1983a) and guides the identification of acts that will count as prototypical instances of the disposition being assessed. The aggregation of manifested acts of an individual over a period of observation to yield an act trend index for assessment purposes follows from the theoretical assumption that dispositional assertions are summarizing statements concerning human conduct (Buss & Craik, 1983a). The optimal

TABLE 2: *Asymmetries in Dominant and Quarrelsome Act Categorization*

Quarrelsome Acts Also Sorted into
Dominance Category by Majority of Judges

Quarrelsome	Dominant	Acts Initially Nominated as Quarrelsome
90%	50%	She got angry when her friend expressed the opposite point of view.
80%	70%	She condemned others for overindulging in food and drinks.
65%	80%	She was furious when the group's attention wandered from what she was saying.
85%	55%	She refused to listen to her friend's side of the story.
70%	50%	She made fun of his driving ability.
60%	80%	She refused to change her mind on the issue.
80%	65%	She got angry when someone tried to offer her advice.
65%	65%	She criticized someone for her clothes.

Dominant Acts Not Sorted into
Quarrelsome Category by Majority of Judges

Quarrelsome	Dominant	Acts Initially Nominated as Dominant
5%	90%	She set goals for the group.
10%	80%	She gave advice, although none was requested.
25%	95%	She demanded that he run an errand.
00%	63%	She made a bold sexual advance.
15%	90%	She chose to sit at the head of the table.
25%	90%	She demanded a backrub.
25%	95%	She decided which programs they would watch on TV.
16%	84%	She asked someone else to wash the dishes.

Note: Numbers reflect the percentage of judges (*N* = 20) who sorted the acts into the quarrelsome and dominant act categories. Half of the judges sorted the "he..." acts and half of the judges sorted the "she..." acts. The acts in this Table are presented in the "she..." form, but the percentages reflect the total placement regardless of whether a "he..." or "she..." act was being categorized.

conditions for dispositional assessment of persons within the act frequency approach are now being formulated and explored. A basic standard is that the monitoring of act trends will constitute a stratified representative sampling of an individual's everyday conduct within the person's natural ecology. Selecting dimensions of stratification raises a number of issues that warrant systematic conceptual analysis and field testing. The recording methods for monitoring act trends involve one of three sources: self-reports, observer reports, and mechanical recording devices. The strengths and weaknesses of each method are discussed by Buss and Craik (1984a).

Monitoring specific acts in the course of a person's conduct is an interpretive process. Provisional conceptual specification of our construct of the *act* is congruent with recent discourse in analytic philosophy (Buss & Craik. 1984b). The act is a concrete, individual event that entails intentionality and can have diverse descriptions (Davidson, 1969, 1971, 1976; Stoutland, 1976). Descriptions of an act can be expanded or contracted as if the act description were an accordion, to encompass greater or fewer aspects and consequences (Davidson, 1971; Feinberg, 1965). Acts can be described in terms of intentions and consequences rather than in reference to desires and other putative causes of acts (Stoutland, 1976; Thalberg, 1971). The on-line delineation of acts also involves the perceptual units of social action (Buss & Craik, 1983a). In this sense, the identification of an act within the course of a person's conduct (e.g., "taking charge of the situation after the accident") is a social construction.

This interpretive process must be seen as embedded within the full process of deriving act trend indices based on representatively monitored conduct as a basis for dispositional assessments within the act frequency approach. This set of operations is quite distinct from the recourse to dispositional constructs as spontaneous attributions made by actors and lay observers within the context of everyday life. Assessment of act trends takes place entirely without reference to such spontaneous dispositional attributions.

Furthermore, the causal potency of act trends found in the separate and aggregated consequences and impacts of an individual's acts can be considered without recourse to such spontaneous lay attributions at the dispositional level. High frequencies of acts such as "working late into the night on the report" and "seeking more demanding assignments" can affect organizational effectiveness, group accomplishments, and personal status and income. The causal chain includes linkages that are consequences of the acts (e.g., the report is ready and the next day's meeting is productive; the person takes on more responsible tasks) that are relatively independent of observer's spontaneous attributions at the dispositional level (e.g., Louis is ambitious). Of course, these lay attributions at the dispositional level may also appear in the causal chain (e.g., as performance appraisals; reputation).

Because the research program of the act frequency approach is not intrinsically tied to immediate on-line social constructions in dispositional terms by lay persons (actors and observers), it raises the intriguing question: What *are* the linkages between systematically assessed manifested act trends and the dispositional constructions spontaneously invoked by actors and observers? Although research is clearly needed here, several considerations suggest that assessed act trends and social constructions by lay persons will diverge, or at least display less than unity in their correspondence. First, social constructions held by lay observers may be based on factors other than direct apperception of act trends. Reputation, observer characteristics, and the vividness or cognitive salience of certain acts all may influence social judgments of dominance which thereby diverge from assessed act trend for dominance.

Second, any particular observer can see only a fraction of the relevant acts, and these subsets may not be representative. A supervisor may be excluded from relevant dominant acts performed in the presence of a peer. Non-representative act samples noted by lay persons can be expected to cause divergence between observer constructions and systematically assessed act trends for each disposition based on representative time and place sampling.

It would be surprising, however, if act trends and observer judgments of dispositional standing were unrelated. Indeed, there is already evidence that moderate correspondence exists between act trends and observer judgments - a correspondence that is stronger when the observer is in an intimate position (i.e., the spouse of the actor) than when the observer is a relative stranger in an interview context.

FROM ACTS TO CONSTRUCTS

An intriguing issue concerns the processes by which dispositional terms, as socio-cultural products, emerge, evolve, and spread throughout a culture. Perhaps there has been no other time in history when cultural evolution has been so rapid as at present. The introduction of technology, for example, directly produces new categories of acts that were previously unperformed. Each cultural change can be expected to influence the nature and frequency of acts performed in everyday life. These acts, in turn, are often described by the invention of nouns and adjectives that subsume and categorize performance. Examples surrounding technology include "technocrat," "computer nerd," and "video jock." Similarly, other classes of acts may decrease in relative frequency, may become less salient as important cultural categories, and their corresponding constructs may fade from everyday use. "Honor," for example, (including personal honor, family honor, and preserving a maiden's honor) was by some reports once a more prominent dispositional construct (honorable) than it is today, with perhaps a previously higher frequency of corresponding act performance.

Other shifts in constructs may be more subtle, involving the introduction of synonyms that may capture the essence of a differently described act category but alter its meaning and emphasis. There has never been a lack of dispositional constructs to describe acts that are weak and submissive. But novel constructs such as "whimpy" can introduce nuances of meaning that perhaps were previously less salient - in this case, connotations of weak sexual potency.

Certain categories of acts, and their corresponding constructs, may show remarkable stability, transcending different cultures and historical eras. These might involve universal human problems, or issues that all individuals in all cultures must somehow negotiate. Gough (1968; see also John, Goldberg, & Angleitner, 1984) uses the term "folk concepts" to describe features of human conduct that are universal - applicable to all societies everywhere. Since all cultures appear to possess status hierarchies (Lopreato, 1984), for example, all societies will evolve dispositional constructs such as "dominant" to describe the acts that correspond to relative position in the hierarchy.

Although the presence or absence of universal dispositional constructs is centrally an empirical issue, this consideration points to an important qualification of a constructivist position - one that stems from a consideration of the origins of social constructions. Are existing constructions arbitrary, time-bound, and culturally driven? Or does there exist only a limited set of reasonable constructions, a set of constructs that all societies everywhere must evolve to subsume universally relevant categories of acts? Do existing patterns of conduct in everyday life hold the range of possible constructions on a leash? If so, then the current constructivist positions that stress the relative and culture-bound aspects of constructions must be seriously softened.

FROM CONSTRUCTS TO ACTS

We have outlined several methods by which dispositional constructs, as socio-cultural emergents, can be studied. Reference to the acts that members of a culture believe to be subsumed by them, ratings of the status of each act within the category to which it is nominated, and the multiple dispositional classification of acts are methods that begin to reveal the nature and use of dispositional constructs for the scientific analysis of personality.

There is a sense in which these procedures yield an overly simplified portrait of dispositional constructs in their application to everyday conduct. Specifically, these empirical procedures are oriented toward uncovering the *shared* meaning of constructs. In taking the average or mean prototypicality rating for each act and the average category placement taken from the multiple dispositional sortings, individual variations in the use and application of dispositional constructs are implicitly treated as error.

The consensual level of analyzing dispositional constructs is central to both the act frequency approach and to the constructivist position as advanced by Berger and Luckmann (1967) and by Hampson (1984). Adequate composite agreement can be obtained for panels in their dispositional classifications and prototypicality judgments. The magnitude of the between-rater agreement, however, varies from disposition to disposition, suggesting that constructs themselves can differ in the degree of semantic consensus they accrue. And although several factors may even attenuate the observed between-rater agreement, such as transient mood states and other situational factors, there is some evidence that individual variation in the application of dispositional constructs to acts may be systematic. This possibility suggests two levels of analysis beyond the consensual level: individual differences and idiographic analysis (Buss & Craik, 1983b).

A vivid illustration of individual differences in the application of dispositional constructs emerged in analysing sex differences in the prototypicality ratings of dominant acts (Buss, 1981). Specifically, female judges tended to rate acts such as "asked others to perform menial tasks" as more prototypically dominant than did male judges. Males, in contrast, tended to rate acts such as "settling a dispute among members of a group" as more prototypically dominant. That is, females tended to emphasize the domineering component of the dominance construct (and hence viewed dominance as more socially undesirable), while males tended to emphasize the leadership component. In addition to sex differences, individuals can also differ in the range or breadth of act exemplars that are considered to fall within the boundaries of each disposition, just as differences are found even in the use of color categories such as the boundaries of "blue" (Block, Buss, Block, & Gjerde, 1981).

A final, and perhaps unresolvable, level of analysis concerns the unique (idiographic) use and application of dispositional constructs. Assimilation of cultural constructs is unavoidably an individual experience. The specific acts subsumed by dispositional constructs that each person encounters and observes in everyday life are unquestionably unique. Thus, individual constructions, containing shades of meaning and connotations not held by others, are an inevitable consequence of the processes entailed by assimilating cultural constructs.

Although the consensual level of analysis is basic to the act frequency approach to dispositional analysis and assessment, the study of individual differences and idiographic analyses also form part of its research agenda. Indeed, this approach offers several novel directions of investigation at each level of analysis (Buss & Craik, 1983b, 1984).

DISCUSSION

This brief review of the act frequency approach to personality provides a context for considering the "construction of personality" (Hampson, 1982b). In an insightful treatment of the current field of personality, Hampson identifies three perspectives from which personality can be viewed: the personality theorist's perspective, the lay observer's perspective, and the self perspective. She concludes that "personality is best regarded as a construction made up of contributions from all three perspectives" (p. 279).

We propose a slightly but importantly revised formulation. Our field of inquiry holds a stake in 1) personological theories about *human conduct*; 2) theories about the notions lay persons hold about other people's personalities; and 3) theories about the notions lay persons hold about their own personalities. That is, there are three distinct, but perhaps related, subject matters about which scientific theories are formulated. Such theories are all, or course, cognitive constructions – a recognition generally shared and relatively uninteresting.

Each of these three kinds of theories has a different focus because they are theories about different things. Hampson's formulation of personality as a construction composed of three perspectives seems implicitly to place scientific theories of human conduct on the same conceptual plane with lay "notions" about the self and about others. From our perspective, the *data* about which theories are formulated (human conduct, lay notions of self, lay notions of others) must be distinguished from the *scientific theories* about those respective data. That is, we view act trends, observer attributions, and self-referential statements as the basic data to be analyzed and explained. The scientific theories proposed to account for these different types of data, as well as the relations among them, occupy a separate arena of discourse and should not be confused with lay "notions" that form one data sub-type.

In this context, the act frequency approach is a contribution to the scientific theory of personality. The approach seeks to understand trends in human conduct as well as the shared socio-cultural dispositional constructs that are used to capture regularities in these trends. Because the act frequency approach advances explicit procedures for systematically assessing the act trends of persons and for unpacking the shared socio-cultural forms of dispositional constructs, it is distinct from other theoretical formulations that are directed toward understanding informal and spontaneous impression formations, trait attributions, and self-referential statements.

In conclusion, there are five basic points we would like to make:
(1) One basic goal of personality psychology is to account for regularities in everyday conduct of persons.
(2) Dispositional constructs, as constructions, are useful in the scientific analysis of everyday conduct.
(3) Constructions are also imposed spontaneously by actors and by observers on behavior in the social world and they constitute interesting subject matter for scientific inquiry.
(4) The two uses of dispositional constructions, one for the scientific analysis of personality and the other by actors and observers, are conceptually separate.
(5) Assessed act trends subsumed by dispositional constructs have *causal potency* in their consequences and impacts, quite apart from any dispositional constructions imposed by actors, by observers, or by personality psychologists.

ACKNOWLEDGEMENT

The authors thank Lewis R. Goldberg, Sarah E. Hampson, and Oliver P. John for insightful comments on an earlier version of this chapter.

REFERENCES

Abelson, R.P. (1981). Psychological status of the script concept. *American Psychologist, 36,* 715-729.
Allport, G.W. (1937). *Personality: A psychological interpretation.* New York: Holt.
Allport, G.W., & Odbert, H.S. (1936). Trait-names: A psycholexical study. *Psychological Monographs, 47,* (Whole No. 211).
Barker, R.G., & Wright, H.F. (1951). *One boy's day.* New York: Harper & Row.
Berger, P.L., & Luckmann, T. (1967). *The social construction of reality.* Harmondsworth: Penguin Books.

Block, J., Buss, D.M., Block, J.H., & Gjerde, P.F. (1981). The cognitive style of breadth of categorization: Longitudinal consistency of personality correlates. *Journal of Personality and Social Psychology*, *41*, 401–408.

Buss, D.M. (1981). Sex differences in the evaluation and performance of dominant acts. *Journal of Personality and Social Psychology*, *40*, 147–154.

Buss, D.M., & Craik, K.H. (1980). The frequency concept of disposition: Dominance and prototypically dominant acts. *Journal of Personality*, *48*, 379–392.

Buss, D.M., & Craik, K.H. (1981). The act frequency analysis of interpersonal dispositions: Aloofness, gregariousness, dominance and submissiveness. *Journal of Personality*, *49*, 174–192.

Buss, D.M., & Craik, K.H. (1983a). The act frequency approach to personality. *Psychological Review*, *90*, 105–126.

Buss, D.M., & Craik, K.H. (1983b). The dispositional analysis of everyday conduct. *Journal of Personality*, *51*, 393–412.

Buss, D.M., & Craik, K.H. (1983c). Act prediction and the conceptual analysis of personality scales: Indices of act density, bipolarity, and extensity. *Journal of Personality and Social Psychology*, *45*, 1081–1095.

Buss, D.M., & Craik, K.H. (1984a). Acts, dispositions, and personality. In B.A. Maher & W.B. Maher (Eds.), *Progress in experimental personality research: Vol. 13. Normal personality processes* (pp. 241–301). New York: Academic Press.

Buss, D.M., & Craik, K.H. (1984b). *The act: Notes*. Berkeley, CA: Institute of Personality Assessment and Research, University of California.

Buss, D.M., & Craik, K.H. (1985). Why *not* measure that trait? Alternative criteria for identifying important dispositions. *Journal of Personality and Social Psychology*, *48*, 934–946.

Buss, D.M., & Craik, K.H. (Note 1). *The multiple dispositional categorization of acts*. Manuscript in preparation.

Cattell, R.B. (1946). *Description and measurement of personality*. Yonkers-on-Hudson, NY: World Book Company.

Craik, K.H. (1976). The personality research paradigm in environmental psychology. In S. Wapner, S.B. Cohen, & B. Kaplan (Eds.), *Experiencing the environment* (pp. 55–79). New York: Plenum.

Davidson, D. (1969). The individuation of events. In N. Rescher (Ed.), *Essays in honor of Carl G. Hempel* (pp. 216–234). Boston: D. Reidel.

Davidson, D. (1971). Agency. In R. Brinkley, R. Bronaugh, & A. Marras (Eds.), *Agent, action and reason* (pp. 3–37). Toronto: University of Toronto Press.

Davidson, D (1973). Freedom to act. In T. Honderich (Ed.), *Essays on freedom of action*. London: Routledge and Kegan Paul.

Feinberg, J. (1965). Action and responsibility. In M. Blank (Ed.), *Philosophy in America* (pp. 134–160). London: George Allen & Unwin.

Goldberg, L.R. (1982). From ace to zombie: Some explorations in the language of personality. In C.D. Spielberger & N.J. Butcher (Eds.), *Advances in personality assessment* (Vol. 1, pp. 203–234). Hillsdale, NJ: Erlbaum.

Gough, H.G. (1968). An interpreter's syllabus for the California Psychological Inventory. In P. McReynolds (Ed.), *Advances in psychological assessment* (Vol. 1, pp. 1-28). Palo Alto, CA: Science and Behavior Books.

Hampson, S.E. (1982a). Person memory: A semantic category model of personality traits. *British Journal of Psychology, 73*, 1-11.

Hampson, S.E. (1982b). *The construction of personality: An introduction*. London: Routledge & Kegan Paul.

Hampson, S.E. (1984). The social construction of personality. In H. Bonarius, G. Van Heck, & N. Smid (Eds.), *Personality psychology in Europe: Theoretical and empirical developments* (pp. 3-14). Lisse, The Netherlands: Swets & Zeitlinger.

Harré, R. (1979). *Social being*. Oxford: Blackwell.

John, O.P., Goldberg, L.R., & Angleitner, A. (1984). Better than the alphabet: Taxonomies of personality-descriptive terms in English, Dutch, and German. In H. Bonarius, G. Van Heck, & N. Smid (Eds.), *Personality psychology in Europe: Theoretical and empirical developments* (pp. 83-100). Lisse, The Netherlands: Swets & Zeitlinger.

Little, B.R. (1983). Personal projects: A rationale and method for investigation. *Environment and Behavior, 15*, 273-309.

Lopreato, J. (1984). *Human nature and biocultural evolution*. Boston: Allen & Unwin.

McClelland, D.C. (1980). Motive dispositions: The merits of operant and respondent measures. In L. Wheeler (Ed.), *Review of personality and social psychology* (Vol. 1, pp. 10-41). Beverly Hills, CA: Sage.

Murray, H.A. (1938). *Explorations in personality*. New York and London: Oxford University Press.

Norman, W.T. (1963). Toward an adequate taxonomy of personality attributes: Replicated factor structure in peer nomination personality ratings. *Journal of Abnormal and Social Psychology, 66*, 574-583.

Pervin, L.A. (1983). The stasis and flow of behavior: Toward a theory of goals. In M.M. Page & R. Dienstbier (Eds.), *Nebraska Symposium on Motivation* (pp. 1-53). Lincoln, NE: University of Nebraska Press.

Rosch, E. (1975). Cognitive reference points. *Cognitive Psychology, 7*, 532-547.

Rosch, E., & Mervis, C.B. (1975). Family resemblances: Studies in the internal structure of categories. *Cognitive Psychology, 7*, 573-605.

Rosch, E., Simpson, C., & Miller, R.S. (1976). Structural bases of typicality effects. *Journal of Experimental Psychology: Human Perception and Performance, 2*, 491-502.

Stoutland, F. (1976). The causal theory of action. In J. Manninen & R. Tuomela (Eds.), *Essays on explanation and understanding: Studies in the foundations of humanities and social sciences* (pp. 271-304). Boston: D. Reidel.

Thalberg, I. (1971). Two problems about reasons for actions: Comments. In R. Binkley, R. Bronaugh, & A. Marras (Eds.), *Agent, action and reason*. (pp. 154-166). Toronto: University of Toronto Press.

Wiggins, J.S. (1979). A psychological taxonomy of trait descriptive terms: The interpersonal domain. *Journal of Personality and Social Psychology, 37,* 395–412.

Zadeh, L.A., Fu, K.S., Tanaka, K., & Shimura, M. (Eds.). (1975). *Fuzzy sets and their application to cognitive and decision processes.* New York: Academic Press.

PART IV

TRAIT INFERENCES: ATTRIBUTION,
DISTORTIONS AND PREDICTION

THE ATTRIBUTION OF PERSONALITY TRAITS

Ivan Mervielde

University of Ghent
Belgium

For some years now the value of personality questionnaires as predictors of behaviour, implied by the traits they intend to measure, has been questionned (Fiske, 1974; Mischel, 1968; Peterson, 1968). In the past decade much attention has been paid to the conceptualization of situations as determinants of behaviour (Barker, 1968; Moos, 1973), and especially to the interaction between traits and situational factors (Endler & Magnusson, 1976). Taking into account situational factors and interactions between traits and situations, may increase the predictive value of trait measures, but it is doubtful that this will be sufficient to predict the occurrence of specific behaviours.

It is somewhat surprising that this attack on trait psychology did not have a major impact on the way in which personality psychologists conceptualise traits. The impetus for challenging the view that traits are global dispositions, however, came from cognitive psychology. Cantor and Mischel (1977) demonstrated that some traits operate as prototypes, which direct the attention to certain stimuli and influence the selection and organization of information. According to Markus (1977), traits can be a component of the person's self-schemata and as such organise and guide the processing of self-related information.

However, these new developments did not yet alter the way in which traits are measured. Presumably the fact that there were no dramatic new developments in test theory which are applicable to this new conceptualization has prevented a change in the way traits are measured. It should also be emphasized that this new conceptualization stresses the role of traits as cognitive structures, directing the way in which information is processed. How information processing is related to specific behaviours, remains largely unspecified, and this may also explain why personality assessment has not been affected by these new developments.

A considerable number of personality inventories still require from the respondent that he or she attributes trait adjectives to the self or to people in general. Typical examples of such instruments are the Bem Sex Role Inventory (Bem, 1973) and the Adjective Check List (Gough & Heilbrun, 1965). Many personality questionnaires have a mixture of items formulated in trait adjective style and items pointing to behaviours which are typically implied by certain traits. Moreover, Burisch (1984), provided some evidence that direct trait ratings which are frequently used in observational and clinical studies, have the same predictive value as trait scores derived from personality questionnaires.

Furthermore, Furnham reported significant correlations between actual (test-derived) and self-estimated scores for extraversion, neuroticism, psychoticism, self-monitoring and social anxiety (Furnham,

1984; Furnham & Henderson, 1982). If these results are widely confirmed by other research this could significantly increase the use of direct trait ratings as a method for personality assessment.

Although the conception of traits as measures of global disposition has been attacked at a theoretical level, one cannot deny that direct or indirect attribution of traits still remains an important aspect of personality assessment. Therefore, a better understanding of the processes involved in trait attribution may be useful to further improve and refine trait measurement.

THREE TYPES OF TRAIT ATTRIBUTION

The elaboration of a comprehensive theory of trait attribution requires a conceptual analysis of trait attributional processes. Three functionally different types of trait attribution will be distinguished: descriptive trait attribution, explanatory trait attribution, and inferential trait attribution.

Descriptive trait attribution

People can attribute a trait to themselves or to others, in order to summarize, describe or label a series of observed behavioural episodes. When someone offers me a cup of coffee or gives me a lift when my car has broken down, I will be inclined to label this person as friendly or perhaps as helpful. Offering someone a cup of coffee or giving someone in trouble a lift are considered to be instances of friendly of helpful behaviour.

Although descriptive trait attribution may seem to be a fairly trivial process, it is by no means obvious *when* certain behavioural episodes will be considered as instances of a particular class, *why* some instances belong to a given category and, last but not least, *which* behavioural instances can be subsumed under a given trait label. Traits as descriptors of a class of behaviours are a typical example of so-called fuzzy sets (Zadeh, 1965). A given behavioural episode may be assigned to different categories, by different persons and even by the same person depending on the context of the trait attribution. Receiving a cup of coffee may be seen as an instance of friendly behaviour, or as an instance of social behaviour and perhaps as an instance of helpful behaviour.

To which category the behavioural episode will be assigned is often difficult to predict. Kelly (1955), among others, has provided ample evidence for the fact that people depend on their personal constructs or categories to segment the ongoing stream of behaviour. The assignment of a behavioural episode to a particular category is thus likely to be influenced by the personal constructs of the perceiver.

The situational context is also an important determinant of descriptive trait attribution. Given that the situation or context is rather ambiguous, personal constructs may have a decisive influence on which category will be available, but when the perceiver operates in a context which makes certain categories more salient, he or she will probably assign the observed episode to the trait category which is made salient by the context. For example, someone who receives a cup of coffee after jumping in ice cold water to save someone from drowning, will probably attribute receiving coffee to the category of helpful behaviours since at that moment the helpfulness category will be very salient. On the other hand, someone who is sitting alone on an isolated table in a cafetaria and who is offered a cup of coffee by a stranger, may be more inclined to see this act as an instance of friendliness or sociability.

Some behavioural episodes can be ordered on a continuum. Athletic performances, for example, can be ordered from *very good* to *very bad*. Many of the behavioural episodes which reflect some from of ability can be ordered along such a continuum. A student's performance is another example of a behavioural episode that can be located somewhere on a continuum from *very good* to *very bad performance*. Reeder and Brewer (1979) noticed the following interesting asymmetry in the attribution of such behavioural episodes. A good performance on a difficult exam will normally be attributed to the intelligence or high ability of the student. A bad performance on the other hand, may be seen as the result of low ability but can also be attributed to situational or context factors. A highly intelligent student will normally perform very well on exams but he can have an occasional bad performance. A student with low ability, however, will be expected to perform badly all the time.

This asymmetrical relation between good and bad performance on the one hand, and the attribution of high or low ability on the other hand has consequences for the *certainty* of the inference. Observing a good performance will make the perceiver feel confident that the behaviour should be attributed to high ability. However, given a bad performance, the perceiver may feel less confident about the level of ability he should attribute to the performer.

This asymmetrical relation also has implications for the effects of situational demands and context factors on the trait attribution. Messick and Reeder (1972, 1974) asked observers to watch a videotape of an actor who portrayed himself as *introverted* during a job interview. The context of the interview was varied so that the behavioural episode was either consistent (the person was interviewed for a job as nightwatchman, which requires the ability to be alone for long periods) or inconsistent (the job required rather extraverted behaviour, e.g., salesman) with situational demands. As expected, observers judged the actor to be more introverted when the introverted performance was inconsistent with situational demands (salesman condition) than when it was consistent with the situational demands (nightwatchman).

In a second study the observers were presented a videotape of someone who protrayed himself as *extraverted* during the job interview. Again, the situational demands or context were varied to make it either consistent or inconsistent with the observed behavioural episode. In contrast to the previous study with introverted behaviour, the extraverted performance led observers to attribute a relatively high degree of extraversion to the actor *regardless* of the situational demands.

Attributions based on observation of an introverted behavioural episode were context-dependent, whereas attributions based on observation of extraverted behaviour were not affected by situational demands or context information. Since context effects only occurred at one end of the continuum (i.e., for introverted performance) these results suggest a similarity between the introversion-extraversion dimension and the attribution of ability. Observers may believe that an extraverted person can portray behaviour that ranges from extraverted to introverted. Therefore, when the situational context requires introverted behaviour (job interview for nightwatchman,) the extravert could portray introverted behaviour and hence the attribution of the behavioural episode to introversion becomes less certain. If an introverted person is believed to be incapable of portraying extraverted behaviour, then perception of extraverted behaviour will lead to the attribution of extraversion, regardless of the situational demands.

Explanatory trait attribution

The second type of trait attribution that will be distinguished is explanatory trait attribution. Traits may be attributed to persons in order to explain a certain behavioural episode. Explaining a behavioural episode usually means that the perceiver relates the observed behaviour to one or more causes. The basic question that the perceiver wants to answer is *why* the behavioural episode has occurred. Recently, there has been a growing interest among social psychologists in causal attribution (Harvey & Weary, 1984; Kelley & Michela, 1980). Attribution theorists classify the perceived causes of behaviour on a number of dimensions such as internal-external, stable-unstable, and controllable-uncontrollable causes (Weiner, 1979) and global versus specific causes (Abramson, Seligman, & Teasdale, 1978). According to this classification, traits are examples of internal, stable, global, and uncontrollable causes of behaviour.

An influential model for causal attribution has been developed by Kelley (1967, 1973). According to his model, people attribute behavioural episodes to three main causal categories. When I perceive that a person named John performs badly or fails on a psychology exam, I can attribute that failure to three main causal categories:
1) The failure may be attributed to something about the person John. I may think, for example, that he is lazy or lacks the necessary skills.
2) I could also attribute the failure to the difficulty of that psychology exam. In this case the entity to which the person responds (the psychology exam) is seen as the cause.
3) Finally, I can think that the particular situation in which the exam took place explains the failure. I can think that it was extremely hot that afternoon or that there was to much noise in the room, etc.
Whether the failure will be attributed to something about the person, something about the exam, or something about the situation will, according to Kelley, be a function of three types of information: (a) *Consensus information:* this is information about the number of persons failing on that exam. Consensus is said to be low when only John fails on the exam. The consensus is high when several students fail on that psychology exam. (b) *Consistency information:* this is information about

the frequency of failure in different situations. John may fail consistently across different situations or he may only fail in one particular situation. (c) *Distinctiveness information:* this is information about the failure rate on other exam's, or to use Kelley's general term, other entities. The failure is said to be distinctive if John only fails on the psychology exam. The effect is not distinctive when there is evidence that John also fails on other exams.

Attribution of behaviours to traits is an example of what in Kelley's model are called person-type attributions. The question that concerns us here is of course what type of information pattern will lead to a person attribution. An effect such as failure on a psychology exam, will be attributed to something within the person, when the person believes or is told that the consensus for the effect is low (only John fails), the consistency is high (he fails in different situations) and the distinctiveness is low (he fails on different exams).

Attribution theories are of course models for the attributional behaviour of lay persons or people in general. The concepts which attribution theory provides may nevertheless turn out to be useful for the study of individual differences. The classification of causes in internal-external, stable-unstable, controllable-uncontrollable, and global-specific, could be a good starting point for the construction of attributional style measures.

Kelley's three types of information could prove to be useful for the study of individual differences in social information processing style. It seems at least plausible to suggest that some people will be more sensitive to consensus information, while others may be more influenced by distinctiveness or consistency information.

Inferential trait attribution

The third type of trait attribution to be distinguished is inferential trait attribution. Once a number of traits are attributed to a person, the perceiver may infer the presence of additional traits without further observation of behavioural episodes. If I meet someone who is intelligent, warm, and social, I may consider that person to be honest as well. In this case the judgement of honesty is not based on observation of relevant behaviour but is inferred directly from the presence of other traits.

Inferential trait attribution is only possible if the perceiver has an implicit theory about the relationships between traits (Schneider, 1973). Maps of such implicit networks of perceived relationships have been published, for instance, by Rosenberg and Sedlak (1972).

Maps of implicit personality theories are useful to predict pairwise or trait-trait attributions, because the distance or proximity between any pair of traits provides an estimate of the perceived degree of relationship between the traits. However, the task of the attributor is often more complicated. When the target person is perceived as having more than one trait, then the attributional problem requires an inference or attribution of one or more response traits to a conglomerate of stimulus traits.

To what extent a person who is intelligent, warm and social, will be considered as honest, depends on the perceived distance between the trait *honest* and the other three traits. Implicit personality theory, however, is not very clear on how the perceiver might assess the distance between the response trait (honest) and the stimulus traits (intelligent, social, and warm). To get a better idea of how the perceiver accomplishes this task, two studies were performed. In the first study, subjects were asked to judge the rate of co-occurrence for 14 traits. These ratings were converted to a multidimensional representation and a hierarchical clustering tree. The pairwise distances and proximities from these analyses were subsequently used in the second study to test the predictive value of four attributional rules.

STUDY 1

The main purpose of this study was to collect information about the implicit perceived structure of 14 trait adjectives. Implicit personality structures can be represented either as a multidimensional trait space or as a series of hierarchically ordered trait clusters. Both methods are based on different assumptions about the way trait information is organised. Little is known about the relative efficiency of both methods for representing implicit personality theories. Therefore, it was decided to use both methods and to compare their relative efficiency for predicting trait attribution.

Method

Subjects and instructions. Forty eight first year psychology students (24 male and 24 female), rated the degree of co-occurrence of 14 traits. Ratings were made on a seven-point scale ranging from *one* to *seven*. The subjects were carefully instructed to use the entire range of the scale. Subjects completed the task in groups of twelve and were seated at separate tables.

Traits. The 14 traits were arranged in a lower-triangular matrix format. The subjects were instructed to fill the matrix column after column. Traits were selected from a list of 100 traits which had been rated on a likableness scale by a similar sample of 88 subjects (Mervielde, 1977a, 1977b). The likableness of the selected traits ranged from 4.64 to 6.21 on a seven-point rating scale and the mean likableness of the 14 traits was 5.79. The selected traits and their likableness value are reported in Table 1.

Scaling and clustering algoritm. A matrix with proximities for all pairwise combinations of the 14 traits was constructed by averaging the ratings provided by the 48 subjects. This matrix was analyzed with Johnson's (1967) hierarchical clustering algorithm. Distances between a cluster and another element were computed according to the diameter or complete linkage method (Johnson, 1967).

The same proximity matrix was also used as input for the multidimensional scaling routine, MINISSA-1, developed by Roskam and Lingoes (1970). This analysis produced configurations with a dimensionality ranging from 1 to 13 dmensions. The badness of fit of these solutions was evaluated with Kruskal's (1964) stress measure.

TABLE 1: *Likableness values of 14 traits which were rated on frequency of co-occurrence.*

Traits	Likableness
Warm (warm)	5.54
Poised (evenwichtig)	5.88
Polite (beleefd)	5.22
Active (actief)	5.91
Honest (eerlijk)	6.46
Patient (geduldig)	5.57
Progressive (progressief)	5.15
Intelligent (intelligent)	5.39
Social (sociaal)	6.21
Friendly (vriendelijk)	6.12
Thrustworthy (betrouwbaar)	6.35
Happy (gelukkig)	6.34
Sincere (oprecht)	6.23
Nonconforming (nonconformistisch)	4.46

Note. The Flemish translation of the traits is indicated between brackets.

Results

Hierarchical clustering. The dendrogram produced by Johnson's (1967) diameter method is represented in Figure 1.

This figure illustrates that the 14 traits can be grouped in various ways. At the highest level two groups emerge: one containing the traits *progressive, active, intelligent,* and *nonconforming,* and a second cluster with the rest of the traits. The proximity between any pair of traits was defined as the value of the highest node connecting them. The correlation between these output proximities and the input proximities was .79.

Multidimensional scaling. The adequacy of the output configuration obtained by applying MINISSA-1 to the proximity matrix, was evaluated with Kruskal's (1964) badness of fit measure. The stress percentages for the solutions with dimensionality 1 to 5 were: 32%, 18%, 7%, 4% and 2%. It was decided that a three-dimensional solution would be adequate to represent the data, because the stress percentages did not decline sharply for configurations with a higher dimensionality. The values for the 14 traits on the three dimensions are reported in Table 2.

STUDY 2

The clustering analysis and the multidimensional scaling reported in the first study can be used to predict the perceived relationship between pairs of traits. In many instances, however, the impression of the perceiver consists of more than one trait. A perceiver may think of a particular person as being social, polite, and intelligent. When

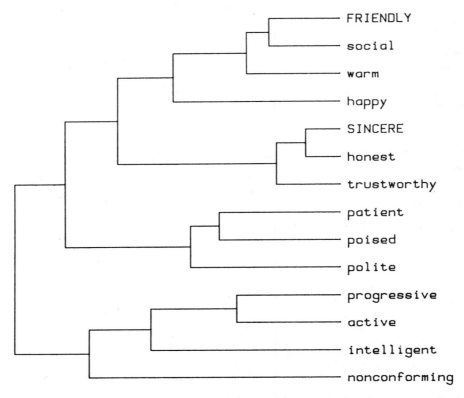

Figure 1: *Dendrogram resulting from hierarchical cluster analysis according to Johnson's diameter method. Traits listed in capital letters served as response traits in Study 2.*

such a perceiver is asked whether the target person will also be sincere, then the perceiver must somehow calculate the distance between the response trait (sincere) and the three stimulus traits.

The calculation of the distance between the response trait and the conglomerate can be seen as an information integration task. According to Anderson (1974), impression formation is a form of information integration which can be best represented by a weighted averaging model. Anderson's research, however, is restricted to one response scale, that is, likableness judgements. Therefore, Anderson's weighted averaging model was extended in order to allow for attribution of any trait to a stimulus person (Figure 1).

The attribution of a response trait X to a stimulus person, described by the traits a, b and c, is considered to be a *weighted average* of the *pairwise distances* between the response trait and each of the stimulus traits. The basic difference between this formulation and the one proposed by Anderson is that distances between traits are

TABLE 2: *Loadings of 14 traits on the three dimensions of the MINISSA configuration*

	Dimension		
	1	2	3
Warm	-0.299	0.333	-0.743
Poised	-0.523	-0.248	-0.636
Polite	-1.076	-0.641	-0.165
Active	0.779	-0.359	-0.543
Honest	0.093	0.497	0.536
Patient	-1.148	0.012	0.205
Progressive	0.947	-0.633	-0.304
Intelligent	0.081	-1.011	0.460
Social	-0.086	0.128	-0.457
Friendly	-0.488	0.007	-0.667
Thrustworthy	-0.074	0.392	0.665
Happy	0.128	0.938	-0.388
Sincere	0.222	0.581	0.472
Nonconforming	1.444	0.003	0.292

STIMULUS TRAITS

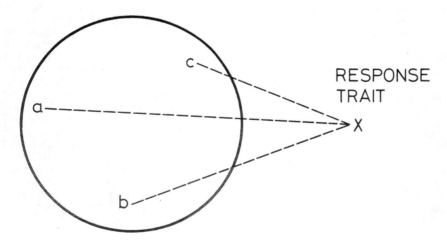

RESPONSE TRAIT

$$\text{ATTRIBUTION OF } X = \frac{w_a r_{ax} + w_b r_{bx} + w_c r_{cx}}{w_a + w_b + w_c}$$

Figure 2: *Schematic representation of attribution of a response trait X to a stimulus conglomerate with traits a, b, and c. (The w's refer to the weights and the r's to the relationships between response and stimulus traits).*

to be averaged and not the likableness values of the traits themselves. Restricting the averaging process to a likableness dimension makes it rather difficult to take into account the descriptive meaning of the traits. Integration of perceived distances, however, assures that descriptive as well as evaluative meaning, can influence the perceived degree of relationship.

Because a weighted averaging model allows for differential weighting of the information, it was decided to assess the effects of various weighting procedures. Attributing a response trait to a target person characterized by three different stimulus traits is a rather complex task. Therefore, it was expected that subjects might try to symplify the task by assigning more weight to the trait which is closest or most similar to the required response trait. In order to test this hypothesis four different rules for assigning weights were constructed:

a) *Smallest distance rule* (SMA): this rule assigns a weight of 1 to the smallest of the three pairwise distances and zero weight to the two others.

b) *Greatest distance rule* (GRE): this rule assigns a weight of 1 to the greatest of the pairwise distances and a zero weight to the other two distances.

c) *Unweighted averaging rule* (UWA): each of the pairwise distances receives a weight of 1.

d) *Proportionally weighted averaging rule* (PWA): each distance receives a weight which is the inverse of the distance.

These four rules differ from one another because they assign greater or lesser weight to the trait which is closest to the response trait. The SMA-rule only takes into account the trait which is closest to the response trait. The PWA-rule assigns the greatest weight to the trait which is closest to the response trait and the smallest weight to the trait with the greatest distance. The UWA-rule assigns an equal weight to all distances and, finally, the GRE-rule only takes into account the trait with the greatest distance to the response trait. The four rules can thus be differentiated according to the weight they assign to the stimulus trait which is closest to the response trait. If subjects reduce the complexity of the integration task by assigning greater weight to the stimulus trait which is closest or most similar to the response trait, then the predictive validity of the four rules will not be the same. More precisely it is expected that the predictive validity will be a function of the weight assigned to the stimulus trait which is closest to the response trait. The validity will be highest for the SMA-rule and lowest for the GRE-rule. Furthermore, it is expected that the predictive validity of the PWA-rule will be higher than that for the UWA-rule.

Method

Subjects and instructions. A group of 96 first year psychology students (48 male, 48 female) was asked to rate, on a seven-point scale, the degree of sincerity and friendliness of 40 stimulus persons. Each stimulus person was described by three traits a, b, and c. The task was completed in groups of twelve and each subject was seated at a separate table in the experimental room.

Stimulus and response traits. The 14 traits from Study 1 were divided in three groups: a group with two response traits (i.c., sincere and friendly, a group of six traits with the most extreme loadings on the three-dimensional MINISSA configuration, and a group with the six remaining traits. This procedure made it possible to create trait triplets with varying degrees of *redundancy*. Redundancy was defined as the mean of all pairwise distances *(ab, ac, bc)* among traits of a triplet. The distances necessary to compute the redundancy were taken from the three-dimensional MINISSA configuration. Twenty trait triplets were constructed with each of the two groups of six traits. The 40 triplets were subsequently grouped in four categories, according to their degree of redundancy. It was thought that the redundancy of the stimulus conglomerate could affect the predictive validity of the four rules, because differential weighting might be less pronounced for stimulus triplets which are close to each other.

Results

Redundancy. The mean attribution score (for both response traits) was computed for each of the 40 stimulus triplets. The effect of redundancy of the stimulus configuration was tested by comparing the attribution scores for the four redundancy categories. One-way analysis of variance on these scores showed no significant redundancy effects. For the response trait *sincere,* F (3, 36) = 1.67, and for *friendly,* F (3, 36)= .55.

Predictive validity of the four rules. Attributions of the two response traits, sincere and friendly, were predicted according to the four rules. Moreover, each prediction was made either with multidimensional scaling as input or with the results of the hierarchical clustering. The correlation between predicted and observed trait attribution was used as criterion for the predictive validity of the four rules and also served as an indicator of the relative efficiency of scaling and clustering.

There were no major differences among the predictive validity coefficients based on multidimensional scaling and hierarchical clustering, as is evident from comparison of the correlations reported in the upper and lower part of Table 3.

The main purpose of the study was to compare the predictive validity of the four rules. Table 3 shows that, for the attribution of *sincere,* the lowest correlations are obtained when the predictions are made according to the GRE-rule (-.31 for MD-scaling and .03 for clustering). A similar pattern can be observed for the attribution of the response trait *friendly.* The best predictions are provided by the SMA- and the PWA-rule. Significant but lower correlations are found when the attribution is predicted by the UWA-rule.

Moreover, comparison of the validity coefficients for the four rules, showed that the predictive validity of the GRE-rule is significantly lower than that of the other three rules ($p<.001$). This effect did not depend on the type of input, that is, scaling or clustering, nor on the type of response trait.

The predictive validity of the SMA-rule is significantly higher than that of the UWA-rule, when scaling serves as input and *friendly* as response trait ($p<.01$). Comparison of the validity coefficients for the

I. Mervielde

TABLE 3: *Predictive validity coefficients for four attribution rules*

	Attribution of sincere				Attribution of friendly			
Redundancy	SMA	GRE	UWA	PWA	SMA	GRE	UWA	PWA
	Multidimensional scaling: three dimensions							
H	-.93**	-.61*	-.82**	-.94**	-.76**	-.68*	-.84**	-.84**
MH	-.84**	.39	-.88**	-.88**	-.76**	.15	-.42	-.70*
ML	-.89**	-.61*	-.93**	-.94**	-.79**	-.41	-.41	-.74**
L	-.90**	.25	-.84**	-.92**	-.73**	-.61*	-.16	-.67*
Total	-.86**	-.31*	-.84**	-.89**	-.71**	-.24	-.39**	-.68**
	Hierarchical clustering: diameter method							
H	.91**	-.20	.64*	.82**	.68*	.70*	.92**	.88**
MH	.85**	.35	.85**	.86**	.77**	-.28	.80**	.82**
ML	.89**	.00	.85**	.88**	.75**	.00	.78**	.77**
L	.92**	.00	.95**	.94**	.92**	.00	.85**	.88**
Total	.86**	.03	.75**	.82**	.73**	.09	.70**	.74**

* $p < .05$ ** $p < .01$
H = high; MH = moderately high; ML = moderately low; L = Low
SMA = smallest distance rule
GRE = greatest distance rule
UWA = unweighted average distance rule
PWA = proportionally weighted distance rule

UWA-rule and those for the PWA-rule did not reveal any significant differences.

The main conclusion is that rules, which favour the trait with the smallest distance to the response trait, are better predictors of the observed trait attribution. Subjects seem to base their attributions mainly on the trait which is closest to the response trait. They may use this strategy because it demands less information processing power and reduces an essential multidimensional problem to a rather simple judgement of the distance between two traits. But before this reduction in complexity can be achieved, the subject must somehow know which of the stimulus traits is closest to the response trait. Therefore, it seems likely that the attribution task requires a two stage process: First, the subject selects the stimulus which is closest to the response trait, and then estimates the proximity or distance between that trait and the response trait. Evidence for the fact that inferences based on implicit personality theory, may be best represented by a two-stage model is also provided by Ebbesen and Allen (1979).

Finally, this study indicates that knowledge of implicit personality structure is not sufficient for a precise prediction of trait attribution. Trait attribution involves some form of information integration. Therefore, a precise formulation of information integration rules is required. Furthermore, the results from the second study indicate that the integration of information may be systematically biased. When subjects are asked to predict whether a given person will have a certain trait, they are likely to assign a greater weight or importance to the stimulus trait which is closest or most similar to the response trait.

DISCUSSION

Differentiation among the three processes

The distinction made between the three types of trait attribution illustrates that a lay person may attribute traits for different reasons. Trait attribution can be seen as a process of categorization, as a way of explaining events or as an inference process based on implicit personality theory. Those three functionally different types of trait attribution are probably based on distinct psychological processes, and illustrate the need for a more comprehensive, more integrated theory of trait attribution.

Elaboration of such a theory will require at least some research about the conditions which evoke each type of attributional process. An important factor in this respect may be the *time perspective* of the attributor. Explanatory trait attribution refers to behavioural episodes which have occurred in the past, whereas inferential trait attribution focusses on behavioural episodes which might occur in the future. Descriptive trait attribution involves categorization of behavioural episodes which are presently salient or happened in the past but are presently recalled from long term memory.

The type of problem the attributor faces or the type of question he tries to answer could also determine which process is instigated. Questions such as "what kind of person is he or she?", are likely to prompt descriptive trait attribution. A "why-question", on the other hand, will contribute to explanatory trait attribution. A question about possible future behaviour of a subject will probably stimulate inferential trait attribution.

Implications for personality psychology

Although the study of trait attribution by the lay person is an important part of research on person perception, it seems also interesting to look at some of the implications of this research for personality psychology. The data on which personality theory is based and verified is usually provided by observers who rate the behaviour of other subjects or by subjects who report on their own behaviour. Although in some cases the task of the observers is restricted to reporting behavioural episodes, many researchers go beyond that information by asking more or less qualified judges to sort the data into trait-like categories. This is of course very similar to what has been described as descriptive trait attribution. Clinically oriented personality psychologists on the other hand, may want to know why reported or recorded behaviour has occurred and this requires some

form of explanatory trait attribution. Finally, differential psychologists
will be interested in predicting future behaviour in novel settings and
this often entails some form of inferential trait attribution.

It seems evident that professional personality psychologists rely on
the three types of trait attribution but emphasize them differently.
Moreover, personality psychology as a discipline has historically
shifted and divided its attention among predictive, explanatory, and
descriptive personality theories.

Recently, there has been a growing interest in descriptive
personality theories. A good example of this trend is the act frequency
approach to personality proposed by Buss and Craik (1983). According
to this model dispositional assertions (traits) are "summary statements
about the behavior up to the present; they are not predictions, ...
they do not deal with causal properties nor provide a causal account of
the behavior at issue" (Buss & Craik, 1983, p. 106). Buss and Craik
consider traits as "natural cognitive categories", which summarize or
describe a person's behaviour. Their fundamental measure of an
individual's disposition is a multiple-act composite index, provided by a
frequency summary of acts across a specified period of time.

The basic asymmetric uncertainty described in this chapter as one
of the features of descriptive trait attribution may have some
implications for the act frequency approach. Let's assume that the
asymmetric relation is not a mere judgemental artefact but has a factual
basis. This means that we are prepared to accept, for example, that
high ability students display intelligent behaviour but sometimes
behave in a less intelligent manner. That extraverts can behave in an
introverted manner but that the behaviour of introverts is more
restricted and thus limited to introverted performance. If we observe a
person during a given period and we tally ten extraverted behaviours
and no introverted acts, we will feel confident that this person is an
extravert. If we record for another person a mixture of seven
extraverted and three introverted acts then we might have a problem.
If we accept that extraverts have a flexible behavioural repertoire and
adapt their behaviour to situations which require introverted
performance, then an absolute frequency of seven extraverted acts
does not necessarily indicate a lower degree of extraversion then a
frequency of ten acts. This example shows that absolute frequency of
acts may not automatically be equated with relative dispositional
strength.

In general, the frequency of acts will be problematic as indicator of
dispositional strength, when bipolar dispositions have non-exclusive
classes of acts. If dominant people can behave in a submissive way,
but submissive people are less capable of displaying dominant acts,
then observation of a mixture of dominant and submissive acts will limit
the usefulness of act frequencies as indicators of dispositional
strength. It should be noted, however, that when two dispositional
categories share a subset of acts in a symmetrical way, the frequency
of acts remains a good indicator of dispositional strenght. If the
frequency of stupid acts performed by intelligent people is equal to
the number of intelligent acts performed by unintelligent people then
bias is the same for each dispositional category. It remains to be
tested, however, to what extent dispositional categories share acts in a
symmetric or asymmetric way. Finally, it should be emphasized that
this reasoning is not restricted to bipolar trait pairs. In principle the

reasoning can be applied to any pair of traits which share a set of common acts in an asymmetrical way.

A fundamental task of the act frequency approach is to determine which acts belong to each of the dispositional categories. Buss and Craik (1983) asked subjects to "think of the three most dominant females (males) you know.... write down five acts or behaviors they have performed that reflect or exemplify their dominance" (p. 109). Although subjects are instructed to think about the acts of dominant persons, their attention is directed towards those acts which according to them exemplify dominance. It is highly unlikely that any mixture of dominant and submissive acts will be the outcome of this procedure. This method seems to be well suited to provide acts which are exclusive to one particular dispositional class. Nevertheless, Buss and Craik (this volume) reported that when other subjects were asked to assign the acts back to dispositional categories, misclassification still occurred. This is of course compelling evidence for the multiple significance of acts and stresses the fact that act classes may have a considerable number of acts which belong to more than one dispositional category.

The nomination of acts as instances of trait categories can also be influenced by the implicit personality theory of the judges. When a person thinks that dominance is associated or related to talkativeness, quarrelsomeness, etc., he or she may be inclined to nominate acts which exemplify the related traits as instances of dominant acts. Systematic study, of implicit personality theories may therefore be useful to estimate the extent to which dispositional categories share common acts. Such a strategy would of course emphasize the fact that trait categories are often related and share common acts. This could provide a correction to the traditional act nomination procedure which seems to underestimate the degree of overlap among act categories.

Kelley's (1973) attributional model nicely illustrates that act perception does not automatically leads to trait attribution. Suppose that failure on an exam is an example of an unintelligent act. Perception of failure can be attributed to something within the person (laziness or low intelligence), to the difficulty of the exam, or to the particular circumstances in which the exam took place. A person-type attribution will be most likely when the actor fails in many circumstances (high consistency of act), on different types of exams (low distinctiveness), and when other people do not fail on that exam (low consensus). According to this model, the frequency or consistency of failure in not a sufficient criterion for a person-type attribution. If a person fails frequently on a psychology exam and other people also fail on that exam but nobody fails on other exams, then the failure will be attributed to the difficulty of the psychology exam. Recently, much attention has been paid to the cross-situational consistency of behaviour but it remains an open question to what extent consideration of distinctiveness of acts and consensus information, may be useful for personality assessment.

ACKNOWLEDGEMENTS

I thank P. Borkenau, P. De Boeck, G. De Soete, and E. Pot for their helpful comments.

REFERENCES

Abramson, L.Y., Seligman, M.E.P., & Teasdale, J.D. (1978). Learned
    helplessness in humans: Critique and reformulation. *Journal of
    Abnormal Psychology, 87,* 49–74.
Anderson, N.H. (1974). Cognitive algebra: Integration theory applied
    to social attribution. In L. Berkowitz (Ed.), *Advances in
    experimental social psychology* (Vol. 7, pp. 1–101). New York, NY:
    Academic Press.
Barker, R.G. (1968). *Ecological psychology: Concepts and methods for
    studying the environment of human behaviors.* Stanford, CA:
    Stanford University Press.
Bem, S.L. (1973). The measurement of psychological androgyny.
    Journal of Consulting and Clinical Psychology, 42, 155–162.
Burisch, M. (1984). Approaches to personality inventory construction:
    A comparison of merits. *American Psychologist, 39,* 214–227.
Buss, D.M., & Craik, K.H. (1983). The act frequency approach to
    personality. *Psychological Review, 90,* 105–126.
Cantor, N., & Mischel, W. (1977). Traits as prototypes: Effects on
    recognition memory. *Journal of Personality and Social Psychology,
    35,* 38–48.
Ebbesen, E.B., & Allen, R.B. (1979). Cognitive processes in implicit
    personality trait inferences. *Journal of Personality and Social
    Psychology, 37,* 471–488.
Endler, N.S., & Magnusson, D. (1976). (Eds.). *Interactional
    psychology and personality.* Washington D.C.: Hemisphere.
Fiske, D.W. (1974). The limits of the conventional science of
    personality. *Journal of Personality, 42,* 1–11.
Furnham, A. (1984). Lay conceptions of neuroticism. *Personality and
    Individual Differences, 5,* 95–103.
Furnham, A., & Henderson, M. (1982). The good, the bad and the
    mad: Response bias in self-report measures. *Personality and
    Individual Differences, 3,* 311–320.
Gough, H.G., & Heilbrun, H.B. (1965). *The adjective check list
    manual.* Palo Alto, CA: Consulting Psychologist Press.
Harvey, J.H., & Weary G. (1984). Current issues in attribution theory
    and research. *Annual Review of Psychology, 35,* 427–459.
Johnson, S.C. (1967). Hierarchical clustering schemes. *Psychometrika,
    32,* 241–254.
Kelley, H.H. (1967). Attribution theory in social psychology. In D.
    Levine (Ed.), *Nebraska Symposium on Motivation* (pp. 192–240).
    Lincoln, NE: University of Nebraska Press.
Kelley, H.H. (1973). The process of causal attributions. *American
    Psychologist, 28,* 107–128.
Kelley, H.H., & Michela, J.L. (1980). Attribution theory and
    research. *Annual Review of Psychology, 31,* 457–501.
Kelly, G.A. (1955). *The psychology of personal constructs.* New York,
    NY: Norton.
Kruskal, J.B. (1964). Multidimensional scaling by optimising goodness
    of fit to a nonmetric hypothesis. *Psychometrika, 29,* 1–27.
Markus, H. (1977). Self-schemata and processing information about the
    self. *Journal of Personality and Social Psychology, 35,* 63–78.

Mervielde, I. (1977a). Ratings for likableness and subjective frequency of personality traits and interpersonal behaviors. *Psychologica Belgica, 17,* 143–156.

Mervielde, I. (1977b). *Persoonsperceptie als informatieverwerking* [Person perception as information processing]. Unpublished doctoral dissertation. University of Ghent, Belgium.

Messick, D.M., & Reeder, G.D. (1972). Perceived motivation, role variations, and the attribution of personal characteristics. *Journal of Experimental Social Psychology, 8,* 482–491.

Messick, D.M., & Reeder, G.D. (1974). Roles, occupations, behaviors and attributions. *Journal of Experimental Social Psychology, 10,* 126–132.

Mischel, W. (1968). *Personality and assessment.* New York: Wiley.

Moos, R.H. (1973). Conceptualization of human environments. *American Psychologist, 28,* 652–665.

Peterson, D.R. (1968). *The clinical study of social behavior.* New York, NY: Appleton-Century-Crofts.

Reeder, G.D., & Brewer, M.B. (1979). A schematic model of dispositional attribution in interpersonal perception. *Psychological Review, 86,* 61–79.

Rosenberg, S., & Sedlak, A. (1972). Structural representations of implicit personality theory. In L. Berkowitz (Ed.), *Advances in experimental social psychology* (Vol. 6, pp. 235–297). New York, NY: Academic Press.

Roskam, E.E., & Lingoes, J.C. (1970). MINISSA-1: A Fortran IV (G) program for the smallest space analysis of square symmetric matrices. *Behavioral Science, 15,* 204–205.

Schneider, D.J. (1973). Implicit personality theory: A review. *Psychological Bulletin, 79,* 294–309.

Weiner, B. (1979). A theory of motivation for some classroom experiences. *Journal of Educational Psychology, 71,* 3–25.

Zadeh, L. (1965). Fuzzy sets. *Information and Control, 8,* 338–353.

SYSTEMATIC DISTORTIONS IN THE RECOGNITION
OF TRAIT INFORMATION

Peter Borkenau

University of Bielefeld
Federal Republic of Germany

Human observers and judges have for a long time been important sources from which psychologists gather their data. Their ability to structure highly complex information and to grasp the gist of people's behaviour is beyond the feasibility of mechanical coding devices. Therefore, human raters have been employed in almost every field of psychology. Most popular are global ratings within the field of personality, where self-ratings and judgements by knowledgeable informants turned out to be useful tools in prediction (Moskowitz & Schwartz, 1982; Sawyer, 1966; Shrauger & Osberg, 1981; Wiggins, 1973) and are among the most widely used data sources.

The use of raters is controversial, however, since the early days of scientific psychology. As early as 1920, Thorndike pointed to a phenomenon which he called "halo-effect". He established suspiciously high correlations between ratings comprising evaluative connotations. Thus, for example, several ability ratings were significantly more highly correlated than comparable objective test scores. Results by Newcomb (1931) and by Asch (1946) indicated that the "halo-effect" is not only due to the influence of evaluation. Newcomb (1931) assumed that logical predispositions in the minds of the raters might be responsible for the higher correlations within the retrospective judgements. This argument was later on pursued by several authors (Chapman & Chapman, 1967, 1969; D'Andrade, 1965; Fiske, 1978; Mischel, 1968; Shweder, 1975, 1982; Shweder & D'Andrade, 1979, 1980) arguing strongly against the reliance on global trait ratings or memory-based reports within studies on the structure of personality.

Research on "implicit personality theory" (Bruner & Tagiuri, 1954; Cronbach, 1955) elaborated the structure and impact of these predispositions. Thus, for example, subjects were asked how likely a person exhibiting the behaviour A will also exhibit the behaviour B. Substantial agreement is found between these co-occurrence expectancies and the empirical inter-item correlations within pertinent personality inventories (Jackson, Chan, & Stricker, 1979; Lay & Jackson, 1969; Stricker, Jacobs, & Kogan, 1974). Moreover, the factor structure obtained from self-ratings and ratings by knowledgeable informants is very similar to the structure obtained if the ratings are done by strangers (Newcomb, 1931; Norman & Goldberg, 1966; Passini & Norman, 1966). Finally, implicit personality theory and the factor structure of self- and observer-ratings show high correspondences to the semantic similarity structure of the trait-descriptive terms (D'Andrade, 1965, 1974; Ebbesen & Allen, 1979; Gara & Rosenberg,

1981; Hakel, 1969; Mulaik, 1964; Shweder, 1975; Shweder & D'Andrade, 1980).

Thus, it may be concluded that there are expectancies with regard to the co-occurrence of traits and behaviours that are widely shared in our culture (Norman & Goldberg, 1966; Shweder, 1977). These expectancies unambiguously influence the intercorrelations of trait ratings in first impression studies. Moreover, they relate systematically to the semantic similarities of the trait-words.

It is controversial, however, whether implicit personality theory accurately mirrors the trait and behaviour interrelationships (Block, Weiss, & Thorne, 1979; Jackson, 1982; Jackson, Chan, & Stricker, 1979; Jackson & Stricker, 1982; Lamiell, Foss, & Cavenee, 1980; Lay & Jackson, 1969; Rowe, 1982; Stricker, Jacobs, & Kogan, 1974). On the other hand, it has been suggested that implicit personality theory mirrors the semantic similarities of the trait-descriptive terms showing little correspondence to the covariations in behaviour (D'Andrade, 1965, 1974; Mirels, 1976, 1982; Mischel, 1968; Schneider, 1973; Shweder, 1975, 1977, 1982; Shweder & D'Andrade, 1979, 1980). Shweder and D'Andrade supported their hypothesis in several empirical studies, but these were severely criticized on methodological grounds. Thus, Block, Weiss, and Thorne (1979) emphasized the poor correspondence between actual behaviour and rated behaviour categories, the former indices being insufficient operationalizations of the rated psychological concepts. Moreover, they argued that the amount of distortion should *usually* be quite small as evidenced by the high temporal stability of trait-ratings. Lamiell, Foss, and Cavenee (1980) reported results indicating that people are *capable* of generating behaviour reports which do not correspond highly to their conceptual schemes. Thus, the topic whether rating intercorrelations *usually* distort the structure of actual behavior has not yet been resolved.

However, even if implicit personality theory and the structure of trait-ratings would accurately mirror *usual* covariations in behaviour, there will exist subject samples and situational circumstances wherein the actual trait-covariations deviate from the assumed structure of personality (Buse, 1980; Lamiell, Foss, & Cavenee, 1980). Using artificial character descriptions, such a divergence is easily constructed and may help to clarify *how* implicit personality theory influences personality ratings and how it's distorting impact might be reduced. Thus, Ebbesen and Allen (1979) studied reaction times to get information about the cognitive processes taking place in implicit personality trait inferences. Berman, Read, and Kenny (1983), Cantor and Mischel (1977, 1979a), Crocker, Hannah, and Weber (1983), Erber and Fiske (1984), Hastie (1980, 1984), Hastie and Kumar (1979), Snyder and Uranowitz (1978), and Wyer and Gordon (1982), among others, investigated the memory for consistent and inconsistent information about persons. From their results, Berman, Read, and Kenny (1983) drew conclusions for the administration of observer ratings and suggested that "future attempts to develop correction techniques for rating will need to focus on the early stages of the rating process when raters are actually observing or encoding social events" (p. 1223).

Most studies in person memory investigated the *accuracy* of recognition or recall of the presented material. Berman and Kenny

(1976), however, studied the co-occurrences within recognized trait information. They constructed artificial characters wherein the actual correlations between trait pairs were varied in a systematic fashion but independently of the assumed covariations among the traits. These had been established in advance using another subject sample. Subjects were instructed to learn and later on to recognize the trait information given. Significant main effects for actual correlations and assumed correlations were found for the co-occurrences within the subjects' responses. Moreover, the effect of actual correlations was reduced under conditions of high memory load.

Following arguments by Bellezza and Bower (1981), it is debatable whether distortions in recognition are due to differences in availability of the information given or to a guessing bias. However, a guessing bias may also be operative in observer ratings, and thus the arguments by Bellezza and Bower (1981) are not very relevant regarding the existence of systematic distortions in judgements about personality. Another criticism of the Berman and Kenny study stems from Block (1977a). He argued that some of the trait pairs presented to the subjects had been synonyms (e.g., friendly - sociable) or antonyms (e.g., shy - domineering) being *by definition correlated* to a high degree. Thus, the subjects were confused by negative correlations between synonyms and positive correlations between antonyms. Moreover, according to Block, the subjects had been given insufficient opportunity to learn the empirical covariations and thus to modify their expectations. Finally, he suggested to average the responses of several subjects, because in this way "the actual correlation effect becomes relatively much more important vis-a-vis the assumed correlation effect" (Block, 1977a, p. 878).

The present studies were designed to investigate, whether a consideration of Block's (1977a) arguments results in a reduced correlational error.

PRELIMINARY STUDIES[1]

Semantic Similarities

Within one preliminary study, the semantic similarities were assessed for the trait-descriptive terms used in the subsequent experiments. The traits selected for study are primary factors of extraversion, according to Eysenck and Eysenck (1969), and are usually correlated to a substantial degree. However, they are distinct factors and not tautological. Thus, zero or negative correlations between these primary factors within a subject sample are *infrequent but not impossible* (Buse, 1980).

Method. Subjects were ten psychology sophomores of the University of Bielefeld, West Germany. They rated the meaning-similarity

[1]) The research reported in this chapter was supported by a grant from the University of Bielefield (OZ 2743)

180   P. Borkenau

relationships between 16 trait-descriptive terms on seven-point scales ranging from −3 *(completely contradictory)* to +3 *(identical in meaning)*. The English translation of the German words[1] used is *gregarious, lively, active, jocular, impulsive, enthusiastic, talkative, friendly, uncommunicative, quiet, passive, serious, deliberate, aloof, taciturn,* and *unfriendly*. The 120 paired comparisons between these words were alloted to two booklets comprising 60 comparisons each. Each subject was administered only one booklet and thus the meaning–similarity ratings were done by five subjects for each trait pair. The order of presentation of the comparisons was randomized.

Results. First, intraclass correlations were calculated to estimate the rater agreement concerning the similarity ratings. The coefficients amounted to $\rho_1 = .65$ for the single scores and $\rho_1 = .90$ for the average rating of the five judges. Subsequently, the terms *enthusiastic, friendly, uncommunicative,* and *unfriendly* were eliminated from further analyses due to ambiguous similarity patterns. Within the remaining "extraverted terms", the mean similarity rating was 1.3 and within the realm of introversion it was 0.8. The average similarity between "extraverted terms". on the one hand, and introverted ones on the other hand, was −1.0. Thus, the expected similarity structure emerged within the remaining twelve trait-descriptive terms.

Item intercorrelations

In order to investigate the external structure, the terms were first combined into six pairs, that is, *gregarious - aloof, lively - quiet, active - passive, jocular -serious, impulsive - deliberate,* and *talkative - taciturn*. Thirty-six male students of the Bielefeld University were then asked to indicate, which term out of each pair was more appropriate to describe their personality. Subsequently, the "extraverted term" of each pair was coded *one* and the "introverted term" *zero*. Positive correlations emerged for 12 out of the 15 possible trait-combinations, eight of them being significantly different from zero ($r \geqslant .32$) None of the negative coefficients was significant. The average correlation amounted to $\bar{r} = .25$. Thus, there is independent evidence that the extraverted or introverted trait-ratings used in our experiments are usually positively intercorrelated. However, the highest correlation amounting to $r = .55$, no synonyms seem to be present.

EXPERIMENT 1

Method

Subjects of the first main experiment were 14 introductory psychology students who had not participated in the preliminary studies. They were repeatedly tested during a one-week period.

---

[1]) The original German words were *gesellig, lebendig, aktiv, witzig, impulsiv, begeisterungsfaehig, gespraechig, freundlich, verschlossen, still, passiv, ernst, ueberlegt, reserviert, schweigsam,* and *unfreundlich*.

Material. Eight characters having male Christian names were constructed being characterized by one and only one word out of each of the six mentioned pairs of trait-descriptive terms. The combination of traits was done in such a way that, over the eight characters, all traits were completely uncorrelated. More precisely: Each of the four quadrants of the 15 fourfold tabels contained two characters. For example, two characters were gregarious and lively, two were gregarious and quiet, two were aloof and lively, and two were aloof and quiet. Thus, the base rate of all traits was 50 per cent. The characters were presented in a randomized order being different for each subject.

In order to test for recognition memory, a second booklet was made available. Herein, the subject were instructed to indicate which of the two traits of each pair applied to the several characters. The items were formulated like

    Karl was   a) aloof........b) gregarious
                a) jocular.......b) serious

etc. The order of presentation was also randomized and varied for each subject.

Procedure. First, the artificial characters were presented to the subjects who were instructed to form an impression of the eight persons depicted. An impression instruction was chosen in order to enhance the ecological validity of the study. It was assumed that an instruction to learn the characters would have limited the generalizability of the findings for usual rating tasks. The subjects were paced through the booklet twice: In the first round, they were given 1.5 minutes per character and in the second round one minute. After completion of the second round, the learning material was collected and the second booklet was distributed. The questions were then answered without time limitations. One week later the subjects were surprised by a delayed test for recognition memory using the same questions as before.

Results

All data analyses were done using Pearson and phi coefficients. First, for each subject and each of the six trait pairs, the correlation over the eight characters was calculated between the presented and reproduced specifications. The resulting 84 "validities of the single ratings" indicate the accuracy of the recognized information separately for each subject and each trait dimension. Second, for each subject 15 correlations were computed between the six dichotomous dimensions over the eight characters. As all these correlations had been zero in the presented material, the 210 reported "intercorrelations of the single ratings" indicate the amount of correlational error. Coefficients with a positive sign imply a co-occurence of extraverted or introverted attributes, respectively. Third, all specifications in the reported characters were averaged over the 14 subjects and these averaged scores were correlated with the presented specifications resulting in six "validities of the averaged ratings". Finally, all averaged scores were correlated over the eight characters resulting in 15 "intercorrelations of the averaged ratings". All coefficients were

182   P. Borkenau

TABLE 1: *Averaged correlations and Chi-square statistics in the first main experiment*

	Immediate test for recognition	Delayed test for recognition
Validity of single ratings	$.25^a$	$.03^a$
Intercorrelation of single ratings	$.07^b$ $\chi^2 = 8.99**$	$.17^b$ $\chi^2 = 23.17**$
Validity of averaged ratings	$.71^c$	$.03^c$
Intercorrelation of averaged ratings	$.38^d$ $\chi^2 = 8.07**$	$.32^d$ $\chi^2 = 4.57*$

Note: a = Average of 84 correlations each one being based on eight observations; b = average of 210 correlations each one being based on eight observations; c = average of six correlations each one being based on eight observations; d = average of 15 correlations each one being based on eight observations.
* $p < .05$ ** $p < .01$

calculated separately for immediate and delayed recognition memory. Table 1 presents the respective mean correlations[1].

Although the sample size for the single correlations is small ($N = 8$), the mean correlations being the average of 6 to 210 coefficients can be assumed to be sufficiently reliable. Concerning the correlational error, it was tested whether the number of positive correlations significantly exceeded the number of negative correlations using a Chi-square statistic. As there is one degree of freedom, the Chi-square values reported in Table 1 are all significant and indicate that the correlational error is systematically in the direction of the semantic similarity of the trait-descriptive terms. Moreover, the systematic distortions seems to be more pronounced for the averaged ratings compared to the responses of the single subjects. No monotonous relationship, however, is discernible between the accuracy of the reported characters and the time interval between encoding and retrieval on the one hand, and the amount of correlational error on the other hand.

EXPERIMENT 2

Within the first main experiment, one character had been presented to the subjects being a prototypical introvert exhibiting the attributes

---

[1]) As several of the single coefficients amounted to $r = 1.00$, no Fisher r to Z transformation could be performed. Therefore, the average of the raw correlation coefficients was calculated.

aloof, quiet, passive, serious, deliberate, and taciturn. This prototype was more accurately recognized than the other seven characters. Therefore, the reported correlational errors might be due to this prototype only. To avoid this ambiguity, the six trait-pairs were combined into eight new characters being all non-prototypes. The same names for these characters were used as in the first experiment.

Moreover, an attempt was made to control for effects during the encoding stage. Therefore, the subjects had to learn the characters until they were able to recognize them once faultlessly[1]. In addition, a salience manipulation was introduced immediately before recognition.

Method

Subjects of the second experiment were 39 students of the University of Bielefeld who did not study psychology. Twenty-three of them recognized the characters once perfectly. They were tested for delayed recognition two weeks later and were paid for their cooperation.

Material. Whereas the presented characters had been modified as described, the recall task was the same as in the first experiment. The salience manipulation comprised reading a description of one introvert and one extravert prototype and listing for ten minutes characteristic extraverted and introverted acts. It was assumed that the extraversion – introversion dimension would become more salient thereby.

Procedure. The subjects were tested in groups from two to five by another experimenter than in the preceding experiments[2]. First, they were paced by 1.5 minute intervals through the booklet containing the eight artificial characters. After presentation of the last character, the booklet was collected and the other one comprising the recognition task was distributed. The questions, forming the immediate test for recognition memory, were then answered without time limitations.

Subsequently, the booklet including the characters was again distributed and the subjects were asked to learn them until they recognized them perfectly. When a subject believed that he or she had reached this criterion, the booklet was collected and the other one containing the questions was delivered. Upon completion of this recognition test, it was checked by the experimenter whether any faults had been made. If there were one or more mistakes, the first booklet comprising the characters was again distributed, etc. Subjects who did not recognize the eight characters once faultlessly, were excused from the experiment and their data were not analysed. Subjects fulfilling this learning criterion, however, were instructed to reappear for a second session two weeks later.

During this second session, subjects were randomly allotted to an experimental ($N = 11$) or a control group ($N = 12$). Whereas the control group subjects were immediately administered the questions about the eight characters, the experimental group was first given the

---

[1]) I am indebted to my colleague Rainer Riemann for making this suggestion.

[2]) I am indebted to student Jost Altmeyer for conducting this experiment.

184   P. Borkenau

material prepared for a salience manipulation. Thereafter, the
questions about the characters were given to the experimental group
also. There were no time limitations during this delayed test for
recognition memory.

Results

The data were analysed in the same way as in the first experiment:
Coefficients of accuracy and trait-interrelations were calculated for
each subject across the eight characters. Moreover, the average score
for all subjects was computed and accuracy and interrelation
coefficients were calculated for the average scores. First, the data
analyses were done separately for the experimental and control group.
No significant discrepancies, however, could be detected and the
results reported here are those of the whole group comprising 23
subjects. Table 2 gives the average correlations and the Chi-square
statistics indicating if significantly more positive than negative
correlations prevailed within the reproduced characters.
  Correlational error could be established within the immediate and
delayed tests for recognition memory when the scores averaged over
subjects were analysed. For the scores of the single subjects this held
true only for the delayed test. Correlational error ($\bar{r}$ = .15; minimum =
-.08, maximum = .79) could be established in the delayed test for the
averaged ratings although their accuracy was very high ($\bar{r}$ = .96;
minimum = .92, maximum = .98).

TABLE 2: *Averaged correlations and Chi-square statistics in the
second main experiment*

	Immediate test for recognition	Delayed test for recognition
Validity of single ratings	.23[a]	.57[a]
Intercorrelations of single ratings	.00[b] χ^2 = 0.01	.09[b] χ^2 = 25.19**
Validity of averaged ratings	.85[c]	.96[c]
Intercorrelation of averaged ratings	.30[d] χ^2 = 11.27**	.15[d] χ^2 = 8.07**

Note: a = Average of 138 correlations each one being based on eight
observations; b = average of 345 correlations each one being based
on eight observations; c = average of six correlations each one
being based on eight observations; d = average of 15 correlations
each one being based on eight observations.
* p < .05   ** p < .01

GENERAL DISCUSSION

Most striking in our results is the ubiquity of the correlational error which can be found using immediate *and* delayed tests for recognition, analysing the responses of single subjects *as well as* the average scores of many subjects, investigating the interrelations between reproduced attributes being completely invalid *and* those showing nearly perfect accuracy. The one exception to this pattern in the second experiment (immediate test for recognition; intercorrelation of the single ratings) is difficult to interpret because correlational bias was found under very similar conditions in the first experiment and it also arises in the second experiment when averaging over raters takes place.

Furthermore, aggregating the responses of the subjects *increases* the correlational error. Thus, the combination of several subjects' scores is no useful tool for diminishing the systematic distortion. This results is in contradiction to Block's (1977a) arguments and to the model proposed by Kenny and Berman (1980). The most reasonable cause for this phenomenon is that the implicit theories of personality are *shared* by the subjects and thus the correlational errors do not cancel out when averaging is performed. Thus, this error seems to be systematic in two respects: First, it seems to be predominantly in line with the usual covariation and semantic similarity of the trait-ratings studied, and, second, it seems to be shared by individuals within our culture. Therefore, averaging over judges is no useful tool for coping with this kind of bias although this method may be helpful for many problems encountered by personality researchers (Block, 1977b; Epstein, 1979; Horowitz, Inouye, & Siegelman, 1979; Rushton, Jackson, & Paunonen, 1981).

The correlational errors established within the immediate tests for recognition memory in both experiments indicate that systematic correlational bias takes place even when retention intervals last as short as 10 minutes only. Moreover, there is *no* clear tendency for systematic distortion to increase when the storage interval is extended from 10 minutes to one or two weeks. Such a trend can be seen for the responses of the single subjects. By averaging over subjects, however, this tendency is reversed: Surprisingly, the correlational error gets smaller the longer the retention interval. No test for the statistical significance of these tendencies is available, however, and thus it can only be stated that there is no unequivocal tendency for correlational bias to increase with the duration of the retention interval. This finding is in agreement with results reported by Cantor and Mischel (1979a) and by Berman and Kenny (1977). Taken together, the evidence seriously questions Shweder and D'Andrade's assumption that the systematic distortion increases with decay of the memory for the original information. Moreover, the lack of a negative relationship between recognition accuracy and the amount of correlational error is in contradiction to the assumption of a "reverse error of attenuation" operative in personality ratings. This formulation assumes that the illusory correlation increases in a reciprocal relationship to the reliability of the data (Shweder, 1982; Thorndike, 1920).

The salience manipulation may have turned out to be ineffective since extraversion – introversion had already been a salient dimension for the classification of persons. Thus, a ceiling effect may have arisen preventing a strengthening of correlational bias (see Schneider & Blankmeyer, 1983); but our data do not contain any direct evidence for this explanation. Moreover, our experiments are mute with regard to the question whether the systematic distortions stem from differences in accessibility of the trait words or from a guessing bias. However, for the science of personality, the question which source correlational errors stem from is less important than the problem how to reduce or eliminate its distorting influence.

What then *is* the *significance of this study for personality psychology?* It could be shown that judges make systematic errors when uncertain about the real state of affairs and when the real state of affairs deviates from their lay theory of personality. Thus, when covariations of traits deviate from implicit personality theory within a subject sample, these discrepancies will not be fully mirrored in the structure of the trait-ratings. Their intercorrelations can be assumed to be a "compromise" between observed and expected co-occurences (Alloy & Tabachnik, 1984; Cantor & Mischel, 1977, 1979a; Berman & Kenny, 1976).

Regarding the administration of observer ratings, it was shown that, contrary to Block's (1977a) suggestions, *averaging over raters is no suitable method for the reduction of correlational error.* Completely different methods may be needed for increasing the validity of trait-ratings and for reducing correlational error as long as the validity coefficients do not reach unity. Substantial systematic distortions were encountered in our second study (delayed recognition; averaged ratings) in spite of very high validity coefficients of about $r = .96$. This demonstrates the relevance of independent efforts to reduce correlational bias in addition to the more common studies on the improvement of prediction (see Amelang & Borkenau, 1986, for a review).

Moreover, our results suggest to qualify the suggestion by Berman, Read, and Kenny (1983) to focus on the early stages of the rating process when raters are actually observing or encoding social events. Within our second study, it could be demonstrated that even after a faultless recognition of the original material correlational bias emerged.

Regarding Shweder and D'Andrade's systematic distortion hypothesis, the present study is arguing against their formulations. As far as we *constructed artificial characters* wherein actual trait-covariations deviated from the assumed ones, the study is mute with respect to the problem whether the assumed structure of personality is dissimilar to *usual* covariations in actual behaviour. The distortions found in our study emerged *when* such a discrepancy was present but it was not shown *that* such a dissimilarity is very common. On the other hand, our results are in disagreement with Shweder and D'Andrade's assumption that memory based ratings are distorted but behaviour recorded on-line (within ten minutes after observation; D'Andrade, 1974) is not distorted. Other explanations seem to be necessary for the reported discrepancies in correlational structure between actual behaviour and rated behaviour matrices (D'Andrade, 1974; Shweder, 1975; Shweder & D'Andrade, 1980; Thorndike, 1920). I am currently conducting studies in order to investigate, if acts being indicating several behaviour categories (i.e., "act-overlap") are responsible for the structure of retrospective ratings in addition to behaviour co-occurences.

The ecological validity of our results for the study of personality might be questioned on the grounds that in our experiments trait lists were presented to the subjects in a verbal mode and were not the result of a trait-attribution process resting on the observation of numerous instances of behaviour, as is usually the case in self- and peer ratings. Indeed, when real persons are rated, memory and judgemental processes are interwoven in a highly complex way (Alloy & Tabachnik, 1984; Cooper, 1981; Crocker, 1981, Lingle, 1983). It is very unlikely, however, that the inference processes *adjust* for the bias that takes place during the encoding, storage and retrieval of the pertinent information. More plausible is the assumption that memory *and* judgemental processes are subject to correlational bias. With regard to a guessing bias interpretation of our data (Bellezza & Bower, 1981). I see no argument why such a bias should be operative in the present study *in contrast* to usual (only moderately reliable) personality ratings. Studies being ecologically more valid could be conducted if there would exist a *prescriptive* model which judgements are correct given specific behavioural information. The present models on information integration (e.g., Anderson, 1965; Buss & Craik, 1983; Cantor & Mischel, 1979b; Hampson, 1982; Mervielde, this volume; Reeder & Brewer, 1979) are of a *descriptive* nature. However, the evidence reported by Tversky and Kahneman (1973, 1974) and Nisbett and Ross (1980) concerning domains other than judgements about persons, supports the assumption that the better available or accessible information is more heavily weighted in judgemental processes. Therefore, experiments on person memory may shed light on processes and distortions taking place in the assessment of real persons.

REFERENCES

Alloy, L.B., & Tabachnik, N. (1984). Assessment of covariation by humans and animals: The joint influence of prior expectations and current situational information. *Psychological Review, 91,* 112-149.

Amelang, M., & Borkenau, P. (1986). The trait concept: Current theoretical considerations, empirical facts, and implications for personality inventory construction. In A. Angleitner & J.S. Wiggins (Eds.), *Personality assessment via questionnaires.* New York: Springer.

Anderson, N.H. (1965). Adding versus averaging as a stimulus combination rule in impression formation. *Journal of Experimental Psychology, 70,* 394-400.

Asch, S.E. (1946). Forming impressions of personality. *Journal of Abnormal and Social Psychology, 41,* 258-290.

Bellezza, F.S., & Bower, G.H. (1981). Person stereotypes and memory for people. *Journal of Personality and Social Psychology, 41,* 856-865.

Berman, J.S., & Kenny, D.A. (1976). Correlational bias in observer ratings. *Journal of Personality and Social Psychology, 34,* 263-273.

Berman, J.S., & Kenny, D.A. (1977). Correlational bias: Not gone and not to be forgotten. *Journal of Personality and Social Psychology, 35,* 882-887.

Berman, J.S., Read, S.J., & Kenny, D.A. (1983). Processing inconsistent social information. *Journal of Personality and Social Psychology, 45,* 1211-1224.

Block, J. (1977a). Correlational bias in observer ratings. Another perspective on the Berman and Kenny study. *Journal of Personality and Social Psychology, 35,* 873-880.

Block, J. (1977b). Advancing the psychology of personality: Paradigmatic shift or improving the quality of research. In D. Magnusson & N.S. Endler (Eds.), *Personality at the crossroads: Current issues in interactional psychology* (pp. 37-63). Hillsdale, NJ: Erlbaum.

Block, J., Weiss, D.S., & Thorne, A. (1979). How relevant is a semantic similarity interpretation of personality ratings? *Journal of Personality and Social Psychology, 37,* 1055-1074.

Bruner, J.S., Tagiuri, R. (1954). The perception of people. In G. Lindzey (Ed.), *Handbook of social psychology* (Vol. 2, pp. 643-654). Cambridge, MA: Addison-Wesley.

Buse, L. (1980). Intraindividuelle Merkmalsvariation und Validität eines Extraversionsfragebogens. Eine Untersuchung zur Gültigkeit des Eigenschaftsbegriffs. *Zeitschrift für Differentielle und Diagnostische Psychologie, 1,* 35-42.

Buss, D.M., & Craik, K.H. (1983). The act frequency approach to personality. *Psychological Review, 90,* 105-126.

Cantor, N., & Mischel, W. (1977). Traits as prototypes: Effects on recognition memory. *Journal of Personality and Social Psychology, 35,* 38-48.

Cantor, N., & Mischel, W. (1979a). Prototypicality and personality: Effects on free recall and personality impressions. *Journal of Research in Personality, 13,* 187-205.

Cantor, N., & Mischel, W. (1979b). Prototypes in person perception. In. L. Berkowitz (Ed.), *Advances in experimental social psychology* (Vol. 12, pp. 3-52). New York, NY: Academic Press.

Chapman, L.J., & Chapman, J.P. (1967). Genesis of popular but erroneous psychodiagnostic observations. *Journal of Abnormal Psychology, 72,* 193-204.

Chapman, L.J., & Chapman, J.P. (1969). Illusory correlation as an obstacle to the use of valid psychodiagnostic signs. *Journal of Abnormal Psychology, 74,* 271-280.

Cooper, W.H. (1981). Ubiquitous halo. *Psychological Bulletin, 90,* 218-244.

Crocker, J. (1981). Judgment of covariation by social perceivers. *Psychological Bulletin, 90,* 272-292.

Crocker, J., Hannah, D.B., & Weber, R. (1983). Person memory and causal attributions. *Journal of Personality and Social Psychology, 44,* 55-66.

Cronbach, L.J. (1955). Processes affecting scores on understanding of others and assumed similarity. *Psychological Bulletin, 52,* 177-193.

D'Andrade, R.G. (1965). Trait psychology and componential analysis. *American Anthropologist, 67,* 215-228.

D'Andrade, R.G. (1974). Memory and the assessment of behavior. In

H.M. Blalock (Ed.), *Measurement in the social sciences* (pp. 159-186). Chicago: Aldine-Atherton.

Ebbesen, E.B.. & Allen, R.B. (1979). Cognitive processes in implicit personality trait inferences. *Journal of Personality and Social Psychology, 37,* 471-488.

Epstein, S (1979). The stability of behavior: I. On predicting most of the people much of the time. *Journal of Personality and Social Psychology, 37,* 1097-1126.

Erber, R., & Fiske, S.T. (1984). Outcome dependency and attention to inconsistent information. *Journal of Personality and Social Psychology, 47,* 709-726.

Eysenck, H.J., & Eysenck, S.B.G. (1969). *Personality structure and measurement.* London: Routledge & Kegan Paul.

Fiske, D.W. (1978). *Strategies for personality research.* San Francisco, CA: Jossey-Bass.

Gara, M.A., & Rosenberg, S. (1981). Linguistic factors in implicit personality theory. *Journal of Personality and Social Psychology, 41,* 450-457.

Hakel, M.D. (1969). Significance of implicit personality theories for personality research and theory. *Proceedings of the 77th Convention of the American Psychological Association.*

Hampson, S.E. (1982). Person memory: A semantic category model of personality traits. *British Journal of Psychology, 73,* 1-11.

Hastie, R. (1980). Memory for behavioral information that confirms or contradicts a personality impression. In R. Hastie, T.M. Ostrom, E.B. Ebbesen, R.S. Wyer, Jr., D.L. Hamilton, & D.E. Carlston (Eds.), *Person memory: The cognitive basis of social perception* (pp. 155-177). Hillsdale, NJ: Erlbaum.

Hastie, R. (1984). Causes and effects of causal attribution. *Journal of Personality and Social Psychology, 46,* 44-56.

Hastie, R., & Kumar, P.A. (1979). Person memory: Personality traits as organizing principles in memory for behaviors. *Journal of Personality and Social Psychology, 37,* 25-38.

Horowitz, L.M., Inouye, D., & Siegelmann, E.Y. (1979). On averaging judges' ratings to increase their correlation with an external criterion. *Journal of Consulting and Clinical Psychology, 47,* 453-458.

Jackson, D.N. (1982). Some preconditions for valid person perception. In M.B. Zanna, E.T. Higgins, & C.P. Herman (Eds.), *Consistency in social behavior: The Ontario symposium* (Vol. 2, pp. 251-279). Hillsdale: NJ: Erlbaum.

Jackson, D.N., Chan, D.W., & Stricker, L.J. (1979). Implicit personality theory: Is it illusory? *Journal of Personality, 47,* 1-10.

Jackson, D.N., & Stricker, L.J. (1982). Is implicit personality theory illusory? Armchair criticism versus replicated empirical research. *Journal of Personality, 50,* 240-244.

Kenny, D.A., & Berman, J.S. (1980). Statistical approaches to the correction of correlational bias. *Psychological Bulletin, 88,* 288-295.

Lamiell, J.T., Foss, M.A., & Cavenee, P. (1980). On the relationship between conceptual schemes and behavior reports. *Journal of Personality, 48,* 54-73.

Lay, C.H., & Jackson, D.N. (1969). Analysis of the generality or trait-inferential relationships. *Journal of Personality and Social Psychology, 12,* 12-21.

Lingle, J.H. (1983). Tracing memory-structure activation during person judgments. *Journal of Experimental Social Psychology*, *19*, 480-496.

Mirels, H.L. (1976). Implicit personality theory and inferential illusions. *Journal of Personality*, *44*, 467-487.

Mirels, H.L. (1982). The illusory nature of implicit personality theory: Logical and empirical considerations. *Journal of Personality*, *50*, 203-222.

Mischel, W. (1968). *Personality and assessment*. New York: Wiley.

Moskowitz, D.S., & Schwarz, J.C. (1982). Validity comparison of behavior counts and ratings by knowledgeable informants. *Journal of Personality and Social Psychology*, *42*, 518-528.

Mulaik, S.A. (1964). Are personality factors raters' conceptual factors? *Journal of Consulting Psychology*, *28*, 506-511.

Newcomb, T.M. (1931). An experiment designed to test the validity of a rating technique. *Journal of Educational Psychology*, *32*, 279-289.

Nisbett, R.E., & Ross, L. (1980). *Human inference: Strategies and shortcomings of social judgment*. Englewood Cliffs, NJ: Prentice Hall.

Norman, W.T., & Goldberg, L.R. (1966). Raters, ratees, and randomness in personality structure. *Journal of Personality and Social Psychology*, *4*, 681-691.

Passini, F.T., & Norman, W.T. (1966). A universal conception of personality structure? *Journal of Personality and Social Psychology*, *4*, 44-49.

Reeder, G.D., & Brewer, M.B. (1979). A schematic model of dispositional attribution in interpersonal perception. *Psychological Review*, *86*, 61-79.

Rowe, D.C. (1982). Monozygotic twin cross-correlations as a validation of personality structure: A test of the semantic bias hypothesis. *Journal of Personality and Social Psychology*, *43*, 1072-1079.

Rushton, J.P., Jackson, D.N., & Paunonen, S.V. (1981). Personality: Nomothetic or idiographic? A response to Kenrick and Stringfield. *Psychological Review*, *88*, 582-589.

Sawyer, J. (1966). Measurement and prediction, clinical and statistical. *Psychological Bulletin*, *66*, 178-200.

Schneider, D.J. (1973). Implicit personality theory: A review. *Psychological Bulletin*, *79*, 294-309.

Schneider, D.J., & Blankmeyer, B.L. (1983). Prototype salience and implicit personality theories. *Journal of Personality and Social Psychology*, *44*, 712-722.

Shrauger, J.S., & Osberg, T.M. (1981). The relative accuracy of self-predictions and judgments by others in psychological assessment. *Psychological Bulletin*, *90*, 322-351.

Shweder, R.A. (1975). How relevant is an individual difference theory of personality? *Journal of Personality*, *43*, 455-484.

Shweder, R.A. (1977). Illusory correlation and the MMPI controversy. *Journal of Consulting and Clinical Psychology*, *45*, 917-924.

Shweder, R.A. (1982). Fact and artifact in trait perception: The systematic distortion hypothesis. In D.A. Maher (Ed.), *Progress in experimental personality research* (Vol. 11, pp. 65-100). New York, NY: Academic Press.

Shweder, R.A., & D'Andrade, R.G. (1979). Accurate reflection or systematic distortion? A reply to Block, Weiss and Thorne. *Journal of Personality and Social Psychology, 37,* 1075-1084.

Shweder, R.A., & D'Andrade, R.G. (1980). The systematic distortion hypothesis. In R.A. Shweder (Ed.), *Fallible judgment in behavioral research. New directions for methodology of social and behavioral science, No. 4* (pp. 37-58). San Francisco, CA: Jossey-Bass.

Snyder, M., & Uranowitz, S.W. (1978). Reconstructing the past: Some cognitive consequences of person perception. *Journal of Personality and Social Psychology, 36,* 941-950.

Stricker, L.J., Jacobs, P.I., & Kogan, N. (1974). Trait interrelations in implicit personality theories and questionnaire data. *Journal of Personality and Social Psychology, 30,* 198-207.

Thorndike, E.L. (1920). A constant error in psychological ratings. *Journal of Applied Psychology, 4,* 25-29.

Tversky, A., & Kahneman, D. (1973). Availability: A heuristic for judging frequency and probability. *Cognitive Psychology, 5,* 207-232.

Tversky, A., & Kahneman, D. (1974). Judgment under uncertainty: Heuristic and biases. *Science, 185,* 1124-1131.

Wiggins, J.S. (1973). *Personality and prediction.* Reading, MA: Addison-Wesley.

Wyer, R.S., & Gordon, S.E. (1982). The recall of information about persons and groups. *Journal of Experimental Social Psychology, 18,* 128-164.

PREDICTING INDIVIDUAL DIFFERENCES IN PERSONALITY RATINGS

Nico G. Smid

and

Frank B. Brokken

University of Groningen
The Netherlands

About thirty years ago Cronbach (1955) already drew attention to the fact that differences in global personality ratings may not only reflect reliable differences between the ratees, but may also reflect systematic differences in the ways in which subjects use rating scales. Personality ratings are often used as a dependent variable in research on personality psychology. Theoretically, person perception research investigates how personality ratings depend on specific characteristics of a ratee. Individual differences between judges limit the generalizability of common person perception principles. Within the applied context of assessment, personality ratings are usually part of decision procedures with respect to the rated persons. Predicting individual differences between raters is of course important when false decisions are to be minimized.

After Cronbach's (1955) article individual differences between judges have not been extensively studied. Sophisticated psychometric analyses concerning the structure of personality ratings mainly referred to people in general (cf. Brokken, 1978; John, Goldberg & Angleitner, 1984; Wiggins, 1980). Only in various cases the focus has been on differences between judges (cf. Wiggins, 1973). Within the more experimentally oriented research on person perception, started – among others – by Asch (1946), Heider (1958), Jones and Davis (1965) and Anderson (1974), mainly common perceptual tendencies have been studied. However, the research on different perspectives of actors and observers (cf. Jones & Nisbett, 1971) can be interpreted as research on differences between judges. Furthermore, the social construction of personality-view (cf. Hampson, 1984), focusses more on general symbolic interactionistic principles in studying ratings of personality than on individual differences between judges.

Yet, specific pieces of information about a ratee are not equally relevant to different judges providing personality ratings. The present research focusses upon such differences between raters. In particular it is investigated whether the prediction of personality ratings can be improved by taking into account individual differences in the judged relevance of information.

In order to delineate what is meant by *personality rating* the concepts *cue* and *trait* will be used from now on. A *cue* is defined to be any piece of distinguishable information a judge may use to base a

personality rating upon. A *trait* refers to any personality descriptive
concept that defines a specific personality rating scale. Thus, any
personality rating task is conceived of as a trait rating on the basis of
one or more cues.

Following Brunswik (1956) it has been tried to build linear models
for individual judges, e.g., in predicting the differential diagnosis
neurotic versus *psychotic* from specific MMPI-profiles (Goldberg, 1970;
Dawes, 1979). Within the present context the single MMPI-scale scores
are *cues*, and *neurotic* and *psychotic* are the poles of a *trait*
dimension. Such a linear model of a judge is built by regressing the
differential diagnoses on a large set of MMPI-profiles, which have been
successively presented as cues to the judge. The resulting regression
weights represent the model and may thus be conceived of as a set of
individual scale relevance values. Generally, the predictive validity of
the model is higher than the predictive validity of the judge.
Therefore, constructing linear prediction models for different judges
may be helpful in comparing and controlling for individual differences
in trait ratings.

The mentioned linear models are psychometrically *inferred* from
actual judgments. It is well known that many judgments are needed to
secure reliable estimates of the regression weights of the models. For
example, in the data used by Goldberg (1970) each judge had to rate
861 MMPI-profiles. The disadvantages of the procedure are clear: it is
time-consuming, costly, and boring. Still, the advantage seems
obvious: the regression weights, i.e., the judgmental policy, is
inferred from real ratings, rather than *asked* from the judge.
However, why should the judge *not* be asked for his or her judgmental
policy? If the judge could simply be asked, the disadvantages of the
procedure would clearly disappear. Goldberg's judges would have had
to provide only ten scale weights or scale relevance values, rather
than to process 861 profiles. The price to pay, however, is
introspection. Having been considered an invalid data source for a
long time, introspection has (re)gained its status as a data source
within the above mentioned person perception research tradition (cf.
Kahnemann, Slovic & Tversky, 1982; Nisbett & Ross, 1980). However,
within the same research tradition quite a number of pitfalls and biases
in human judgments have been documented.

The present research *does* use an introspective method to collect
individual relevance values for cues to infer traits. This method is,
however, provided with several safeguards against common errors that
frequently occur in human judgment. Thus, following the person
perception research tradition, for each of a number of judges
individual relevance values were introspectively assessed for a number
of combinations of cues and traits that were considered relevant with
respect to personality ratings. At the same time, however, following
the psychometric research tradition, different "profiles" of such
cues - defining so-called "stimulus persons" - were presented to each
judge, who had to rate the stimulus persons on the same traits as
used in assessing the relevance values. Thereafter it was investigated
whether introspectively obtained relevance values of cues can fruitfully
be used in prediction models of personality ratings.

Two aspects of using such relevance values may be distinguished.
For a single judge it can be investigated whether those values can be
used equally well or even better than cross-validated individual

regression weights in predicting ratings. This refers to Goldberg's (1970) judge-modeling paradigm. If this is the case, time and money can be saved while the judge remains attentive. Alternatively, in predicting the personality ratings of a random judge out of a group of judges the predictive validity of individual relevance values of the selected judge may be compared with the validity of the common regression equation of the group of judges. The present research is about the latter issue. If the predictive validity of individual relevance values turns out to be equally high or even higher than group-based regression equations, large scale validation research using many judges can be replaced by a simple procedure to find these individual relevance values in order to obtain a model of the randomly chosen judge. Money and time will thus be saved while the often practical problem of not having enough judges to perform validation research is solved too.

Theoretically, a comparison of individual regression weights with introspectively assessed relevance values for a single judge will yield valuable information about the extent to which a personality rating task can be considered cognitively equivalent to judging the relevance of a single cue for a trait. Anderson (1974) seems to imply that such is the case by strictly distinguishing between valuation and integration within a single rating task. In the present study, therefore, regression weights and relevance values are also compared.

Individual differences between judges have been partially attributed to response styles (for a review: see Wiggins, 1980). A specific style which has been extensively studied is the extreme response style (Bonarius, 1971, 1980). Since the present study focusses on personality ratings of individual judges, an individual extreme response style index is used to predict such ratings. From a practical point of view such an index may contribute to the reduction of false decisions. Theoretically, it is interesting to study extreme responses since they may indicate the degree of certainty with which a judge attributes a trait to a ratee. It is reasonable to assume that such certainty at least partially depends on the judged relevance of specific cues, which is a main variable within the present research.

Within assessment situations personality ratings are generally provided by professional people. For reasons of generalizability professionals might be preferred to laymen as subjects for this study. However, from a theoretical person perception view a less specific sample of subjects was preferred. Furthermore, studies in applied settings at a later stage may profit from the results of this research by comparing the judgmental behavior of the present sample of judges with that of specific professional groups.

METHOD

Subjects

The subjects were 103 paid volunteers, mainly undergraduates from various faculties. The sample consisted of 48 men and 55 women. 95 subjects completed their tasks. Data obtained from these 95 subjects were used in the analyses. The subjects' mean age was 22.3 years, ranging from 17 to 36.

Rating materials

Starting point for the selection of traits and cues to be used in this research were existing taxonomic studies.

Traits. Hofstee, Brokken, and Land (1981) constructed a Dutch list of personality-descriptive adjectives, the S.P.E.L. (Standard Personality Adjective List), which has been shown to be fairly exhaustive (Brokken, 1978). This list contains seven relatively independent scales. Each scale of the S.P.E.L. consists of a number of groups of nearly synonymous adjectives. The rater has to rate the ratee on the *common* meaning of each group. In order to reduce the amount of work for the subjects a much shorter version of the S.P.E.L. was constructed, having only one group of adjectives per scale. The meaning of the original scale was maximally preserved in each single group of adjectives. In Table 1 the English translation of the adjectives in the resulting list is presented.

Cues. The cues are short sentences describing a certain behavior of a person in a specific situation. The sentences are intended to represent behavior which is both concrete and intersubjectively observable and which is not uniformly regarded as either highly desirable or highly undesirable. An existing taxonomy of ten independent situation factors (Van Heck, 1984) was used as a guideline to formulate the cues. For each factor the first author and a few colleagues constructed a cue that might represent one of the situations loading on that factor. No combination of two or more cues were formed that were incompatible within one stimulus person. Of course, the resulting list only partially represents the situation factors. Complete coverage of situations by cues, however, is not the main issue in this study. The list of cues is presented in Table 2, the cue numbers therein correspond to the numbers of the factors given by Van Heck (1984).

Design and procedure

Relevance values. Intuitively, individual relevance values of cues for inferring traits may be considered *diagnostic values* within a Bayesian framework. Indeed, Ajzen and Fishbein (1975) explicitly did so in proposing the log likelihood ratio (LLR) as a measure of cue diagnosticity in the realm of attribution processes. Within the present context this means that a relevance value for a specific *cue* (C) - *trait* (T) combination is given by the following LLR:

$$\log [p \; (C \mid T)] - \log [p \; (C \mid \text{not } T)].$$

In which

$p \; (C \mid T)$ represents the subjective probability that the behavior described by the cue C will be performed, given that the actor possesses the trait T.

$p \; (C \mid \text{not } T)$ represents the subjective probability that the behavior described by the cue C will be performed, given that the actor possesses the opposite of trait T.

TABLE 1: *The shortened version of the S.P.E.L.-scales*

    I. Contemplative, shy, reserved
   II. Cheerful, sociable, enthusiastic
  III. Dutiful, thrifty, industrious
  IV. Certain, independent, self-supporting
    V. Uncivilized, impolite, banal
  VI. Hot-tempered, offensive, domineering
 VII. Progressive, liberal, radical

TABLE 2: *The list of cues*

---

1. At political meetings (s)he compares the own arguments with those of the discussion-partners

2. During consultation on labor organization (s)he presents feasible solutions to most of the problems

3. At parties (s)he regularly finds a bedpartner

4. At receptions (s)he often starts to talk with strangers

5. In the train (s)he regularly tips the barman

6. During a cremation (s)he rejects critical remarks about the deceased

7. As a member of a sports club (s)he often assists at organizing the competition

8. At the yearly party with the colleagues (s)he is one of the last people to leave

9. In a busy restaurant (s)he invites strangers at the table

10. During shopping (s)he regularly asks for the quality of the commodities

---

Of course, it is easier to define an LLR than to assess it properly. People often are quite unreliable and inconsistent when they are asked to give direct subjective probability estimates (Lourens, 1984; Tversky & Kahnemann, 1974). Furthermore, people are not used to predict a specific behavior in the presence of a trait. Usually – as is amply demonstrated by attribution research – lay people go the other way around. They infer traits from actual behavior. McCauley and Stitt (1978) approached this latter problem as follows. They defined "idiosyncratic individual stereotypes" or "personal stereotypes" (Secord & Backman, 1964) as diagnostic ratios of the form

$$p\,(T \mid C)\,/\,p\,(T),$$

in which
$p\,(T \mid C)$ represents the subjective probability that a specific trait is present given that an actor performs a specific behavior, described by cue C, and

N.G.Smid/F.B.Brokken

p (T)   represents the subjective probability that *people in general* possess the trait T. Or, shortly, the *subjective base rate* of the trait T.

As can be seen, the inferential direction is as desired. Furthermore, Smid (1984) shows that McCauley and Stitt's conceptualization may lead to a framework encompassing various lines of attribution and trait rating research. In particular, Ajzen and Fishbein's (1975) proposal may be subsumed under it since, according to Bayes' theorem, the LLR defined above is identical to

$$LLR = \log [p(T|C) / p(T)] - \log [p(\text{not } T|C) / p(\text{not } T)].$$

Thus, an LLR within the present context is interpreted as the difference between the *personal stereotypes* related to a pair of opposite traits. This implies that the diagnostic value of a cue, i.e., its relevance value for an individual, is represented by the *change of belief* about the presence of a trait when the individual is informed about the cue. Thus this diagnostic value is not merely interpreted as the conditional probability of the trait given the cue. A similar argument made by McCauley and Stitt (1978) and by Ajzen and Fishbein (1975) emphasizes that this change in belief notion is the proper way to represent diagnostic value. The assessment procedure used in the present research (to be described below) in fact capitalizes on this notion.

McCauley and Stitt (1978) propose to assess subjective probabilities directly. Considering the problems that may be encountered in using a direct estimation procedure, it was decided here not to estimate them directly, but to use so-called "betting odds" (Winkler, 1967). Betting odds seem less liable to common biases of probability estimation (Vlek & Wagenaar, 1979). In particular, our subjects were asked to divide ten points between the presence of a trait and its opposite. First, each subject was asked to generate for each group of adjectives representing a S.P.E.L.-scale another group of adjectives, representing the opposite meaning of the given group of adjectives. Consequently, each subject created seven *semi-personal* constructs (Kelly, 1955), consisting of a *common* S.P.E.L.-scale and its opposite *as generated by the subject*. This procedure should make the forced choice betting odds task as natural as possible. Moreover, the present Bayesian framework demands for each subject strictly opposite poles. Common bipolar scales for all subjects may introduce unwanted error in the betting-odds data. For each subject the generated set of seven semi-personal constructs was used as the dependent variable throughout this study.

To illustrate the procedure an example of the instruction with respect to the first S.P.E.L.-scale and the first cue is given here.

To assess p(T), i.e., the subjective base rate, the subject was asked to "divide ten points, as if you were to bet, over the applicability of the common meaning of *contemplative, shy,* and *reserved* to people in general, compared to the applicability of the set of opposites of *contemplative, shy* and *reserved*". To assess p(T|C) the subject was asked "how do your betting odds just given, *change* if you know that at political meetings a person compares his/her own arguments with those of the discussion partners? Give your new betting odds".

As can be seen this procedure tries to minimize two common biases in both probability estimation and trait rating tasks. First, people tend to neglect base rates (Nisbett & Ross, 1980). The base rates, however, were made maximally salient here. Second, people often neglect the alternative hypothesis implied by a single probability statement of the form $p(T|C)$ or $p(T)$ (Beyth-Marom & Fischhoff, 1983). It was tried to minimize this error by the explicit bipolarity of the betting odds task. Beyth-Marom and Fischhoff (1983) also document that a structured judgment task, in which implied judgments are made explicit, greatly improves the calibration and achievement of the subjects.

After the transformation of the betting odds into subjective probabilities $p(T)$, $p(\text{not } T)$, $p(T|C$, and $p(\text{not } T|C)$, the LLRs were constructed for further use in this study.

Data structure. Two data sets were collected. First, each subject had to rate 64 stimulus persons on all seven S.P.E.L.-scales. These scales were in the form of six-point semi-personal constructs as defined above. The lower pole (score = 1) invariably designated the common S.P.E.L.-scale, the higher pole (score = 6) designated the individual opposite of the common S.P.E.L.-scale. A stimulus person consisted of a random subset of one ore more cues out of the set of ten cues given in Table 2. Out of the 2^{10} = 1024 possible stimulus persons each subject rated a unique and randomly chosen set of 64 stimulus persons who were presented in a random order to the subjects. The subjects were allowed to take the stimulus materials - presented on computer printout - home and were requested to return their ratings within a week. They were instructed to work carefully during several short periods. In order to simulate a real life situation they were instructed to imagine that they were expecting a new close colleague about whom they had accidently overheard the information as represented by the stimulus person. Thus, the first data set (generated by 95 subjects) consisted of 6080 (95 x 64) vectors of seven six-point S.P.E.L.-ratings.

The second data set, collected several weeks later, consisted of 10 (cues) x 7 (S.P.E.L.-scales) x 95 (subjects) = 6650 LLRs, which were collected according to the procedure described earlier. Again, these data were collected in a unique and random order per subject.

Finally, for each subject all 64 stimulus persons were either described as males or as females. After separating the male and female *subjects* a crossed Sex of Rater x Sex of Ratee design was thus constructed.

Research questions. For each subject, actual $p(T)$ and $p(T|C)$ values may be computed from the ratings of the 64 stimulus persons. A high degree of correspondence between these values and the subjective values obtained at the betting-odds task will be obtained if - as seems to be implied by Anderson (1974) - valuation of single cues is essentially the same process in isolated tasks (betting odds) as in information integration tasks (rating).

The main question is the differential validity of individual relevance values versus common regression weights. This question may be investigated by comparing a linear model of the average subject that is only based on the presence or absence of cues within stimulus persons with a model that uses individual LLRs for each subject. Should the latter show a higher validity than the former, a three way Rater x Ratee x Rating scale interaction is established as a function of personal stereotypes.

The additional predictive power of extreme response style tendencies can be computed by comparing a model including an extreme response style index for each subject with a model that is based on individual LLRs.

RESULTS

On the average, cue diagnostic values that were inferred from the rating data were only moderately predictable from the subjective diagnostic values based on the betting odds. However, the linear models in which individual LLRs are used as predictors, perform at least as well as the common linear model of the average subject. A remarkable increase of the predictive validity with respect to the seven S.P.E.L.-scales was obtained after using an individual extreme response style index.

Reliabilities

Since subjective $p(T)$-values were collected during the first and the second part of the data collection, it was possible to compute for each subject Spearman-rho test-retest coefficients of reliability. The mean rho-coefficient equals .48. As 10% of the subjective $p(T|C)$-values were random replications for each subject, it was also possible to estimate Spearman-rho coefficients of reliability for these data. Here the mean coefficient of reliability equals .66. The reliability of the LLRs was considered acceptable for the present purposes.

Within the rating task also 10% of the stimulus persons were replicated for each subject. The mean test-retest correlation over subjects is .66 and reduces to .29 after correcting for the mean differences between S.P.E.L.-ratings within subjects. Because of the fact that the S.P.E.L.-version used in this research had a length of only one third of the original S.P.E.L., the obtained coefficient of reliability is considered acceptable, compared to a mean between-subjects reliability of .80 for the original S.P.E.L.-scales (Brokken & Smid, 1984).

Subjective versus actual diagnostic values

For every subject 70 log-diagnostic ratios $(\log[p(T|C) / p(T)])$ computed from the actual rating data were correlated with the 70 log-diagnostic ratios computed from the subjective betting odds. The mean over subjects of these 95 correlations equals .26 (.45 corrected for attenuation). The correlations themselves are neither correlated with common biographical variables, nor with the crossed Sex of Rater x Sex of Ratee structure of the data (Wesselink & Fokkema, 1984). Therefore, this latter structure was not further investigated here.

However, subjective and actual LLRs are only partially exchangeable. Thus, contrary to what seems to be implied by Anderson's (1974) model, cue valuation by means of a betting odds task produces different results than cue valuation by means of an information integration task as occurs, e.g., in personality rating tasks.

Predicting from cues and from LLRs

In order to cross-validate the results the entire sample of 6080 ratings was divided into two random halves. However, the Sex of Rater and Sex of Ratee variables were counterbalanced between both subsamples.

First, the S.P.E.L.-ratings were regressed using straightforward main effects multiple regression on ten binary variables, representing the presence (1) or absence (0) of each of the ten cues within a stimulus person. In this regression process mean rating differences between raters were not corrected. Since in a normal assessment practice there is generally no control over which rater rates which ratee, this procedure provides a baseline of the predictability of the average rater against which more complicated prediction models – including those using LLRs – can be validated.

Following the same cross-validation design a prediction model using LLRs was constructed. The most simple LLR-model is the classical linear log-Bayesian one. Thus, each scale score is interpreted as a linear function of the sum of the pertinent LLRs. I.e., the LLRs with respect to both the scale to be modelled and the cues creating the rated stimulus person. Using this simple model for each S.P.E.L.-scale the ones in the predictor matrix of the first main effects analysis were replaced by the corresponding LLRs, while the zeros remained unchanged. In fact, the desired Rater x Ratee x Rating-scale interaction was incorporated into the prediction model.

The first line of Table 3 presents the cross-validated multiple correlations per S.P.E.L.-scale, using only the binary coded cues as predictors. Therefore, these correlations form the baseline model of the average judge. On the second line the cross-validated multiple correlations using the individual LLRs as predictors are shown. Ratings on six S.P.E.L.-scales are predicted at least as well by the LLRs as by the linear model of the average judge. In particular, it is noted that the baseline model is remarkably exceeded by the LLR-model in predicting S.P.E.L.-scale VI (*hot-tempered, offensive, domineering*). The obtained multiple correlations are .16 and .35, respectively. Although the mean level of the correlations is not high, it is acceptable considering the moderate reliabilities of the S.P.E.L.-scales and of the LLRs.

It is concluded that in predicting a personality rating of a randomly chosen rater, having available data of the present kind, a guided asking method (like "betting odds") may actually improve the prediction obtained using the results of large sample validation research. Sometimes the improvement may even be appreciable, such as occurred with scale VI, which scale seems to be primarily rated on the basis of personal (instead of common) stereotypes.

TABLE 3: *Cross-validated validities for two models with mean and standard-deviation per S.P.E.L.-scale*

	S.P.E.L.-scales						
	I	II	III	IV	V	VI	VII
Validities							
Cues-model	.30	.29	.40	.19	.29	.16	.23
LLR –model	.31	.33	.34	.22	.33	.35	.29
Means	4.43	2.16	2.81	1.93	4.55	3.81	3.02
Standard deviations	1.30	1.06	1.14	.97	1.24	1.20	1.09

Note: Sample sizes are 3040 (=½ x (95 x 64))

One final point should be mentioned. It is possible that the specific cues used in this study actually created the specific position of scale VI. By using other cue-sets other scales might show the predictive advantage of personal over common stereotypes. Considering the content of the cues in Table 2 it seems that the selection criteria used in formulating the cues have produced cues describing moderately agreeable, assertive, independent behavior, to which the rated concept *hot-tempered, offensive, domineering* might be differently related for different persons. This interpretation is supported by the mean rating values on the six-point scales given on the third line of Table 3. Generally, stimulus persons are described as moderately *cheerful, sociable, enthousiastic, certain, independent, self-supporting,* while they are not described as *contemplative, shy, reserved* or *uncivilized, impolite, banal.* These effects are quite consistent, as is shown by the mean standard deviation of 1.14, computed from the last line of Table 3.

An index for extremity of rating

In order to investigate the predictive power of individual differences in extremity of rating a double cross-validation design was used. This design was based on a selected sample from the original 6080 rating vectors. Again, the analyses were carried out for each separate S.P.E.L.-scale. In each analysis a different sample of ratings was selected. In particular, only those ratings were analyzed for which the stimulus persons contained merely cues that were according to the LLRs subjectively relevant for the S.P.E.L.-pole of the rating scale. Consequently, no selected stimulus person contained for any subject contradictory cues for any rating task. This selection was performed to prevent unwanted distortions of an extremity of rating effect from occurring. Contradictions might, e.g., lead to discounting effects (Hampson, 1982). Moreover, relevance of cues for the *personal* pole of the semi-personal constructs might introduce individual differences, which should be separately studied. Finally, as noted by Bonarius (1980), extremity of rating might be a qualitatively different variable when it pertains to a negative instead of a positive pole of a personal construct. Therefore, only the common pole was used in this analysis.

For each of the seven selected samples the double cross-validation was carried out by computing for each subject two extremity of rating indices. One index was computed on his or her odd numbered stimulus persons and the other index was computed on his or her even numbered stimulus persons. Each index was cross-validated on the other subsample. After the cross-validation one index to represent the extremity of rating was formed for each subject by averaging both cross-validated indices. The results of this cross-validation are presented below.

The indices for extremity of rating themselves were constructed as follows. It will be recalled that the used LLR-model is a simple weighted sum of a number of LLRs. LLRs have a meaningful zero-point (as implied by their definition), indicating that a cue has no diagnostic value for a trait. Consequently, using the LLR-model a predicted scale score may be computed for each combination of S.P.E.L.-scale, stimulus person and subject. For a single S.P.E.L.-scale and a single subject all actual scale scores can then be regressed through the origin on the scale scores that are predicted by the LLR-model. The regression coefficient computed separately for each S.P.E.L.-scale and subject, is interpreted as an index of extremity of rating. This interpretation is founded on two considerations. On the one hand, no contradictory cues are present, so every LLR is multiplied *in the same direction*, on the other hand, the LLR-model remains consistent, since the zero-point is not altered.

The results of the double cross-validation, presented in Table 4, are encouraging. The first line shows the multiple correlations reached using the simple LLR-model on each selected sample. These correlations turn out to be virtually identical to those of the unrestricted sample given in Table 3. Therefore, the selection did not alter the validity of the LLR-model. However, when new predicted S.P.E.L.-scales were computed for each combination of S.P.E.L.-scale and subject, using the previously described indices for extremity of rating cross-validated predictive validities increased impressively. These validities are presented in the second line of Table 4. Note, however, the relatively low coefficient of validity obtained for S.P.E.L.-scale I. The common pole of this scale also has a rather low applicability to the stimulus

TABLE 4: *Cross-validated validities of the LLR-model in the selected samples, without and with extremity of rating index*

	S.P.E.L.-scales						
	I	II	III	IV	V	VI	VII
LLR-model							
Without	.32	.38	.38	.26	.31	.31	.34
With	.44	.66	.52	.60	.62	.59	.58
Observations:	506	3111	1792	3945	1131	1961	3036
Subjects:	31	81	73	91	54	70	84

persons in general (see Table 3, third line). Moreover, only 31 subjects (out of the 95) were used in the selected sample for S.P.E.L.-scale I, compared to a range of 54 (scale V) to 91 (scale IV) subjects used in the other samples. Thus, also for the predictive utility of the extremity of rating index the substantive content of the cues seems to be important and to rule out a purely stylistic interpretation of the results.

It may be concluded that the inclusion of an index for the extremity of rating into a model for predicting individual differences in personality ratings improves the predictive power of either a simple linear model of the average judge or a model that incorporates personal stereotypes as predictors. This result was obtained with each S.P.E.L.-scale. Also it is noted that correction for attenuation would produce validities of .7 to .9. This implies that a reliable index for extremity of rating has been defined explaining most of the predictable rating variance. In fact, in the present data it explains much more variance than personal stereotypes of trait concepts as represented by LLRs.

DISCUSSION

The present analyses suggest that a carefully guided asking method may be used to assess personal stereotypes of subjects, while it is not necessary to infer these stereotypes from actual rating data. Therefore, introspection has proven to be a useful information collecting procedure here. In particular, it has been shown for one S.P.E.L.-scale that the prediction of rating data could be markedly improved using the LLR-model instead of the model of the average subject. Using the LLR-model, individual differences in rating data could be related to individual differences in the diagnostic values of cues. For the other S.P.E.L.-scales no such improvement of the predictability of ratings was observed. Since in the latter case personal stereotypes did not result in an improvement of the prediction compared to common stereotypes, Hampson's (1982) hypothesis that in the personality domain people share similar constructs for understanding and predicting each other's behavior was supported. However, it remains to be shown whether such a commonness holds true when another set of cues than the present set is used. In particular, cues seem to vary not only with respect to different situation factors (cf. Van Heck, 1984), but also seem to vary with respect to the shared relevance for each trait scale. In order to investigate the predictive value of personal (compared to common) stereotypes for the entire trait domain a more thorough taxonomic study of the cue domain in relation to different trait factors and to different situation factors is needed. This suggests to take seriously the plea for studying situations "as perceived" (Magnusson, 1981; Smid, 1984). A good starting point for investigating communalities and individual differences in the structure of cue-trait relationships seems to be the act-frequency approach to personality as advocated by Buss and Craik (1983). Individual judges may be asked for any combination of a trait- and a situation-factor to generate a list of *behaviors in a situation* which in their opinion are more or less prototypical for the display of the trait in question.

It can be stated on the basis of the present results that the betting odds method provides LLRs that may be regarded as a good replacement of common stereotypes in cases where an extensive validation study is impractical. Moreover, the method itself implies a relatively short task for the judge, although it seems to be a rather complex way of assessment. However, it is precisely the complexity that should minimize both biases to which Beyth-Marom and Fischhoff (1983) have directed the attention, i.e., subjects' tendencies to neglect base rates and alternative hypotheses. Nevertheless, it will be valuable to know against which simplifications the predictive power of the method will remain robust. In particular, the status of the implied bipolarity of trait concepts and the assumed personal specificity of the opposites of common trait concepts deserve further attention (cf., Bonarius, 1984).

A salient result is the imperfect agreement between the diagnostic value of cues as inferred from rating data and the diagnostic value of cues as directly estimated by subjects. Precisely here the difference between a psychometric approach and an experimentally oriented approach of rating data becomes apparent. Within the latter approach real *valuation* (Anderson, 1974) of cues is assessed, i.e., a conscious cognitive activity of the judge. However, the inferred diagnostic values resulting from the former approach should not be equated with valuation in the cognitive sense. Inferred diagnostic values *only* pertain to psychometrically assessed scale values based on data from stimulus integration rating tasks, as obtained in Anderson's (1974) "functional measurement". Confounding such scale values with a cognitive activity (as Anderson does in distinguishing between valuation and integration) is an unnecessary reification of a psychometric model, which leads to the expectation of similarities between data from different tasks. Such similarities, however, do not have to occur and in fact do only very partially occur within the present data.

Of course, the most important empirical result of this study is the high predictive value of the index for extremity of rating. This result is important since it occurred with every S.P.E.L.-scale, and was only weakly moderated by the specificity of the cue-set. The impression is formed that most of the reliable individual differences in rating data may be attributed to systematic differences in extremity of rating. This extremity of rating can be properly assessed once a prediction model of calibrated diagnostic values (e.g., LLR-data) is available. Earlier in this chapter it was suggested that a purely stylistic interpretation of extremity does not seem to be warranted. However, it might be worthwhile to try to predict extremity of rating from cognitive data pertaining to the relation between an actual stimulus person on the one hand and the individual meaning of the trait rating concept for the judge on the other hand. This refers to an interaction model for extremity of rating. Studies by Bonarius (1971) contain valuable suggestions with respect to this model. In particular it appeared that judges give more extreme ratings on personal constructs than on constructs provided by the researcher. Moreover, this effect was stronger to the extent that the rated object had a more personal meaning for the judge. Using Kelly's (1955) notion that personal constructs have a broader range of convenience than provided ones, one might state the hypothesis that traits for which many cues show non-zero diagnostic values (i.e., traits which are *rich* in content) will on the average lead to more extreme judgments than trait concepts for which few cues show non-zero diagnostic values (i.e., traits which are *poor* in content). With respect to individual differences in ratings this hypothesis predicts that for a particular trait concept judges for whom this trait concept is *rich* will rate a specific set of stimulus persons more extremely than judges for whom this trait concept is *poor*. Preliminary analyses on the present data suggested that such is the case for at least five S.P.E.L.-scales. Though tentative, the results are encouraging enough to suggest further research. The same holds true for an operationalization of Bonarius' (1971) result that personally meaningful objects will trigger relatively more extreme ratings than objects that are less meaningful to the judge's cognitive system. Within the present context it was predicted that for a specific stimulus person and a specific trait concept ratings will become more extreme as the actual stimulus person more closely matches the judge's concept of the so called "prototypical person" (cf. Cantor & Mischel, 1979). In general, the present data suggest that this is the case, but further research is needed here too.

Positive results from the research proposed in the foregoing paragraph would imply that it might be feasible to estimate extremity of rating from cognitive data like LLRs instead of inferring it from a large body of rating data. Again, this might enable us to predict individual differences in personality ratings at the relatively low costs of collecting LLRs.

For the near future of the present research project generalizability studies are in order. Questions to be investigated here are the facets (cues, traits, rating tasks, occasions, time intervals) over which and to what extent extremity of rating generalizes. This information is important if one is interested in using the LLR-method in applied settings. Similarly, it is important to know whether simplifications of the LLR-method itself can be realized.

Two applications are immediately suggested. First, in the area of employee performance, it is important to have available proper rating instruments. Normally, extensive and costly research on actual rating data is needed to get the proper selection of cues used in predicting criteria, where the results have to be exchangeable over raters and conditions. However, by using a guided introspection procedure, e.g., the LLR-method, the researcher can simply carry out psychometric analyses on LLR-data. From these data those cues can thereupon be selected that have a high exchangeability of both raters and rating conditions. Also, cues can be selected that are relatively unaffected by differences between the subjects in extremity of rating. It is clear that LLR-data are collected easier, faster and cheaper than actual rating data. Second, a more theoretical application is the comparison of different cognitive processes that underlie on the one hand the task of the valuation of single cues and on the other hand the task of integrating a number of single cues in one single rating. The results of this latter study will help to clarify what goes on in people's minds when they make judgments about either abstract personality relevant information or about concrete persons.

Thus, the present research shows several routes for advancing personality psychology. Theoretically, it shows the importance of accounting for individual differences in perspectives on the personality of concrete persons. Studying the determinants of the tendency to respond extremely looks promising to that end. At the same time, the somewhat vague concept of personal stereotypes has been operationalized in a way yielding predictive validity. The LLR-measure may therefore profitably be used in a further investigation of idiosyncrasies and communalities with respect to cues and traits. From a practical point of view the present results indicate the possibility of getting useful information about predictive validities from small scale rating settings. This substantially broadens the range of applicability of empirical methods within personality assessment. Of course, introspection has an important place in that enterprise. Furthermore, as shown by this study, introspective and psychometric methods may – not surprising – differ in results. Therefore, a combined research strategy in which both methods control and complete each other is wanted. This research can be seen as an example of such a strategy. Although the present authors are in no way among the first to emphasize a fruitful marriage between the two "disciplines of scientific psychology" (Cronbach, 1957), it is their hope that the present highlighting of that liaison may increase the willingness of at least some more personality psychologists to foster its fertility.

ACKNOWLEDGEMENT

The authors gratefully acknowledge the assistance of Gertie Wesselink and Fokke Fokkema during the data collection and data analysis phases of this study. Willem Hofstee is acknowledged for his insightful comments on an earlier version of this chapter.

REFERENCES

Ajzen, I., & Fishbein, M. (1975). A Bayesian analysis of attribution processes. *Psychological Bulletin, 82,* 261-277.

Anderson, N.H. (1974). Cognitive Algebra: Integration theory applied to social attribution. In L. Berkowitz (Ed.), *Advances in experimental social psychology* (Vol. 7, pp. 1-101). New York: Academic press.

Asch, S.E. (1946). Forming impressions of personality. *Journal of Abnormal and Social Psychology, 41,* 258-290.

Beyth-Marom, R., & Fischhoff, B. (1983). Diagnosticity and pseudo-diagnosticity. *Journal of Personality and Social Psychology, 45,* 1185-1195.

Bonarius, J.C.J. (1971). *Personal construct psychology and extreme response style: An interaction model of meaningfulness, maladjustment and communication.* Amsterdam: Swets & Zeitlinger.

Bonarius, H. (1980). *Persoonlijke psychologie, deel II: Ontwikkelingen in de theorie en praktijk van constructen-psychologie* [Personal psychology, Vol. II: Developments in the theory and practice of construct psychology]. Deventer: Van Loghum Slaterus.

Bonarius, H. (1984). Personal construct psychology: A reappraisal of basic theory and its application. In H. Bonarius, G. Van Heck, & N. Smid (Eds.), *Personality psychology in Europe: Theoretical and empirical developments* (pp. 195-218). Lisse: Swets & Zeitlinger.

Brokken, F.B. (1978). *The language of personality*. Unpublished doctoral dissertation. University of Groningen.

Brokken, F.B., & Smid, N.G. (1984). Een uitbreiding van de Standaard Persoonlijkheids Eigenschappenlijst [An extension of the standard list of personality traits]. *Nederlands Tijdschrift voor de Psychologie, 39*, 348-352.

Brunswik, E. (1956). *Perception and the repesentative design of psychological experiments*. Berkeley: University of California Press.

Buss, D.M., & Craik, K.H. (1983). The act frequency approach to personality. *Psychological Review, 90*, 105-126.

Cantor, N., & Mischel, W. (1979). Prototypes in person perception. In L. Berkowitz (Ed.), *Advances in experimental social psychology* (Vol. 12, pp. 3-52). New York: Academic Press.

Cronbach, L.J. (1955). Processes affecting scores of 'understanding of others' and 'assumed similarity'. *Psychological Bulletin, 52*, 177-193.

Cronbach, L.J. (1957). The two disciplines of scientific psychology. *American Psychologist, 12*, 671-684.

Dawes, R.M. (1979). The robust beauty of improper linear models in decision making. *American Psychologist, 34*, 571-582.

Goldberg, L.R. (1970). Man versus model of man: A rationale plus evidence for a method of improving on clinical inferences. *Psychological Bulletin, 73*, 422-432.

Hampson, S.E. (1982). *The construction of personality: An introduction*. London: Routledge & Kegan Paul.

Hampson, S.E. (1984). The social construction of personality. In H. Bonarius, G. Van Heck, & N. Smid (Eds.), *Personality Psychology in Europe: Theoretical and empirical developments* (pp. 3-14). Lisse: Swets & Zeitlinger.

Heider, F. (1958). *The psychology of interpersonal relations*. New York: Wiley.

Hofstee, W.K.B., Brokken, F.B., & Land, H. (1981). Constructie van een Standaard-Persoonlijkheids-Eigenschappenlijst (S.P.E.L.) [The construction of a standard list of personality traits]. *Nederlands Tijdschrift voor de Psychology, 36*, 443-452.

John, O.P., Goldberg, L.R., & Angleitner, A. (1984). Better than the alphabet: Taxonomies of personality-descriptive terms in English, Dutch and German. In H. Bonarius, G. van Heck, & N. Smid (Eds.), *Personality psychology in Europe: Theoretical and empirical developments* (pp. 83-100). Lisse: Swets & Zeitlinger.

Jones, E.E., & Davis, K.E. (1965). From acts to dispositions: The attribution process in person perception. In L. Berkowitz (Ed.), *Advances in experimental social psychology* (Vol. 2, pp. 220-226). New York: Academic Press.

Jones, E.E., & Nisbett, R.E. (1971). The actor and the observer: Divergent perceptions of the causes of behavior. In E.E. Jones, D.E. Kanouse, H.H. Kelley, R.E. Nisbett, S. Valins, & B. Weiner (Eds.), *Attribution: Perceiving the causes of behavior* (pp. 79-94). Morristown: General Learning Press.

Kahneman, D., Slovic, P., & Tversky, A. (1982). *Judgment under uncertainty: Heuristics and biases.* Cambridge: Cambridge University Press.

Kelly, G.A. (1955). *The psychology of personal constructs.* Vols. I & II. New York: Norton.

Lourens, P.F. (1984). *The formalization of knowledge by specification of subjective probability distributions.* Unpublished doctoral dissertation. University of Groningen.

Magnusson, D. (1981). Wanted: A psychology of situations. In D. Magnusson (Ed.), *Toward a psychology of situations: An interactional perspective* (pp. 9-32). Hillsdale, NJ: Erlbaum.

McCauley, C., & Stitt, C.L. (1978). An individual and quantitative measure of stereotypes. *Journal of Personality and Social Psychology, 36,* 929-940.

Nisbett, R., & Ross, L. (1980). *Human inference: strategies and shortcomings of social judgment.* Englewood Cliffs, NJ: Prentice-Hall.

Secord, P.F., & Backman, C.W. (1964). *Social Psychology.* New York: McGraw Hill.

Smid, N.G. (1984). A judgmental framework of personality data with some research applications. In H. Bonarius, G. Van Heck, & N. Smid (Eds.), *Personality psychology in Europe: Theoretical and empirical developments* (pp. 15-30). Lisse: Swets & Zeitlinger.

Tversky, A., & Kahneman, D. (1974). Judgment under uncertainty: Heuristics and biases. *Science, 185,* 1124-1131.

Van Heck, G.L. (1984). The construction of a general taxonomy of situations. In H. Bonarius, G. Van Heck, & N. Smid (Eds.), *Personality psychology in Europe: Theoretical and empirical developments* (pp. 149-164). Lisse: Swets & Zeitlinger.

Vlek, C.A.J., & Wagenaar, W.A. (1979). Judgment and decision making under uncertainty. In J.A. Michon, E.G. Eijkman, & L.F.W. de Klerk (Eds.), *Handbook of psychonomics* (Vol. 2, pp. 253-345). Amsterdam: North Holland Publishing Company.

Wesselink, G., & Fokkema, F. (1984). *De meting van persoonlijke stereotypen: Een methodologische analyse.* (HB-84-687 SW) [The measurement of personal stereotypes: A methodological analysis]. Groningen: University of Groningen, Department of Personality Psychology.

Wiggins, J.S. (1980). *Personality and prediction: Principles of personality assessment* (2nd. ed.). Reading, MA: Addison-Wesley.

Wiggins, N. (1973). Individual differences in human judgments: A multivariate approach. In L. Rappoport, & D.A. Summers. (Eds.), *Human judgment and social interaction* (pp. 110-142). New York: Holt, Rinehart, & Winston.

Winkler, R.L. (1967). The quantification of judgment: Some methodological suggestions. *Journal of the American Statistical Association, 62,* 1105-1120.

PART V

PERSONALITY AND TEMPERAMENT

MODELS AND PARADIGMS IN PERSONALITY RESEARCH

Hans J. Eysenck

Institute of Psychiatry
University of London
England

In a previous paper (Eysenck, 1983), I have raised the question: "Is there a paradigm in personality research?", and given the provisional answer that such a paradigm does indeed exist, even though only in embryonic form. In a later publication, Eysenck and Eysenck (1985) have examined the evidence, both on the descriptive and the causal side, in very considerable detail, with a similar conclusion. In this chapter I wish to consider the various conditions which have to be fulfilled before a model can be accepted as a paradigm in this field, and to consider the degree to which the three dimensional model of psychoticism versus ego control, extraversion as opposed to introversion, and neuroticism as opposed to emotional stability comes up to these exacting standards.

It is true, of course, that Kuhn (1962, 1970, 1974) considers the social sciences to be pre-paradigmatic, in the sense that they have not advanced to the point where paradigms become possible. One may doubt whether such a judgement, by someone not versed in the social sciences, is actually valid, and Barnes (1982) advances some of the reasons why Kuhn's pessimism may be misplaced. Yet it is important to realise certain limitations of a paradigm which are not always appreciated by psychologists. The concept of the paradigm does not entail the postulation of a perfect theory, exhibiting no anomalies, and making predictions all of which are verified.

Quite the opposite is true. As Kuhn indicates so clearly, the existence of a paradigm gives rise to "normal science" activity, i.e., puzzle-solving behaviour. All this is indicative of the fact that the paradigm is far from perfect. As Barnes (1982) puts it: "how does acceptance of a paradigm indicate problems for research; and how does a paradigm itself serve as a resource for the scientist? Curiously, the answer lies in the perceived inadequacy of a paradigm as it is initially formulated and accepted, in its crudity, its unsatisfactory predictive power, and its limited scope, which may in some cases amount to but a single application. In agreeing upon a paradigm, scientists do not accept the finished product: rather, they agree to accept the bases for future work, and to treat as illusory or eliminable all its apparent inadequacies and defects. Paradigms are refined and elaborated in normal science. And they are used in the development of further problem-solutions, thus extending the scope of scientific competences and procedures." (p. 46).

If we thus encounter anomalies, problems and difficulties in our model, this does not indicate that it lacks the features of a true paradigm. The existence of such weaknesses merely indicates that we are truly dealing with a paradigm, not with a law of nature; we may hope that the paradigm will develop into such a law, but there can of course be no guarantee of that. Looked at from the point of view of personality theory, what would be required before a given model, such as that advocated by the writer (Eysenck, 1981), can be regarded as a paradigm?

First and foremost, it is an absolutely essential requirement that the same or similar factors should emerge from analyses undertaken by many different authors, in many different countries, using many different questionnaires, and different methods of analysis. If we did not find identical or similar factors emerging from studies of the MMPI, the 16 PF, the CPI and other widely used questionnaires, we might indeed doubt whether on the descriptive side there was enough unanimity to assert the existence of a paradigm. Royce and Powell (1983) have carefully gone through all existing studies of correlational factor analytic questionnaire investigations, and have come to the conclusion that three major super-factors or dimensisons emerge again and again, with sufficient frequency to state that these are indeed stable features of the descriptive analysis of personality. They use different nomenclature to the one used here, but there is little doubting the essential identity of their three factors, and those labeled P, E and N by the writer. For the sake of clarity and future reference, the traits the intercorrelations between which define these three super-factors are shown in Figures 1, 2 and 3.

In a more detailed analysis of the various correlational studies made of the items in the major personality inventories widely used at the moment, Eysenck and Eysenck (1985) collected a large body of data indicating that in each case E and N were clearly recognisable, and that P, while encountered less regularly, could also be demonstrated to be present in the great majority of analyses. Readers are referred for details to these two publications; they leave little doubt that whenever a reasonable sample of personality trait is canvassed, the intercorrelations define the three super-factors constituting our model,

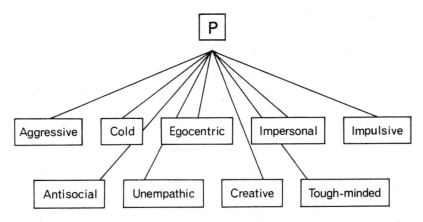

Figure 1: *Traits defining Psychoticism. (Eysenck & Eysenck, 1985.)*

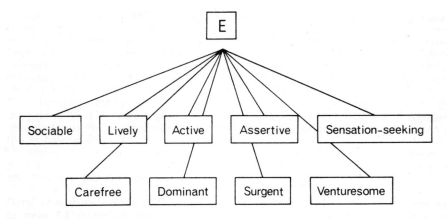

Figure 2: *Traits defining Extraversion. (Eysenck & Eysenck, 1985.)*

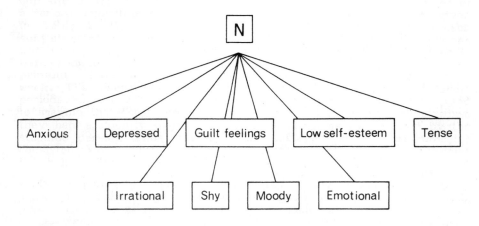

Figure 3: *Traits defining Neuroticism. (Eysenck & Eysenck, 1985.)*

as well, of course, as a number of primary factors usually different from investigation to investigation.

It might be argued that all these studies were carried out in the context of Western civilization, i.e., using subjects mainly from the European Continent, the United States of America, Canada, Australia, etc. The possibility cannot be ruled out that non-Western populations might show quite different combinations of personality traits, and unless the general applicability of the model to all types of cultures can be demonstrated, it cannot be claimed to constitute a paradigm in the most general sense. Barrett and Eysenck (1984) have carried out large-scale comparative studies on 25 widely different populations, ranging from Uganda to Japan, from Mainland China to Sri Lanka, and from Nigeria to Bangla Desh, as well of course as including many Western countries, both communist and non-communist. In these studies, groups of not less than 500 males and 500 females were administered translations of the Eysenck Personality Questionnaire (Eysenck & Eysenck, 1975); intercorrelations were then ran, for males and females separately, for each country, and factor analyses performed. Finally, the resulting factors were compared (a) with the original English norms, and (b) with each of the other 24 countries. It was found that the mean index of factor comparison was better than .98, indicating very close similarity, if not identity, of factor structure between countries. Indeed, it was found that the similarity of one culture with another, as far as structure of personality was concerned, was as good as the comparison of males and females *within* any one nation or culture. Similar findings were made with the smaller number of studies using children (Eysenck & Eysenck, 1985); here too there seemed to be considerable consistency between one culture and another.

Are personality factors like P, E and N consistent over time? If people change their position to any marked extent from one year to another, then one might be wary of believing in the importance and paradigmatic quality of these factors. Conley (1984) has carried out a survey of the very large literature existing in this field, with some studies extending over 50 years of follow-up, with particular reference to P, E and N. He used the standard formula

$$C = Rs^n$$

where C is the observed retest coefficient, R the internal consistency of period-free reliability of the measuring instrument, s the annual stability and n the interval in years over which the coefficient was calculated.

Conley found that for intelligence, s was .99, whereas for P, E and N it was .98, indicating a very high degree of consistency, almost as marked for personality as it was for intelligence. For details his excellent account should be consulted.

In the context of a Darwinian framework, considering these dimensions as fundamental and hence biologically determined, one might expect that similar dimensions could also be found in the animal field. Chamove, Eysenck, and Harlow (1972) observed the social behaviour of Rhesus monkeys over a period of two years, rating that behaviour and intercorrelating the highly reliable behaviour so found, They discovered three major dimensions, bearing remarkable similarity to P, E and N, characterised by aggressive and hostile behaviour, sociable and playful behaviour, and fearful and anxious behaviour. Indeed, it seems difficult to think of any other major aggregations of behaviour patterns than these in the social intercourse between animals, or between humans. ·

In a long continued series of studies with rats, Garcia-Sevilla (1984) has attempted to demonstrate the importance of neuroticism and extraversion in rats, and the possibility of measuring these. Apart from interpreting and predicting behaviour patterns of this kind in tests such as the open-field situation, he and his colleagues carried out many studies to test the view that the behaviours observed were actually characteristic of extraverted or neurotic behaviour. While not without anomalies, on the whole these studies showed remarkable agreement between prediction and outcome, suggesting that we have here indeed the beginnings of very fruitful investigation of animal analogues of human personality. The third dimension, psychoticism, which is characterised by aggressive and hostile behaviour, has so often been the subject of animal investigation that there can be little doubt about its replication in this field also.

If there is any truth in the suggestion that there is a biological foundation for the observed patterns of behaviour, then it would surely seem to follow that genetic factors would have a powerful determining influence on individual differences along the lines of factors P, E and N. The early work of Newman, Freeman, and Holzinger (1937) give little evidence for strong genetic dispositions in this field, but their work was faulty both methodologically and statistically, and has been criticised in detail by Eysenck (1967). Eysenck (1956), Eysenck and Prell (1951), and Eaves and Eysenck (1975, 1977) have empirically demonstrated the great importance of genetic factors in accounting for individual differences in personality. Fulker (1981) and Eaves and Eysenck (1985) have given summaries of what is now a very large and growing literature.

Before summarising the major results, it is important to recognise certain changes that have taken place in the past dozen years or so. In the first place, methods of analysis have improved dramatically. Interest is no longer simply in the heritability of a given trait, but rather in the architecture of that trait, i.e., the contribution to the phenotypic variance of additive genetic material, dominance, assortative-mating, epistasis, etc. On the environmental side, a clear distinction is now made between within-family and between-family environmental variance, with suitable quantitative estimates of both. Finally, various types of interaction are considered and where possible quantified. We thus do not have simply a genetic model; the genetic model inevitably takes into account environmental and interactional factors as well as purely genetic ones, and within each category seeks to apportion the variance to different contributory factors.

In the second place, it has been found that very large numbers of twins and other groups are necessary in order to be able to test the fit of the data to a given model, and groups of 10,000 or 12,000 pairs of twins have now been studied in efforts to arrive at a better estimate of the various parameters in this field. In addition to MZ and DZ twin comparisons, we now have MZ twins reared in isolation, the study of adopted children, the study of family consanguinity, and other methods of empirical investigation and biometrical genetical analysis. Here we only have space of discuss the major findings.

First, and most important, is the fact that genetic factors contribute between one-half and two-thirds of the phenotypic variance; this is true equally of P, E and N. Thus, genetic factors are very much involved in the causation of individual differences and personality, and constitute the strongest single element. When it is realised that the measuring instruments are usually much less reliable than those used in intelligence testing, it will become clear that personality is determined almost as much by genetic factors as is intelligence, very much contrary to the original views of Newman, Freeman, and Holzinger (1937).

While in the importance of genetic factors for phenotypic differences personality resembles intelligence, there are also important differences. There is a high degree of assortative mating as far as intelligence is concerned, with like marrying like, but very little with respect to personality. Correlations are usually positive, but very low, and in general it may be said that the system of mating resembles panmixia with a considerable degree of closeness. This is unexpected and rather odd, but the data are pretty compelling.

Even more interesting and important from the psychological point of view, is the fact that environmental factors are almost entirely of the within-family kind, with practically no contribution at all of between-family environmental factors. This is exactly the opposite to what is found in the intelligence field, where between-family environmental factors are much more important than within-family environmental factors. In other words, as far as personality is concerned, the differences in upbringing, socio-economic status, educational facilities, etc. which distinguish one family from another exert no influence at all; environmental factors determining differences in personality are the accidental differences found as different children in the same family grow up, one contracting a disease, another one not, one finding a good teacher the other not, and one falling in love with a "good woman", another one not.

From the point of developmental theory this is a most important finding, as it rules out in one stroke the usual hypotheses advanced by child psychologists, psychiatrists and psychoanalysts, making parental treatment of the child responsible for observed differences. Clearly such differences in upbringing, whether in regard to toilet-training, weaning, or more direct socialising procedures, fall into the between-family environmental set of influences, and must hence be ruled out as determinants of individual differences in personality.

Granted, then, that biological determinants are relevant to the concept of individual differences in P, E and N, we may ask for another proof of the applicability of the notion of a paradigm in this field. If such a paradigm exists, then it would seem to require that the personality dimension singled out should have important social consequences, in a variety of different fields. This has indeed been found to be so. Personality differences are of great relevance in the field of abnormal and clinical psychology (Eysenck, 1973; Eysenck & Eysenck, 1976). Personality factors have been found to be of considerable relevance in the field of sexual behaviour and marital satisfaction (Eysenck, 1976b; Eysenck & Wakefield, 1981). Personality differences have been found to be of equal importance in relation to criminal and anti-social behaviour (Eysenck, 1977, 1985). In sport, too, personality differences have been found relevant (Eysenck, Nias, & Cox, 1982). This list could be extended indefinately, but it will suffice to indicate the relevance of personality factors to important social problems.

There are a number of ways in which personality has been found to be relevant to various other areas of social behaviour (Wilson, 1981), and these may just be listed in order to indicate the general area over which the influence of personality extends. Wilson lists the following: Affiliation and personal space; birth order; group interaction and social skill; speech pattern; expressive behaviour and person perception; expression control; field dependance; suggestibility; conflict handling; attraction; attitudes and values; recreational interests; occupational choice and aptitude; industrial performance; academic aptitude and achievement; drug use and abuse; and many more. It is clear that personality is intimately related to social psychology in all its manifestations.

Hitherto we have been dealing mainly with the descriptive side of personality research, although our analysis of the genetic determinance is already shading over into the causal sector. Causal hypotheses of a biological nature have been advanced in this field (e.g., Eysenck, 1967, 1981), and these have been followed up and tested along two different lines. On the one hand, psychophysiological experiments have tried to investigate directly the hypothesis advanced, such as that, extraversion is characterised by, and causally related to, low cortical arousal, itself induced by the sluggish activity of the reticular activating system. The large body of research that has resulted from this work cannot be reviewed here; an excellent summary will be found in Stelmack (1981). On the whole the data are undoubtedly supportive of the various theories in question, although obviously anomalies still remain to be cleared up by the puzzle-solving process of normal science. Indeed, it might be said to be one of the most attractive features of the paradigm that it generates a large number of specific hypotheses, each of which can be experimentally tested; few other personality theories have this advantage.

In addition to the physiological type of theory discussed by Stelmack, we also have a growing body of information regarding the relationship between personality and bodily secretions such as hormones, peptides, and enzymes. A good survey of this large literature is given by Zuckerman, Ballinger, and Post (1984). To take but one example, we may consider the enzyme MAO (monoamine oxidase), which is present in all tissues, including brain, with the highest brain concentration in the hypothalamus. Studies of humans have relied largely on measurement of MAO from blood platelets. It is generally found that high levels of MAO are correlated with high introversion, low levels with extraversion and sensation-seeking behaviour. Similar relations have been found in animal studies, where injections add another dimension to the possibilities of the investigation. The large literature leaves no doubt that MAO is very relevant indeed to behaviour normally classified as extraverted or sensation-seeking.

Hormones like testosterone and adrenalin have been found to be relevant to psychoticism and neuroticism, respectively, and peptides too, like Vasopressin, ACTH, and the endogenous opiates have all been related to behaviour patterns associated with P, E and N. This whole area of research promises to be of particular interest now that the biological bases of personality are beginning to be investigated and understood.

Last but not least, we must look at laboratory experimental studies which have been carried out to test predications from the model. These are important from the causal point of view as well because they suggest ways in which the biological diathesis can interact with the environment to produce the observed types of behaviour. Thus, for instance, Eysenck's (1976) hypothesis that the high arousal of the introvert would make Pavlovian conditioning easier and quicker for him than for the low-arousal extravert, allows us to integrate these personality differences with social behaviour probably to a large extent determined by conditioning, such as sexual behaviour, neurotic behaviour, and anti-social behaviour (Eysenck, 1973, 1976b, 1977). There is now a very large body of literature on conditioning, learning, perception, vigilance, memory, and many other areas of experimental psychology (Eysenck, 1976a), and the great majority of predictions in this field have been borne out by the resulting experimental studies. This gives considerable "body" to the general theory and suggests that it does indeed constitute a paradigm in the traditional sense of the word.

It is of course inevitable that many anomalies should remain, but some of these at least have been found to be explainable by perfectly general laws which are well-known in experimental psychology. To take but one example, Pavlov's law of transmarginal inhibition, or protective inhibition, also sometimes known as the Yerkes-Dodson law, tells us that increases in the strength of a given stimulus are followed by increases in the strength of the reaction only up to a certain point, beyond which the regression resembles an inverted U and responses become weaker. If we apply this to the statement that introverts, should show stronger and quicker conditioning than extraverts, we would have to add that this would only be true with relatively weak stimuli; with very strong such stimuli we might get a reversal, because of the intervention of the law of transmarginal inhibition. Such a reversal has indeed been found experimentally (Eysenck & Eysenck, 1985). Appeal to the law of transmarginal inhibition is not motivated by an attempt to explain away awkward findings; the law has been found to operate in a predictable manner in many different circumstances, and in relation to many different types of experimental situations.

Another problem that always confronts anyone experimenting with human (or even animal) subjects is the problem of defining the stimulus. As an example, discussed in some detail elsewhere (Eysenck, 1981), consider the fact that some twenty years ago Eysenck postulated (and found) that eye-blink conditioning was correlated with introversion, but not with neuroticism, whereas Spence postulated, and found, that eye-blink conditioning was correlated with neuroticism but not with introversion! For several years both sides accumulated evidence of an experimental nature favouring their stand, without being able to explain the fact that the other side obtained exactly opposite results. The situation was finally clarified by Gregory Kimble, who paid a visit to Spence's laboratory in order to discover any possible differences in procedure that might be responsible. It turned out that while Eysenck (like all other experimentalists in this field) tried his best to reduce the anxiety of subjects by explaining patiently that they would not be exposed to electric shocks or any other painful stimuli, reassured them on all other points of doubt, and kept all the experimental machinery out of sight, Spence did exactly the opposite, increasing the anxiety of his subjects by having all the experimental machinery in the same room as the subject, not giving him any explanations or reassurances, and in all ways raising rather than lowering his anxiety level (Eysenck, 1981).

What happened, accordingly, is that the complex of stimuli (CS, UCS, environmental variables, etc.) were anxiety provoking in Spence's subjects, so that differences in neuroticism played a very important part in their reactions, and swamped the much smaller differences in arousal produced by extraversion-introversion. Eysenck, on the other hand, experimentally ruled out differences in neuroticism determining the conditioning behaviour of the subjects by reducing anxiety to a very low level, so that it would not influence the subject's arousal. These manipulations of the subject's anxiety level did not find their way into print, so that the reader was faced with an apparent contradiction which was incapable of reconciliation until the true facts of the situation were understood.

The many other ways in which anomalies may arise, and a careful theoretical analysis of the situation, including its meaning for the subject, will also be a requisite of any attempt to test deductions from the theory. Even when great care is taken, however, anomalies will undoubtedly remain, and it will be the task of normal science, i.e., puzzle-solving of the usual kind, to try and demonstrate the reasons for these anomalies, and if possible make them reducible to agreement with theory. But even of this should prove impossible, and the remaining anomalies enforce a Kuhnian revolution, this would in no way diminish the claims of the three-factor models to occupy a paradigmatic place in the development of personality theory. It is generally agreed that Dalton was the founder of modern chemistry, with his postulation of an atomic theory which constituted a definite paradigm in that science. Yet all that Dalton said about atoms - apart from the bare fact of their existence, which wasn't novel - was wrong. Atoms are not indestructible, as he thought; atoms of the same element can have very different weights (isotopes), and atoms need not combine in simple whole-number ratios, as he believed. The point about a paradigm, a model, or a wide-ranging theory, is not that it should be entirely or even largely correct; it is, rather, as Lakatos (1970) pointed out, that we should be dealing with a progressive rather than a degenerative research programme. A degenerative research programme, like the Freudian, has constantly to seek for more and more remote reasons for the failure of its predictions; progressive research programmes have a large body of positive results to show, and such explanations as may be forthcoming for anomalous results can be integrated with the theory, and advance it further. This, I would like to suggest, is the essence of a paradigm in science, and by that token, as well as by those listed above, the three-factor model of personality may claim to being a paradigm in the Kuhnian sense.

REFERENCES

Barnes, B. (1982). *T.S. Kuhn and social science*. London: Macmillan.
Barrett, P., & Eysenck, S. (1984). The assessment of personality factors across 25 countries. *Personality and Individual Differences, 5*, 615-632.
Chamove, A.S., Eysenck, H.J., & Harlow, H.P. (1972). Personality in monkeys: Factor analysis of rhesus social behaviour. *Quarterly Journal of Experimental Psychology, 24*, 496-564.
Conley, J.J. (1984). The hierarchy of consistency: A review and model of longitudinal findings on adult individual differences in intelligence, personality and self-opinion. *Personality and Individual Differences, 5*, 11-26.

Eaves, L., & Eysenck, H.J. (1975). The nature of extraversion: A genetical analysis. *Journal of Personality and Social Psychology, 32,* 102-112.

Eaves, L., & Eysenck, H.J. (1977). A genotype-environmental model for psychoticism. *Advances in Behaviour Research and Therapy, 1,* 5-26.

Eaves, L., & Eysenck, H.J. (1985). *The genetics of personality.* New York: Academic Press.

Eysenck, H.J. (1956). The inheritance of extraversion-introversion. *Acta Psychologica, 12,* 95-110.

Eysenck, H.J. (1967). *The biological basis of personality.* Springfield: C.C. Thomas.

Eysenck, H.J. (Ed.). (1973). *Handbook of abnormal psychology.* London: Pitman.

Eysenck, H.J. (Ed.). (1976a). *The measurement of personality.* Lancaster: MTP.

Eysenck, H.J. (1976b). *Sex and personality.* London: Open Books.

Eysenck, H.J. (1977). *Crime and personality.* London: Palladin.

Eysenck, H.J. (Ed.). (1981). *A model for personality.* Berlin-Heidelberg-New York: Springer.

Eysenck, H.J. (1983). Is there a paradigm in personality research? *Journal of Research in Personality, 17,* 369-397.

Eysenck, H.J. (1985). Personality theory and the problem of criminality. In B. McGurk, D. Thornton & M. Williams (Eds.), *Theory and practice: Applying psychology to imprisonment.* London: H.M.S.O.

Eysenck, H.J., & Eysenck, M.W. (1985). *Personality and individual differences.* New York: Plenum Press.

Eysenck, H.J., & Eysenck, S.B.G. (1975). *Manual of the Eysenck Personality Questionnaire.* London: Hodder & Stoughton. San Diego: DIGITS.

Eysenck, H.J., & Eysenck, S.B.G. (1976). *Psychoticism as a dimension of personality.* London: Hodder & Stoughton.

Eysenck, H.J., & Prell, D.B. (1951). The inheritance of neuroticism: An experimental study. *Journal of Mental Science, 97,* 441-465.

Eysenck, H.J., & Wakefield, J.A. (1981). Psychological factors as predictors of marital satisfaction. *Advances in Behaviour Research and Therapy, 3,* 151-192.

Eysenck, H.J., Nias, D., & Cox, D.N. (1982) Sport and personality. *Advances in Behaviour Research and Therapy, 1,* 1-56.

Fulker, D.W. (1981). The genetic and environmental architecture of psychoticism, extraversion and neuroticism. In H.J. Eysenck (Ed.), *A Model for Personality* (pp. 88-122). Berlin-Heidelberg-New York: Springer.

Garcia-Sevilla, L. (1984). Extraversion and neuroticism in rats. *Personality and Individual Differences, 5,* 511-532.

Kuhn, T.S. (1962). *The structure of scientific revolutions.* Chicago: University of Chicago Press.

Kuhn, T.S. (1970). *The structure of scientific revolutions.* Chicago: University of Chicago Press.

Kuhn, T.S. (1974). Second thoughts on paradigms. In F. Suppe (Ed.), *The structure of scientific theories* (pp. 459–482). London: University of Illinois Press.

Lakatos, I. (1970). Falsification and the methodology of scientific research programmes. In I. Lakatos & A. Musgrave (Eds.), *Criticism and the growth of knowledge* (pp. 91–196). New York: Cambridge University Press.

Newman, H.H., Freeman, F.N., & Holzinger, K.J. (1937). *Twins.* Chicago: University Press.

Royce, J.R., & Powell, A. (1983). *Theory of personality and individual differences: Factors, systems, and processes.* Englewood Cliffs, NJ: Prentice-Hall.

Stelmack, R.M. (1981). The psychophysiology of extraversion and neuroticism. In H.J. Eysenck (Ed.), *A model for personality.* Berlin-Heidelberg-New York: Springer.

Wilson, G.D. (1981). Personality, and social behaviour. In H.J. Eysenck (Ed.), *A model for personality* (pp. 210-245). Berlin-Heidelberg-New York: Springer.

Zuckerman, M., Ballinger, J., & Post, R. (1984). The neurobiology of some dimensions of personality. *International Review of Neurobiology, 25,* 391-436.

TEMPERAMENTAL TRAITS AND STRATEGIES OF DECISION-MAKING IN GAMBLING*

by

Ryszard Przymusiński
Academy of Catholic Theology, Warsaw
Poland

and

Jan Strelau
University of Warsaw
Poland

In accordance with the regulative theory of temperament developed by Strelau (1974, 1983a, 1983b) and his students (e.g., Eliasz, 1981; Klonowicz, 1984), there exists a given relation between *reactivity* and *activity* which are both regarded as temperamental traits. Reactivity, conceived as a property responsible for a relatively stable intensity of response to stimuli, co-determines the individual's activity. The latter, regarded as a regulator of stimulation need, is characterized by the amount and range of actions undertaken which have a given stimulatory value.

Reactivity, which reflects to some degree the Pavlovian strength of the nervous system, co-determines sensitivity and the organism's endurance. The weaker the stimulus which elicits a perceptible response (the higher the sensitivity) and the weaker the stimulus which starts with lower efficiency (the lower the endurance) the higher the reactivity. Conversely, a low-reactive person is marked by low sensitivity and high endurance.

It has been proved in several of our studies that high-reactive individuals, who have low need for stimulation in order to maintain an optimal level of activation, display a low level of activity and vice versa. Low-reactive individuals are characterized by a high level of activity (Strelau, 1983a). This relationship holds true if the role of activity is to supply the individual with stimulation (see Matysiak, 1980). Activity may be regarded as a direct *and* non-direct source of stimulation (see for details Strelau, 1983a). Among other things, the individual regulates his/her need for stimulation by choosing activities that are more or less stimulating in themselves, mostly because of different degrees of risk, threat, difficulty, etc. involved.

Examining the relation between reactivity and activity we will limit ourselves in this chapter to the *strategies of behaviour,* by which the individual copes with tasks and everyday situations. It follows from our theory that high-reactive individuals should be inclined to develop relatively unstimulating strategies of behaviour. In turn, low-reactive

---

*) The paper is based on R. Przymusiński's (1982) Ph.D. thesis supervised by J. Strelau. The latter prepared the manuscript during his 1983/84 fellowship at the Netherlands Institute for Advanced Study in the Humanities and Social Sciences (NIAS).

individuals will develop strategies of behaviour which ensure stimulation of high intensity. This hypothesis has been proved in our laboratory by Eliasz (1973) who studied the relation between reactivity and the style of self-regulation (active vs. passive) regarded here as a strategy of behaviour.

Probably one of the best examples of the strategies of behaviour which might be considered as a source of stimulation is the way in which individuals behave in decision-making situations. It has been stated long ago that there exist individual differences in strategies of decision-making. This is expressed, among other things, in the fact that some individuals prefer risk whereas others prefer probability in decision-making in gambling (e.g., Cameron & Myers, 1966; Edwards, 1953; Kozielecki, 1982; Van Der Meer, 1963). According to our hypothesis a risky situation causes emotional tension which has its physiological correlates in a high level of arousal, thus hightening the stimulatory value of the situation.

High-reactive individuals will avoid situations which evoke strong emotional tension, i.e., they avoid risk. This in turn provides for the development of a risk-avoidance strategy of action. The opposite occurs in individuals with a low level of reactivity. For these individuals the situation of risk is a desirable one because of its high stimulative value. This results in the development of a risky strategy of action. The data collected in an experiment conducted in our laboratory by Kozłowski (1977), where reactivity and neuroticism were related to the strategy of decision-making in gambling, support our hypothesis. Also data presented by Zuckerman (1979) show that a risky strategy in gambling is positively correlated with sensation seeking measured by the Sensation Seeking Scale (SSS).

The idea to relate preferences in decision-making to personality traits is not new and was introduced almost thirty years ago by Atkinson (1957), who studied the interrelations between decision-making and individual differences in motivation (see also Messick & McClintock, 1968). Also other traits have been related to strategies of decision-making in risk-taking situations. Attention has been paid, for example, to the system of value (Scodel, Ratoosh, & Minas, 1960), to personality traits as measured by the Edwards Personality Schedule (Cameron & Myers, 1966), to cognitive styles (Nosal, 1984; Wright & Phillips, 1984), extraversion-introversion (e.g., Vestewig, 1977), and personality factors as measured by Cattell's 16PF questionnaire (e.g., Kozielecki, 1982). Most of the studies provide, however, equivocal results.

The present study is based on the assumption that the strategy of decision-making in risky situations is mainly co-determined by personality traits which are related to the need of stimulation. These traits refer often to biological correlates, especially to the level of arousal. Generally speaking one may say that they belong to the category of temperament (see Strelau, 1982), and reactivity, as mentioned above, should be regarded as one of them. However, in the present study we increased the number of traits to 30 in order to examine which of them play a role in regulating the stimulatory value of risk-taking situations.

On the basis of these considerations we adopted the following hypothesis: Individuals who prefer risk over probability in decision-making in gambling situations (risk-takers) are characterized by temperamental traits which refer to a high demand of stimulation. In individuals who prefer in the same situations probability over risk (risk-avoiders) there is a dominance of temperamental traits which express a low need for stimulation.

METHOD

Subjects

Altogether 267 subjects were selected from three different high-schools (122 males and 145 females aged from 17 to 21 years) in order to take part in this experiment. This number decreased to 211 subjects (101 males and 110 females) after incomplete questionnaires were disregarded. The selection of individuals with consistent preferences in strategies of decision-making meant that 84 more subjects were eliminated from further studies. Thus, from a remaining number of 127 subjects, 40 individuals were assigned as risk-takers and 42 individuals as risk-avoiders.

Measurement of Temperamental Traits

The first stage of our study consisted in measuring the traits of temperament. For this purpose the following inventories have been administered: Eysenck's Maudsley Personality Inventory (MPI), Spielberger's State-Trait Anxiety Inventory (STAI), Thurstone Temperament Schedule (TTS), Strelau Temperament Inventory (STI), and Cattell's Sixteen Personality Factor Questionnaire (16PF). All of them -- except the STI -- are well-known and do not need to be described here. They have been adapted to Polish conditions[1]. The STI has been fully described recently for the English speaking reader (see Strelau, 1983a). The STI contains 134 items and is composed on three scales: Strength of Excitation (44 items), Strength of Inhibition (44 items) and Mobility of Nervous Processes (46 items). The quotient of strength of excitation index divided by the strength of inhibition index is used as the measure of the balance (equilibrium) of nervous processes.

Cattell's 16PF is in fact aimed at measuring personality traits such as assertative ego, general inhibition, hypomanic temperament, exuberance, cortertia, capacity to mobilize vs. regression and exvia vs. invia which seem to have much in common with the Pavlovian nervous system properties, especially with strength of the nervous system (see Cattell, 1972). This hypothesis has been studied with a negative result by Orlebeke (1972).

---

[1] The MPI and TTS have been adapted by Choynowski and his co-workers from the Psychometric Laboratory at the Polish Academy of Sciences (see Choynowski, 1977). The MPI is until now the only Eysenck inventory adapted and standardized for the Polish population. The description of the Polish version of the 16PF has been presented by Nowakowska (1970) and that of the STAI by Sosnowski and Wrześniewski (1983).

Many other dimensions recognized as being related to temperament
(see Strelau, 1982) could be included into our study, as for example,
sensation seeking, impulsivity, the augmenting-reducing dimension,
etc. For technical reasons (e.g., the Zuckerman's SSS was not adapted
at that time to Polish conditions) we limited the number of
temperamental personality variables to 30 (see Table 1).

The subjects completed each inventory during a separate meeting,
except the STAI and MPI both of which were administered together.
The sequence of applicated inventories was randomized. Subjects who
scored high on the Lie-scale (taken from the MPI) and/or from whom
incomplete inventory data were obtained did not take part in further
research.

Estimation of Risk vs. Probability Preferences in Gambling

The next stage of the experiment was aimed at estimating the strategy
of decision-making in gambling situations. For this purpose five
"hazardous" games were used. All of them were of the same type and
had a similar structure. In all of the games the subject had to choose
one of the seven alternatives with probabilities of winning, ranging
from 1/8 to 7/8. The number of points to be won varied in each game
from 215 (7/8 probability of winning) to 1500 (1/8 probability of
winning). This procedure allowed a common indicator to be applied to
the distribution of choices made by subjects. The skew coefficient
(SC)[1] which expresses the preference with respect to probabilities was
used as the measure of the subjects' preferences. Five games were
used in the following order:

(1) *Match-boxes* -- matches which differed in colour from the other
    ones were hidden in one of the eight boxes and the subjects
    were asked to guess in which by pointing to 1, 2, 3, 4, 5, 6,
    or 7 boxes;

(2) *Roulette* -- players could bet on any one of the seven sections
    varying in width;

(3) *Cards* -- subjects were asked to guess which one of the eight
    cards was the Queen of Spades;

(4) *Balls* -- four urns contained 80 balls in two colours of varying
    proportion for each colour; subjects were asked to bet on one
    of the eight colours and than to draw a ball from one of the
    urns;

(5) *Ball-boxes* -- balls of white colour were hidden in all of the
    boxes except one which contained a black ball; subjects were
    asked to guess in which of the boxes was the black ball.

To eliminate the influence of success or failure the subjects were
asked to make the five choices one after the other. In order to
measure the preference in strategies of decision-making regarded as an
expression of trait-behaviour, the authors did not make use of the
traditional paradigm in this type of study (i.e., measuring the
dynamics of risk-taking behaviour under success or failure). On the
basis of five choices without feedback, it was believed that it was

---

[1]) The skew coefficient for which the formula is $SC = 1 - 2p/\sqrt{p(1-p)}$ was taken from
Kozielecki (1982).

possible to estimate the consistency of risk-taking behaviour understood as a relatively stable tendency (preference).

Information about the result obtained by each individual was provided after the experiment had finished. To arrange a situation of competition typical for "hazardous" games two subjects took part in each game. No information was given to the subject about the partner's choice. The subject who won more points in the five games taken together was the winner and he/she got a small monetary payment.

Only subjects with consistent choices were considered for further analysis[1]. As it was believed that only consistent choices express preferences. The relation between individual and group scores of the SD from the mean SC-scores was used as the criterion of consistency. These subjects were regarded as expressing clear-cut preferences in decision-making whose SD was smaller than the mean SD for the whole group.

The next step consisted in separating two groups of individuals who differed evidently in strategies of decision-making in gambling. Taking as a criterion the mean skew coefficient (SC = .33) and its standard deviation (SD = .37), individuals who scored higher than .33 + SD/2 (SC = .515) have been considered as preferring low probability, i.e., risk (risk-takers). Individuals whose score was below .33 - SD/2 (SC = .145) were assigned to the group which prefers high probability (risk-avoiders).

RESULTS

Traits which Distinguish Risk-Takers from Risk-Avoiders

The first question concerns whether there exist differences between risk-takers and risk-avoiders in traits measured in this study. For this purpose the arithmetic means as well as variances of inventory scores obtained in both groups separately have been compared. Eight of the 30 traits revealed significant differences. The traits which distinguish risk-takers from risk-avoiders are presented in Table 2.

Six of the traits in which risk-takers had higher scores than risk-avoiders suggest strongly that they have a common denominator which refers to the need for stimulation. This hypothesis is supported by data collected in our laboratory (see Strelau & Terelak, 1974). They show that strength of excitation[2], impulsiveness, and dominance are all loading on one factor related to the energetic level of behaviour.

---

[1] The inconsistent subjects for reasons given below were not considered for further analysis. In another study (Przymusiński, 1982) it has been shown that such characteristics as intelligence (measured by the Raven's Progressive Matrices), E, O and Q_1 factors from Cattell's 16PF and trait-anxiety (as measured by the STAI) differentiated both consistent and inconsistent groups.

[2] It has to be stated that the *Strength of Excitation* scale from the STI is aimed to measure reactivity. The higher the score the lower the reactivity (the stronger the nervous system). The justification of this procedure has been presented in details elsewhere (Strelau, 1983a).

R. Przymusiński/J. Strelau

TABLE 1: *Differences between Risk-Avoiders ($N_1 = 42$) and Risk-Takers ($N_2 = 40$) in temperamental Personality Traits*

Traits	σ^2_1	σ^2_2	F	M_1	M_2	t
STAI						
Trait-anxiety (A)	57.39	39.58	1.450	43.8	42.9	0.189
MPI						
Neuroticism (N)	120.39	65.71	1.832[b]	25.8	29.0	1.499
Extraversion (E)	74.27	71.22	1.043	29.7	31.2	0.807
STI						
Strength of E (SE)	124.86	152.58	1.222	47.7	56.5	3.327[c]
Strength of I (SI)	230.39	229.73	1.003	56.2	58.9	0.790
Balance of NP (B)	0.15	0.75	5.130[c]	0.9	1.1	1.370[b]
Mobility of NP (M)	134.93	77.81	1.734[b]	54.4	60.0	2.480[b]
TTS						
Active (A)	34.77	36.20	1.041	23.7	25.3	1.209[b]
Vigorous (V)	36.19	52.82	1.460	22.2	25.5	2.205[b]
Impulsive (I)	46.69	41.81	1.117	24.4	27.6	2.149
Dominant (D)	64.16	85.79	1.337	19.1	22.0	1.470
Emotionally stable (E)	42.30	50.10	1.184	17.5	16.3	0.797
Sociable (S)	53.04	41.00	1.294	26.2	28.4	1.441
Reflective (R)	32.68	29.10	1.123	21.6	22.3	0.513
16PF						
Affectothymia (A)	49.26	40.42	1.219	19.9	19.9	0.020
Intelligence (B)	9.06	6.63	1.367	14.8	14.8	0.975[b]
Ego strength (C)	29.37	30.14	1.100	19.1	21.8	2.227[b]
Dominance (E)	23.45	30.43	1.298	17.5	19.6	1.801[a]
Surgency (F)	22.70	29.05	1.280	24.0	25.4	1.233
Superego strength (G)	37.85	44.33	1.171	20.5	20.4	0.082
Parmia (H)	67.73	82.28	1.215	21.1	23.4	1.150
Premsia (I)	31.44	28.93	1.087	21.6	20.3	1.030[b]
Paranoid suspicion (L)	11.35	11.48	1.012	23.4	21.7	2.265[b]
Autia (M)	31.38	28.03	1.120	17.6	16.3	1.060
Shrewdness (N)	18.12	19.71	1.088	21.3	21.2	0.089
Guilt proneness (O)	72.83	56.98	1.278	20.3	17.3	1.677[a]
Radicalism (Q_1)	33.86	23.40	1.447	21.1	21.7	0.474
Self-sufficiency (Q_2)	31.29	28.00	1.118	19.8	18.8	0.815
Self-sentiment (Q_3)	39.43	28.35	1.391[b]	19.6	21.5	1.443
Ergic tension (Q_4)	55.94	30.32	1.845[b]	20.2	18.9	0.919

a: $\alpha < 0.10$
b: $\alpha < 0.05$
c: $\alpha < 0.01$

TABLE 2: *Temperamental Traits which differentiate Risk-Takers and Risk-Avoiders*

Trait	Inventory	Risk-takers	Risk-avoiders
Strength of excitation (SE)	STI	+	−
Mobility of NS (M)	STI	+	−
Vigorous (V)	TTS	+	−
Impulsive (I)	TTS	+	−
Ego strength (C)	16PF	+	−
Dominance (E)	16PF	+	−
Paranoid suspicion (L)	16PF	−	+
Guilt proneness (O)	16PF	−	+

TABLE 3: *Intercorrelations of Temperamental Traits which Differentiate Risk-Taking Decisions*

Traits	SE	M	V	I	C	E	L
M	0.614						
V	0.466	0.417					
I	0.567	0.598	0.446				
C	0.534	0.267	0.235	0.309			
E	0.524	0.352	0.305	0.380	0.258		
L	−0.189	−0.159	−0.025	−0.228	−0.260	−0.033	
O	−0.555	−0.305	−0.231	−0.360	−0.704	−0.410	−0.330

For the meaning of symbols see Table 2.

TABLE 4: *Centroid Factor Matrix of Temperament Traits which Differentiate Risk-Taking Decisions*

Traits	Factor loadings	
	Factor I	Factor II
SE	0.782	0.352
M	0.728	0.098
V	0.631	−0.112
I	0.702	0.187
C	0.408	0.581
E	0.577	0.130
L	−0.071	−0.482
O	−0.465	−0.661

For the meaning of symbols see Table 2.

The Configuration of Discriminating Traits

In order to examine whether there exist an interrelation among the traits which differentiate individuals with different strategies of decision-making we intercorrelated the eight discriminating traits of all 211 individuals. As seen from Table 3 all of the traits except paranoid suspicion correlated with each other significantly. It is striking that all of the traits correlated positively with each other expect paranoid suspicion and guilt proneness which -- being positively correlated -- correlated negatively with all the other traits. This is consistent with the results presented in Table 2.

Thereafter we factor analysed the data by means of the centroid method. This resulted in two separate factors. The factor loadings are displayed in Table 4.

Factor I had the highest factor loadings on strength of excitation (reactivity), mobility of the nervous system, impulsivity, vigorousness, and dominance. This is in concordance with the former results. Factor II comprises ego strength and both guilt proneness and paranoid suspicion.

In summary it has to be said that the traits which differentiate risk-takers from risk-avoiders are strongly related to each other. Taking into account the configuration of traits to be found in Factor I, one may conclude that their common denominator consists in the fact that they are related to the *energetic level of behaviour* and to given aspects of *stimulation need*. As regards Factor II the configuration of ego strength with negative scores in guilt proneness and paranoid suspicion suggests that *emotional stability* is the phenomenon linking these traits together.

DISCUSSION

The eight traits in which risk-takers differ from risk-avoiders derive from three different inventories. The strength of excitation, which we prefer to call reactivity, as well as the mobility of nervous processes (in fact mobility of behaviour -- see Strelau, 1983a) are taken from the STI. It has been shown many times (Carlier, 1985; Mangan, 1982; Strelau, 1983a) that both of these traits are strongly correlated and individuals with low reactivity (high score on the Strength of Excitation scale) as well as with high mobility are regarded as stimulation seekers. The content analysis of vigorousness and impulsiveness which have been measured by the TTS inventory goes into the same direction which suggests that individuals who score high on these traits are stimulation seekers. The data collected in our laboratory show that these traits differentiate a stress-resistant group from a non-stress-resistant group in a competition situation (Strelau, 1983a). There is one more trait -- dominance, measured by the 16PF -- which differentiates the risk-takers from the risk-avoiders and which is included in Factor I. If we consider that high dominance is defined by Cattell as "assertive, independent, confident, and stubborn behavior" (1965, p. 369) than it is easy to see why this trait should be a facet of stimulation seeking.

Strangely enough, extraversion which correlates positively with sensation seeking (Eysenck & Zuckerman, 1970; Zuckerman, 1979) as well as with strength of excitation and mobility of the nervous system (Strelau, 1983a), does not differentiate the groups under investigation. This fact needs further examination.

The three remaining discriminatory traits which derive from Cattell's 16PF questionnaire loaded on Factor II. The positive sign of ego strength together with negative signs of both paranoid suspicion and guilt proneness suggests a configuration of traits linked to emotional stability. High scores in paranoid suspicion and in guilt proneness in risk-avoiders as compared with risk-takers and lower scores in ego strength in the former group, suggest that neuroticism is an important variable which influences certain gambling strategies.

The neuroticism dimension, however, as measured by the MPI did not differentiate risk-takers from risk-avoiders. It is possible, that both factors are relevant to gambling. The experiment conducted by Kozłowski (1977), who related the strategy of decision-making in gambling to the combination of two traits -- reactivity and neuroticism -- seems to support our hypothesis. It has been shown in this study that among high-reactive individuals with high scores on neuroticism there is a dominance of risk-avoiders over risk-takers. The opposite is true in the group with low reactivity together with low neuroticism. The number of risk-takers was in this group significantly larger than the number of risk-avoiders. To check whether this regularity may be replicated we analyzed the data from this point of view. From the group of 127 subjects with consistent preferences in decision-making strategies those individuals were selected who obtained high or low scores in both reactivity (measured by the STI) and neuroticism (measured by the MPI)[1].

As seen from Table 5 in the four groups, which result from the possible combinations of high and low scores in both of the dimensions, the distribution of the number of risk-takers and risk-avoiders is to some degree similar to this which was found by Kozłowski. However, the group with low-reactive and low-neurotic (rn) individuals included approximately the same number of risk-takers and risk-avoiders but the dominance of risk-avoiders in the high-reactive and high-neurotic group (RN) was evident.

It is possible that the gambling situation arranged in our experiment had a stimulation threshold to which the high-reactive individuals with a high level of neuroticism were especially sensitive. It has been shown elsewhere (Eliasz, 1973; Strelau, 1983a) that high-reactive individuals which are at the same time high-neurotic have a low need for stimulation. The high level of activation being typical for these individuals meant that the stimulatory value of gambling was too high in order to assess risk as a desired response. This may explain why they preferred the probability strategy of decision-making. This hypothesis is in agreement with the model of risk-taking for individuals differing in sensation seeking and anxiety presented by Zuckerman (1979).

The question must be raised as to the stimulatory value of the

---

[1] As the criterion for selecting high- vs. low-reactive subjects the quartile deviation was used; in case of neuroticism subjects below and above the median were regarded as having low or high neuroticism.

TABLE 5: *Distribution of Risk-Takers and Risk-Avoiders in Groups Differing in Demand of Stimulation*

Stimulation demand	Risk-takers	Risk-avoiders	Σ
(1) rn	7	6	13
(2) rN	12	5	17
(3) Rn	6	12	18
(4) RN	2	12	14
Σ	27	35	62

$\chi^2 = 11.257$ $\qquad$ $\alpha < 0.02$

(1) = Group with high demand for stimulation (low reactivity - r, and low neuroticism - n)

(4) = Group with low demand for stimulation (high reactivity - R, and high neuroticism - N)

(2) and (3) = Intermediate groups.

gambling situation in this experiment. Was risk-taking in the five "hazardous" games highly stimulating or not? The mean skew coefficient, which theoretically should be about zero, had a value of SC = .33 which implies that the distribution of scores is biased in the direction of risk-taking. This might be interpreted by the fact that the subjects, in general, did not perceive this situation as risky.

In order to discover what the interrelations are between temperamental traits related to stimulation seeking and activity expressed in the strategies of gambling decision-making further studies are needed.

REFERENCES

Atkinson, J.W. (1957). Motivational determinants of risk-taking behavior. *Psychological Review, 64,* 359-372.

Cameron, B., & Myers, J. (1966). Some personality correlates of risk taking. *Journal of General Psychology, 74,* 51-60.

Carlier, M. (1985). Factor analysis of Strelau's questionnaire and an attempt to validate some of the factors. In J. Strelau, F.H. Farley, & A. Gale (Eds.), *The biological bases of personality and behavior: Vol. 1. Theories, measurement techniques and development.* Washington: Hemisphere Publishing Corporation.

Cattell, R.B. (1965). *The scientific analysis of personality.* Harmondsworth: Penguin Books.

Cattell, R.B. (1972). The interpretation of Pavlov's typology and the arousal concept, in replicated trait and state factors. In V.D. Nebylitsyn & J.A. Gray (Eds.), *Biological bases of individual behavior* (pp. 141-164). New York: Academic Press.

Choynowski, M. (Ed.). (1977). *Prodręcznik do "Inwentarzo Osobowości" H.J. Eysencka.* [Manual of H.J. Eysenck's "Personality Inventory"]. Warszawa: Państwowe Wydawnictwo Naukowe.
Edwards, W. (1953). Probability preferences in gambling. *American Journal of Psychology, 66,* 349-364.
Eliasz, A. (1973). Temperamental traits and reaction preferences depending on stimulation load. *Polish Psychological Bulletin, 4,* 103-114.
Eliasz, A. (1981). *Temperament a system regulacji stymulacji* [Temperament and the system of regulation of stimulation]. Warszawa: Państwowe Wydawnictwo Naukowe.
Eysenck, S.B.G., & Zuckerman, M. (1970). The relationship between sensation seeking and Eysenck's dimensions of personality. *British Journal of Psychology, 69,* 483-487.
Klonowicz, T. (1984). *Reaktywność a funkcjonowanie człowieka w różnych warunkach stymulacyjnych* [Reactivity and human functioning in situations of different stimulatory value]. Wrocław: Ossolineum.
Kozielecki, J. (1982). *Psychological decision theory.* Dordrecht: Reidel.
Kozłowski, C. (1977). Demand for stimulation and probability preferences in gambling decisions. *Polish Psychological Bulletin, 8,* 67-73.
Mangan, G.L. (1982). *The biology of human conduct.* Oxford: Pergamon Press.
Matysiak, J. (1980). *Różnice indywidualne w zachowaniu zwierząt w świetle koncepcji zapotrzebowania na stymulację* [Individual differences in animal behaviour regarded from the point of view of stimulation need]. Wrocław: Ossolineum.
Messick, D.M., & Mc Clintock, C.G. (1968). Motivational basis of choice in experimental games. *Journal of Experimental and Social Psychology, 4,* 1-25.
Nosal, C.S. (1984). Cognitive styles and probabilistic thinking indices. *Polish Psychological Bulletin, 15,* 31-40.
Nowakowska, M. (1970). Polska adaptacja 16-czynnikowego Kwestionariusza Osobowości R.B. Cattella. [Polish adaptation of R.B. Cattell's 16 F Personality Questionnaire]. *Psychologia Wychowawcza, 13,* 478-500.
Orlebeke, J.F. (1972). *Aktivering, extraversie en sterkte van het zenuwstelsel* [Activation, extraversion, and strength of the nervous system]. Assen: Van Gorcum and Comp.
Przymusiński, R. (1982). *Rola cech indywidualnych decydentów w preferencjach dotyczących wyboru prawdopodobieństwa* [The role of individual traits of decision-makers in preferences of probability choice]. Unpublished doctoral dissertation. University of Warsaw, Warsaw.
Scodel, A., Ratoosh, P.R., & Minas, J.S. (1960). Some personality correlates of decision making under conditions of risk. In D. Willner (Ed.), *Decisions, values and groups.* New York: Pergamon Press.
Sosnowski, T., & Wrześniewski, K. (1983). Polska adaptacja inwentarza STAI do badania stanu i cechy leku [Polish adaptation of the STAI inventory aimed at studying state and trait anxiety]. *Przeglad Psychologiczny, 26,* 393-412.

Strelau, J. (1974). Temperament as an expression of energy level and temporal features of behavior. *Polish Psychological Bulletin, 5,* 119–127.

Strelau, J. (1982). Biological determined dimensions of personality or temperament? *Personality and Individual Differences, 3,* 355–360.

Strelau, J. (1983a). *Temperament – personality – activity.* London: Academic Press.

Strelau, J. (1983b). A regulative theory of temperament. *Australian Journal of Psychology, 35,* 305–317.

Strelau, J., & Terelak, J. (1974). The alpha-index in relation to temperamental traits. *Studia Psychologica, 16,* 40–50.

Van Der Meer, H.C. (1963). Deicision-making: The influence of probability preference, variance preference and expected value on strategy in gambling. *Acta Psychologica, 21,* 231–259.

Vestewig, R.E. (1977). Extraversion and risk preference in portfolio theory. *Journal of Psychology, 97,* 237–245.

Wright, G.N., & Phillips, L.D. (1984). Decison-making: Cognitive style or task-related behaviour? In H. Bonarius, G. Van Heck, & N. Smid (Eds.), *Personality psychology in Europe: Theoretical and empirical developments* (pp. 287–300). Lisse: Swets & Zeitlinger.

Zuckerman, M. (1979). *Sensation seeking: Beyond the optimal level of arousal.* Hillsdale, NJ: Erlbaum.

PART VI

PRECONSCIOUS PERCEPTUAL PROCESSES
IN PERSONALITY FUNCTIONING

SUBLIMINAL PERCEPTION AND MICROGENESIS IN THE CONTEXT OF PERSONALITY RESEARCH

by

Norman F. Dixon
University College
London, England

Uwe Hentschel
University of
Mainz, FRG

Gudmund Smith
University of
Lund, Sweden

Typical views about the nature of human personality are those of trait theorists and situationalists. Whereas the first assumes a bundle of traits consistent over space and time, the second maintains that the way a person looks, what he does, how he feels, and the attitudes he holds, are a function of the context in which he is observed. But these are extreme viewpoints. The compromise position taken here is an interactional one, namely that those characteristics of an individual which together constitute his personality reflect an interaction between a relatively stable core of adaptive responses (themselves a product of genetic disposition and past experience) and demands of specific situations. In other words, his personality is the particular way he has learned to cope with the variety of circumstances that may occur. The second premise of this chapter is that the overt manifestation of personality reflects the operation of underlying processes that are largely unavailable to conscious scrutiny. They include those relating to biological and social needs, long-term memory, complexes (i.e., emotionally charged systems of ideas), defences, and particular ways (or cognitive styles) of processing information. In the present context the operative phrase is 'unavailable to conscious scrutiny'.

For if personality is determined by processes of which the individual is unaware there are good grounds for using research methods which have the advantage of being able to investigate underlying processes without the subject being aware of the fact that he is being stimulated. By so doing they can bypass defences and the restricting effects of awareness (Spence & Holland, 1962). The paradigms in question are those of *subliminal perception* and *microgenesis*. Whereas the first involves evoking responses by stimulation below the conscious threshold, the latter is concerned with the stages of subjective experience from the first impact of external stimuli upon ongoing brain activity to the elaboration of a relatively stable concious percept.

Referring to Figure 1, both techniques, by looking at the effect of stimuli below the conscious threshold, provide evidence as to the nature of such preconscious determinants of personality as needs, emotion, long-term memory, and the mechanisms of defence.

In other words, since it is necessary to discover the unconscious determinants of personality in order fully to understand the latter's structure the use of experimental techniques which reach below the surface of consciousness, would seem to be an indispensable part of the empirical study of personality.

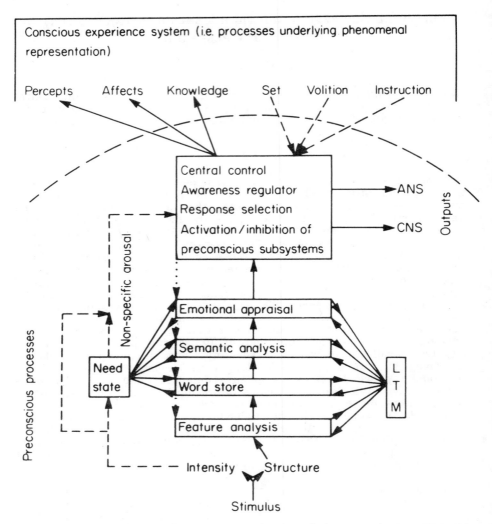

Figure 1: *Relationships between conscious and preconscious processes implied by the data from studies of unconscious perception (from Dixon, 1981).*

Paradigms and methodology

The aim and object of all the paradigms discussed in this section is to affect subjects by stimulation of which they are unconscious. Ideally they remain unaware of the stimulus, of being stimulated, and of the fact that their responses are being influenced by something of which they are not conscious. Through bypassing the monitoring and restrictive functions of awareness these paradigms aim to reveal unconscious pathology, and the unconscious determinants of personality.

In the case of subliminal perception, signal to noise ratios which ensure unawareness are achieved by presenting stimuli, whether these be verbal or pictorial, (a) at intensities or durations below the conscious threshold; (b) in peripheral regions of the visual field; (c) on a sensory channel or modality (as in dichotic listening, dichoptic viewing, or in the course of binocular rivalry) which is, at the time of presentation, not producing any conscious representation; (d) in conjunction with "noise" which is either concurrent or temporally adjacent (as in meta-contrast or other forms of masking).

Many of these ways of reducing the signal to noise ratio are also employed by proponents of microgenesis, the only difference in the latter case being that successive presentations or blocks of presentations differ in terms of progressive increases or decreases in the signal to noise ratio. The subliminal perception dependent variables include: verbal responses (experienced as "guesses" or "free associations"), the selection of pictures, electrodermal responses, reports of dreams subsequent to stimulus presentations, and, in the case of perceptual defence, changes in awareness and recognition thresholds. For microgenesis the main dependent variables are reports of subjective phenomena - descriptions in words or pictures of what the subject sees or thinks he sees - reports of dreams, of after-images and after-effects. It is from such data, considered in relation to other measures, viz. manifest anxiety, changes in regional cerebral blood flow, electrodermal responses, and creativity, that the dynamics of processes underlying personality and linking conscious experience to cerebral activity may be deduced.

Review of typical experiments

Within this chapter we will consider a few of the hundreds of studies carried out by those interested in subliminal perception and microgenesis (see Dixon, 1981; Hentschel & Smith, 1980; Kragh & Smith, 1970; Smith & Westerlundh, 1980). The selection of these typical studies has been governed by three criteria. First, they should relate to individual differences in variables associated with dimensions of personality. Second, they should cover the widest possible range of psychobiological functions, from sensory effects at one end to phenomenal representations at the other. Finally, their results should have been confirmed beyond any reasonable doubt by other comparable investigations. Moreover, microgenesis, though involving subliminal perception in its earlier stages, goes on to explore processes about and above the conscious threshold. Therefore, it provides a more complete picture of perceptual processes. So, it is only logical that under each of the following headings we should start with the simpler antecedent data from studies of subliminal perception.

Individual differences in susceptibility to subliminal stimulation in relation to other personality characteristics

Whereas the work of Libet, Alberts, Wright, and Feinstein (1967) and

Adam (1978) has established, in case of touch and pressure respectively, that it is physiologically possible for the brain to respond to stimuli of which the recipient is unaware, the reality of sensitivity as a function of individual differences has come from the work of Sackeim, Packer, and Gur (1977). These authors have shown that judgements about a neutral face (as to whether it looked happy or sad as a function of the appropriate subliminal label) were significantly more in evidence from subjects displaying *right* hemisphericity, as determined by the eye movement test (Day, 1967), than for those characterised by *left* hemisphericity. Given the other characteristics associated with laterality or hemisphericity differences, this finding is not only consistent with Gordon's (1967) finding that art students were more susceptible to subliminal stimuli than science students, but also with some other studies (e.g., Allison, 1963) which have shown that a relaxed rather than focally alert state of mind increases sensitivity to stimulation below the conscious threshold. Of particular interest in this context is the finding of interactions between susceptibility to subliminal stimuli, defence mechanisms, and creativity (Hentschel & Schneider, 1984). For possible differences in clinical groups one can refer, for example, to Dixon's (1980) postulate of a relationship between subliminal perception and psychosomatic symptoms. In an experiment to investigate the effects of a subliminal auditory verbal stimulus upon free associations, significant differences were found between a control group of normals and patients with either polyarthritis or Chrohn's disease. It was only the control group which responded with emotionally positive or defensive associations. This result was particularly in evidence when the threatening subliminal stimulus had been presented to the left ear (Hentschel & Hickel, 1983). It can be interpreted in terms of a greater lack of symbolizing ability in psychosomatic patients (Hentschel & Kohlmann, 1984). Also relevant in this context are the results from a study by Westerlundh (1984) on conflict activation through subliminal presentation of such phrases as "I am guilty" or "I am ashamed". Administered in the context of perceptgenesis, the treatment resulted in significant differences between the sexes with implications for superego functioning.

Individual personality differences in interaction with situational demands have also been found in psychophysiological processes preceding conscious reactions, i.e., high and low anxiety subjects showed different contingent negative variation patterns in an easy attention task under neutral, ego- and pain-threat conditions. This can be interpreted as covert preconscious changes in effort economy (Fröhlich & Glanzmann, 1984). Event-related evoked potentials with differences for high- and low-interference groups have been interpreted also by Ehlers and Munz (1984) as indicators of preconscious activation in a specific stage of stimulus processing.

Primary process thinking and dreams in the context of personality research

It would be surprising, to say the least, if those memory processes which give rise to an individual's dreams are not also implicated in other aspects of his personality. On the assumption that they are, research paradigms which explore the underlying psychopathology of dreams and of primary process thinking could be of interest to personality theorists. The following examples which, in various ways, support data from earlier work on hypnotically induced dreams (Nachmansohn, 1925; Roffenstein, 1951; Schroetter, 1951) are pertinent to this issue. In the first, subjects are required to draw and describe in words a briefly exposed complex picture. At some later point in time they are requested to give free associations and/or to report any dreams that they might have had in the interim. Data from such studies (Dixon, 1981; Fisher, 1954; Poetzl, 1917) have lead to the following conclusions: (1) Elements of a complex display not consciously perceived (or reported) at the time of the original tachistoscopic presentation tend to occur in subsequently obtained associations or dream reports. (2) These recovered elements, like other "residues of the day's events" tend to appear in the context of representations of unconscious psychopathology. It is as if the brain utilises aspects of preceding sensory inflow, which, either through inhibitory defences or through the very limited capacity of conscious experience, failed to enter awareness at the time of their reception, for the subsequent expression of underlying complexes. In another, simpler paradigm (e.g., Dixon, 1956; Gordon, 1967) it has been found that guesses as to the nature of subliminal words presented either auditory or visually tend to be typical of primary process symbolic associations to the objects or events connoted by the stimulus material. In view of Fonagy's (1977) finding that the symbolising tendency is more pronounced when the subliminal stimulus is directed to the right hemisphere, there might well be individual differences in this phenomenon as a function of the subject's hemisphericity.

The latest paradigm for exploring unconscious psychopathology with subliminal stimuli involves obtaining selections of pictures following the presentation by computer display of critical words in successive presentations of continuously masked super-imposed letter strings (Dixon & Henley, 1984; Dixon, Henley, & Weir, 1984). The following responses to the ambiguous word "Cock" exemplifies the sort of data that can be obtained by this method.

Of the many contributions by proponents of microgenesis to research in this area three are of particular interest. First, there is the relating of the three classes of response - primary process, defensive, and secondary process (concerned with adaptation to reality) - to three levels of stimulation - subliminal, liminal, and supraliminal, respectively (Draguns, 1984). The evidence supporting these distinctions, which were tied in with determinants of personality, supports the view (Dixon, 1981) that, though some structural analysis of sensory inflow must logically precede semantic analysis and emotional appraisal, even the very earliest of these hierarchical stages of processing may be biased centrifugally by pre-existing content of long-term memory and complex-tied emotions. One manifest outcome of this state of affairs is the fact that partial cues (consciously perceived structure) may override semantic analysis in the determining of overt responses. Finally, dream reports have also featured as dependent variables in microgenetic studies involving personality differences. It has, for example, been shown in children (Smith & Carlsson, 1983) and for professional artists (Smith & Danielsson, 1980) that dreaming in colour correlates with a score of creativity in the inverted

TABLE 1: *Identical pictures selected by the same subject on different occasions following the stimulus word "COCK"*

In Experiments 1 & 2		In Experiments 1 & 3	
Teapot		Elephant	Hammer
Cannon		Knife	Ball
Fork		Horse	Pump
Peg		Crane	Dog
Train		Ring	Bike
Combined probabilities of the 5 identical selections		Combined probabilities of the 10 identical selections	
$p < .001$		$p < .00005$	

Note: In three separate experiments, carried out at weekly intervals, the subject was presented with the masked (subliminal) ambiguous stimulus word "COCK" randomly positioned in a sequence of 9 other stimulus words. Following each presentation she reported the names of those pictures in a composite display which caught her eye. The above table shows those pictures which recurred as responses to "cock" and the combined probabilities (based on the number of time each was used over all stimulus presentations) of these repetitions. From the symbolic nature of these picture selections, and their combined probability, it was concluded that, though unaware of the masked stimulus it was determining her selections.

PG test[1]. It is presumed, that people who report without hesitation that they have had a dream are closer to their dream life than those who hesitate or do not know and are therefore more likely to exploit preconscious material.

Memory and personality

It is a truism that, besides genetic predispositions, the single biggest determinant of personality is an individual's store of past experiences. Three qualifications may be made to this statement. First, it is not the reality of past experiences but how these are perceived. Second, the differential effects on manifest personality of different experiences

---

[1] The *inverted PG* (perceptgenetic) method combines a conventional straight microgenetic series with an inverted one, that is, after the straight series has reached its correct stage, the experimenter reverses the procedure and presents the stimulus at gradually decreasing exposure times. Once confronted with the "correct" meaning of the stimulus, would the subject now stick to that meaning and at most "subtract" from it in his reporting while the visibility is diminishing, or will he again make contact with qualitatively different subjective meanings, perhaps the very meanings reported early in his straight microgenesis? If creativity is defined as individuals' inclination to transgress the confines of an established perceptual context, creative individuals would be able to recover many subjective themes (see among other publications, Smith & Carlsson, 1983).

obviously depend on their emotional impact and the conflicts engendered by the events in question. Third, much clinical data suggests that influences of the past are usually greater when what is past has been forgotten rather than consciously remembered.

In the light of these considerations, methodologies which investigate the nature and content of unconscious memory are clearly relevant to understanding the roots of personality. We have already touched on one pertinent line of inquiry, that relating to the phenomenon whereby retrieval of unconscious material is brought about through the access of stimulus material, in a sensory overload situation, to unconscious long-term memory.

In a sense, of course, most, if not all, studies of subliminal perception and microgenesis involve the activation of previously stored information. The preconscious stages of sensory processing (See Fig. 1) - structural analysis, semantic analysis, emotional appraisal, and alerting of defences - are all affected by what has gone before. There is, however, one particular class of microgenetic research which warrants special mention. It is that which supports the notion of micro-macro parallelism, i.e., the hypothesis (Kragh, 1984) of the various stages of microgenesis, from early to late, bearing the hallmarks of parallel stages in ontogenetic development. A specific aspect of this general theory (see Hentschel & Smith, 1980; Kragh & Smith, 1970) that in microgenetic progression it is the early stages which are most likely to reflect the intrusion of early memories, has been demonstrated in a study of young men in their early twenties who had lost their fathers. When presented with the father-son picture it was found that the old male figure identified in early stages of microgenesis, often tended to be replaced at later stages by a female figure. In a recent study of a single subject, using his perceptgenetic Defense Mechanism Technique (DMT) with special anxiety-provoking stimuli, Kragh (1984) has in fact obtained the subject's confirmation of the real chronology of experiences emerging with progressively longer durations of the stimulus material.

Needless to say, this apparent revealing of a temporal ordering relationship between perceptual and memoric processes could be of considerable interest to personality theorists as well as to those concerned with how the brain receives and stores information.

Emotion, need, and personality

Central to any theory of personality is the consideration of subjective states, like affects, feelings, emotions, or moods. The evidence suggests that they in fact have their origins in three sorts of preconscious events: arousal and/or deprivation of an underlying need; the reception, registration, and processing of some need-related or threatening stimulus; and, finally, activation of a pre-existing complex, that is, emotionally charged constellation of ideas. Whether or not they serve to colour conscious experience and to direct behaviour, appears to depend upon four sorts of preconscious process - a two-way interaction with long-term memory, emotional appraisal of sensory inflow, a biasing of perceptual and memoric processes by concurrent need states, and the activation of defences. Techniques of subliminal perception and microgenesis have succeeded in probing all these stages of processing. That concerned with defences will be considered in the next section. For the moment, however, let us consider the case of need and memory. From a series of experiments (Gadlin & Fiss, 1967; Gordon & Spence, 1966; Spence & Ehrenberg, 1964) it has been shown that the combination of three factors - a state of hunger, a priming experience such as self-ratings for feeling hungry or listening to a piece of prose about food or being exposed to the smell of cheese, and, finally, subliminal stimulation with the word "Cheese" -- exercise a selective bias on the recall of previously learned prose. In a comparable study (Spence & Gordon, 1967), feelings of rejection (i.e., frustration of the need to be liked), combined with a characteristic tendency to deal with feelings of depression and anxiety by taking recourse to oral behaviour, and subliminal stimulation with the word "Milk" had a similar effect on retrieval processes. Together, these and other comparable results suggest that individual differences in personality, i.e., in underlying needs, coping mechanisms and content of memory schemata are susceptible to investigation by appropriate stimulation of which the recipient is unaware.

Similar conclusions regarding individual differences in coping with needs has come from studies of perceptual strategies. In a study of the effects of thirst on perception, Klein and his co-workers (Klein, 1970) divided their subjects into two groups on the basis of thirst and non-thirst, and into two independent groups on the basis of the results of Stroop's colour-word test (sensitive and non-sensitive to interference). When thirsty, the two groups used different strategies in situations where thirst symbols, e.g., a glass of beer, interfered with perceptual tasks. The sensitive subjects, presumed to be rigidly defensive against interference, tried to avoid areas in the perceptual field where the thirst symbols were presented, whereas their more flexible counterparts let their eyes wander over the symbols as often as possible while scanning the stimulus.

Defences

A price paid for the evolution of our limited capacity for conscious experience is the psychological (some would say, ego) need to exclude from awareness such information which, were it admitted into consciousness, would occasion dismay. Generally speaking, such unwelcome items of information are of two kinds - those which threaten physical survival, and those which merely threaten peace of mind. Their origins may be external or internal - located in current sensory inflow or long-term memory. They are resisted because of the aversive nature of the affects, anxiety, fear, rage, or guilt, to which they might otherwise give rise. The relevance of all this to personality is three-fold. First, manifestations of particular favourite defences constitute traits which are remarkably consistent over space and time. Secondly, there are marked individual differences in the defence mechanisms which different people employ. Thirdly, the sorts of information defended against, depending as they do upon the person's life-history, differ from individual to individual.

Many studies of subliminal perception and microgenesis have revealed interesting relationships between these various factors. In the case of perceptual defence, for example, Brown (1961) and Dixon (1981), it has been shown that changes in the conscious threshold for anxiety-producing words differ from person to person and also as a function of the particular stimulus words used. The word "Whore", for example, has been found to produce a rise in threshold for women, but not for men (Dixon, 1958). Psychological differences in the defence against acknowledging the possibility of life threatening disease have been found in studies of the responses of people at risk for cervical or breast cancer (Katz, Weiner, Gallagher, Hellman, 1970; Spence, Scarborough, & Ginsberg, 1978; Wirsching, Stierlin, Hoffman, Weber, & Wirsching, 1982). These differences have also been demonstrated by those laboratory studies of perceptual defence (see Dixon, 1981) which involved measuring sensitivity for a neutral stimulus presented to one eye, while the word "Cancer" was presented subliminally to the other eye. In one investigation, using this technique (Henley, 1974), of a habitual smoker with hypochondriacal anxieties about the possible consequences of heavy smoking, repeated daily trials over the period of a week showed no habituation for his defensive response to the same critical word.

Other applications of subliminal stimulation to the study of defence mechanisms have made a special point of looking at brain mechanisms and individual differences in ways of regulating sensory inflow. For example, research by Shevrin (1973) on twins differing in repressiveness has shown significant differences in the compound evoked potential to subliminal visual stimuli. In a study by Dixon and Lear (1962) which compared defensive responses evoked by subliminal stimuli, it was found that, whereas paranoid schizophrenics and depressives showed *involuntary* changes in visual sensitivity towards threatening stimuli, normals tended to control sensory inflow by making *voluntary* alterations in the intensity of the incident stimulus. In another experiment, when led by the subliminally flashed word "Me" to identify with the aggressor, projective-sensitive and borderline patients were confused and even reported perceptual problems (Smith, 1984).

Measures of defence mechanisms

In recent work using subliminal techniques to investigate defence mechanisms, the Defence Mechanism Test (DMT) and the Meta Contrast Technique (MCT) are most prominent.

The DMT uses a special slide-contrivance into which the subject looks through an aperture. The presentation series starts with subliminal values which are geometrically prolonged. The stimulus depicts a central person (the "Hero") and a peripherally placed person constituting a threat to the former. If a threat initiates an anxiety reaction (which remains submanifest because the threat is not directed at the subject himself, but at the projection of his self (the "Hero"), the subject may either: (1) display this anxiety in reports of black or otherwise threatening qualities in what he has seen, or (2) meet the anxiety with defensive reactions. These take the form of transformation of the content of the picture (the hero, the threat, and the relation between them) in a non-threatening direction. The distortions are quite stable phenomena, with forms known from the psychoanalytic theory of defence. The regularity of their form and appearance has allowed - as is the case with other qualitative PG techniques - the construction of a formalized scoring scheme (Kragh, 1969).

Whereas the DMT, in which the person being tested has to draw and describe in words a briefly exposed central figure (the "Hero" figure), provides detailed evidence of defensive organisation activated by the presence in the test material of a peripherally placed "old, ugly, threatening male face", the MCT, though related to the DMT, was originally based on techniques derived from experiments with subliminal perception comprising a rather different paradigm. Two stimuli, A and B, are presented successively on a screen in front of the subject. Stimulus A may be incongruent with B or imply a threat directed at the person depicted in B. The subject is first acquainted with B alone which, throughout the remaining test, is presented at an exposure level making correct identification possible. Without the subject knowing it, A is then introduced immediately before B, at brief exposure times which are gradually prolonged. The presentation series is terminated when the perception of A, developing within the established frame of B, has reached its final, correct stage. If A is threatening, perception of it is often distorted in a way similar to that in the DMT. However, perception of B may also change under the influence of the subliminal perception of A. Observation of the subject's behaviour in the test situation is important in the MCT (Smith & Danielsson, 1982).

Since the "threat" stimulus A is masked by the test stimulus B, the underlying operation of the defensive processes which determine microgenesis of the developing percept is itself usually unconscious and subject to individual differences. From the viewpoint of a personality theorist it is the sensitivity of the DMT and the MCT to individual differences which is of special interest. In the case of the DMT, for example, the so-called "barrier" response, in which the respondent appears to separate the threatening peripheral face from the "Hero" by means of a physical barrier (e.g., he draws a line between the two), is most often to be found in the protocols of compulsive patients, people who are particularly prone to use "isolation" as a defensive strategy (Kragh, 1969). Another comparable example is the predilection of paranoid patients for the "projection" reaction in MCT. For these subjects perception of the threatening first stimulus is delayed, but changes occur in that of the second, masking stimulus, the latter may be altered beyond recognition and all continuity lost. In extreme cases, when defences seem inefficient and the threatening quality of the stimulus is somehow "leaking" through, subjects regress to defensive strategies found in children. They may, for instance, shut their eyes or turn their heads away (Smith & Danielsson, 1982).

The processing of information in microgenetic experiments is often so delayed, that the final stabilized and correct stage of perception is late in coming or is never reached at all. This reaction is typical of many psychopathological groups, but particularly of retarded depressives where the processing, once stuck like the needle on a broken grammophone record, gives rise to a long series of reports just repeating each other in a stereotyped manner. Typical of the many studies showing the effect is an investigation of 95 in-patients by Eberhard, Johnson, Nilsson, and Smith (1965) which involved administering the MCT, the serial colour-word test (CWT), and an assortment of questionnaires. The results from this study have been subsequently confirmed many times, most recently in a group of 62 children, aged 7 - 15, from a children's psychiatric clinic and a comparable group of 69 normal children (Smith & Danielsson, 1982).

As pointed out earlier, microgenetic studies, though involving subliminal perception (in the early stages of microgenesis), are particularly concerned with the gradual development of conscious perceptual experiences. The relation of these to individual differences in anxiety and brain metabolism has been investigated by Johanson, Risberg, Silfverskiold, and Smith (in preparation). In the first part of this study, the MCT was used to pick up signs of anxiety, such as the accounts of dark or broken structures, from patients with anxiety neurosis. The following day these subjects were asked to associate to their MCT anxiety responses, and at the same time their regional changes in cerebral blood flow were measured. All 12 patients, except one, reacted strongly, many of them being close to panic. Simultaneously, their cerebral blood flow pattern changed, showing significant increase in the fronto-orbital area. The fact that this pronounced increase in cerebral blood flow occurs for the left hemisphere could be due to attempts to control anxiety verbally.

As should be clear from the above examples, the DMT and the MCT, although similar in many respects, have proved to reveal different aspects of personality functioning. When applied to the same individual they do not, therefore, necessarily yield analogous results. Each on its own account, however, possesses a high degree of reliability and predictive power as has been described in detail in, for example, Hentschel and Smith (1980).

Behavioural change and personality

According to the situationalist view, behavioural manifestations of personality will change as a function of the situation in which the behaviour occurs.

The question then arises as to whether such behavioural changes reflect deliberate conscious adaptation to given situations or constitute on occasions unconscious effects. Given the evidence for subliminal perception and preconscious determinants of behaviour it seems inherently likely that the latter would be the case. This expectation has in fact been borne out by several researches involving subliminal perception. Zuckerman (1960) has shown that people may be induced, without their knowledge, to write longer or shorter descriptions of TAT cards by concurrent presentations, at subliminal durations, of the exhortations "write more" and "don't write", respectively. More recently, Tyrer, Lee, and Horn (1978) have demonstrated that agoraphobic behaviour can be modified by the reception of subliminal film sequences which depict desensitising scenes of a crowded market place.

Some dramatic examples of behaviour change have come from the researches of Silverman and his co-workers (Silverman, 1976; Silverman, Martin, Ungaro, & Mendelsohn, 1978; see also Dixon, 1981). Supposedly because it gratifies an unconscious symbiotic wish, the subliminal message, "Mommy and I are one" has been found particularly effective in this context. Not only have this and other messages been found to exercise different effects on the psychopathology of different patient groups, but the symbiotic one in particular is also (presumably by reducing anxiety) productive of reduced compulsive eating behaviour in obese women and improved mathematical performance in students (Ariam, 1979). By the same token, the subliminal words "Beating Dad is wrong" and "Beating Dad is OK" have been found to hinder or, respectively, to improve dart-throwing accuracy in normal males (Silverman, Ross, Adler, & Lustig, 1978). Complementing these researches, several studies have used microgenetic techniques to predict and to follow behavioural change during psychotherapy. In one of these researches (Smith, Sjoholm, & Nielzén, 1975), 30 neurotic outpatients suffering from pronounced anxiety were studied before and after a therapeutic period of 1.5 to 2 years. For the subjective scores on two rating scales and two perceptgenetic methods, the MCT and an after-image experiment, it was possible to relate original status with improvement and non-improvement of manifest anxiety. The most positive prognostic sign was sensitivity to subliminal (inner and outer) cues, whereas the most negative signs were pre-psychotic discontinuities, projection, and total lack of defence mechanisms.

Discussion and conclusions

If we define personality as those relatively stable and consistent ways which characterise how a person reacts to his environment, then a crucial determinant of personality must surely be how he or she perceives the environment. Hence, any investigation of personality must profit from an analysis of those factors which shape perceptual experience. Besides genetic dispositions, these factors include past experiences, current needs, complexes, and preferred defence mechanisms. Unfortunately, however, the nature and operation of these factors are largely unconscious. For the most part they act upon sensory inflow during that brief but measurable interval between receipt of a stimulus and emergence of an established stable percept. Apart from such paradigms (with their attendant disadvantages) as hypnotic suggestion or drug administration, the only methods that appear to get at these unconscious processes are those of subliminal perception and microgenesis. The following advantages may be claimed for these approaches: (1) Since subjects are unaware of the stimulus, and sometimes even of being stimulated, they remain ignorant of the contingencies between what they do or report and the sensory inflow which is shaping their response. Hence, they are prevented from consciously concealing or editing information which might otherwise reveal aspects of their psychopathology that they prefer to keep hidden. Moreover, since they cannot know what the experimenter expects or desires as responses, they are not in a position to yield to the demand characteristics of the investigation in question. (2) It is possible, presumably, through the role of cortical activation consequent upon contributions from the non-specific ascending reticular activating system, to find signal to noise ratios for an external stimulus which ensure that the latter acts upon preconscious representation of the external scene. These signal to noise ratios are those employed by the proponents of subliminal perception and microgenesis[1]. (3) In the case of subliminal stimulation where, by definition, there is no awareness of the external stimulus, the data are confined to autonomic (e.g., electrodermal or evoked potentials) responses, behavioural responses (such as writing longer or shorter essays, as in the Zuckerman experiment referred to earlier), free associations experienced as guesses, and reports of such conscious experiences as affects, illusions, and dreams.

In the case of microgenesis, there is the added bonus of obtaining phenomenal data about what the subject sees (or thinks he sees) with gradual increases in stimulation duration. En passant, one of the most interesting outcomes of microgenetic procedure is the discovery that conscious phenomena do not suddenly occur en bloc at the end stage of processing sensory inflow, but may intrude, albeit in a highly distorted form, at quite early stages in the hierarchy of processing operations. Without wishing to labour the point, it is *as if* our capacity to be conscious of the external scene can be used to take fleeting samples of what is coming in. To use an overworked analogy, it is as if a very weak torch can be played over the fragments of the preconscious processing domain. An alternative possibility is that those cerebral processes responsible for subjective perceptual phenomena can actually manufacture percepts purely on a basis of signals, themselves unconscious, from early stages in the hierarchy of preconscious activities. In favour of this latter view is the recognised phenomenon which occurs during sleep, the so-called alarm clock dream. The point about such dreams is that unconsciously perceived signals, whether auditory, tactile, or olfactory, can cause the brain to elaborate some "justifying" perceptual scene which may have nothing whatsoever to do with the actual initiating cause. So much for the rational for subliminal perception in the context of personality research. What conclusions can be drawn from its applications?

(a) Judging from the experiments referred to in this chapter, two approaches have been followed. In the first, the techniques employed have revealed interesting characteristics of those preconscious processes which underlie the overt manifestations of personality. In the second approach, a number of researchers have actually looked at preconscious correlates of individual differences in, for example, sex, hemisphericity, and ego defences.

(b) The specific preconscious determinants of personality so far looked at include: unconscious long-term memory, primary process thinking, complexes, need states, and defensive organisation.

(c) The outcomes of these various investigations include: the detection of accident proneness, the discovery of the symbolic meaning of words and phrases to the individual subject, the manipulation of dreams, the differential activation of different defence mechanisms, the differential increasing or decreasing of psychopathology in different

---

[1]) There is of course a parallel between these techniques and those of ordinary projective tests which also (hopefully) militate against the subject knowing the real reasons for the response data which he produces. The important difference, however, is that in projective tests the subject is aware of the physical characteristics of the stimulus array, whether this be an ink blot or a TAT card. Thus, we cannot be sure that he or she is *unaware* of its psychological implications. We cannot be sure that what (s)he is saying is not a consciously contrived effort to conceal or to please the experimenter.

patient groups, the reducing of phobic tendencies and of compulsive overeating, the testing (and sometimes supporting) of various psychoanalytic hypotheses (see Kline, 1981), the obtaining of data pertaining to the psychodynamic correlates of such miscellaneous phenomena as creativity, anxiety, hemisphericity, psychosomatic disorders, and electro-physiological responses of the brain.

The study of unconscious processing by means of subliminal stimulation, on the one hand, and protraction of perceptual processes ad modum microgenesis, on the other, represent two different research traditions which started to join forces in the middle seventies.

All in all, subliminal perception and microgenesis *could* be to the study of personality and psychopathology what ultrasonics and radiology *have* been to the study of physical pathology – objective methodologies which reveal what was otherwise obscure.

To be more specific, the various paradigms referred to in this paper could be used to investigate the relationship between those personality characteristics/traits which are measured by traditional personality tests and such underlying correlates as those of unconscious complexes, defences, and drive schemata. By the same token microgenetic paradigms, such as that of the Defence Mechanism Test, could be used to investigate relationships between the ontogenesis of personality and the chronology of specific events in the person's life history.

REFERENCES

Adam, G. (1978). Visceroception, awareness and behaviour. In G.E. Schwartz & D. Shapiro (Eds.), *Conscious and self-regulation* (pp. 199-212). Chichester: Wiley.

Allison, J. (1963). Cognitive structure and receptivity to low intensity stimulation. *Journal of Abnormal and Social Psychology, 67,* 132-138.

Ariam, S. (1979). The effects of subliminal symbiotic stimuli in Hebrew on academic performance of Israeli High School students. Unpublished doctoral dissertation. New York University, New York.

Brown, W.P. (1961). Conceptions of perceptual defence. *British Journal of Psychology,* Monograph, Suppl. No. 35.

Day, M.E. (1967). An eye-movement indicator of type and level of anxiety: Some clinical observations. *Journal of Clinical Psychology, 23,* 433-441.

Dixon, N.F. (1956). Symbolic associations following subliminal stimulation. *International Journal of Psychoanalysis, 37,* 159-170.

Dixon, N.F. (1958). Apparent changes in the visual threshold as a function of subliminal stimulation. A preliminary report. *Quarterly Journal of Experimental Psychology, 10,* 211-219.

Dixon, N.F. (1980). Psychosomatische Störungen als ein Spezialfall der unterschwelligen Wahrnehmung? [Psychosomatic disorders as a special case of subliminal perception?]. In U. Hentschel & G.J.W. Smith (Eds.), *Experimentelle Persönlichkeitspsychologie. Die Wahrnehmung als Zugang zu diagnostischen Problemen* [Experimental personality psychology. Perception as the entry to diagnostic

problems]   (pp.   372-394).   Wiesbaden: Akademische
Verlagsgesellschaft.

Dixon, N.F. (1981). *Preconscious processing.* Chichester: Wiley.

Dixon, N.F., & Henley, S.H.A. (1984, May). *Personality factors in subliminal perception.* Paper presented at the 2nd European Conference on Personality. Bielefeld.

Dixon, N.F., Henley, S.H.A., & Weir, C.W. (1984). The extraction of information from continuously masked successive stimuli: An exploratory study. *Current Psychological Reviews, 3,* 1-7.

Dixon, N.F., & Lear, T.E. (1962). Perceptual regulation and mental disorder. *Journal of Mental Science, 108,* 356-361.

Draguns, J.G. (1984, May). *Subliminal perception as the first stage of microgenesis: Can personality be revealed so early in the sequence?* Paper presented at the 2nd European Conference on Personality. Bielefeld.

Eberhard, G., Johnson, G., Nilsson, L., & Smith, G.J.W. (1965). Clinical and experimental approaches to the description of depression and anti-depressive therapy. *Acta Psychiatrica Scandinavica,* Suppl. *186.* Copenhagen: Munksgaard.

Ehlers, W., & Munz, D. (1984, May). *Evoked potentials as unaware indicators of cognitive control.* Paper presented at the 2nd European Conference on Personality. Bielefeld.

Fisher, C. (1954). Dreams and perception. The role of preconscious and primary modes of perception in dream formation. *Journal of the American Psychoanalytic Association, 5,* 5-60.

Fonagy, P. (1977). *The use of subliminal stimuli in highlighting function differences between the two hemispheres.* Paper presented to the Experimental Psychology Association, Birkbeck College, London.

Fröhlich, W.D., & Glanzmann, P. (1984, May). *Anxiety and covert changes in attention control: Subliminal prestages of imbalanced selectivity?* Paper presented at the 2nd European Conference on Personality, Bielefeld.

Gadlin, W., & Fiss, H. (1967). Odor as a facilitator of the effects of subliminal stimulation. *Journal of Personality and Social Psychology, 7,* 95-100.

Gordon, G. (1967). *Semantic determination by subliminal verbal stimuli: A quantitative approach.* Unpublished doctoral dissertation, University of London, London.

Gordon, C.M., & Spence, D.P. (1966). The facilitating effects of food set and food deprivation on responses to subliminal food stimulus. *Journal of Personality, 34,* 406-415.

Henley, S.H.A. (1974). *Preconscious processing in normals and schizophrenics.* Unpublished doctoral dissertation, University of London, London.

Hentschel, U., Hickel, U. (1983, March). *Persönlichkeitsmerkmale in Beziehung zu (psycho-) somatischen Erkrankungen* [Personality characteristics in (psycho) somatic diseases]. Paper presented at the 25. Tagung experimentell arbeitender psychologen. Hamburg.

Hentschel, U., & Kohlmann, C.W. (1984, November). *Pinocchio-Syndrom oder Reaktionsspezifität? Spezifische Verhaltens- und Erlebensweisen bei chronischer Polyarthritis* [Pinocchio-syndrom or reaction specificity? Specific ways of behaving and experiencing in chronic polyarthritis]. Paper presented at the 21. Arbeitstagung des Deutschen Kolegiums für Psychosomatische Medizin.

Hentschel, U., & Schneider, U. (1984, May). *Psychodynamic personality correlates of creativity.* Paper presented at the 2nd European Conference on Personality, Bielefeld.

Hentschel, U., & Smith, G.J.W. (1980). *Experimentelle Persönlichkeitspsychologie. Die Wahrnehmung als Zugang zu diagnostischen Problemen* [Experimental personality psychology. Perception as the entry to diagnostic problems]. Wiesbaden: Akademische Verlagsgesellschaft.

Johanson, A.M., Risberg, J., Silfverskiold, P., & Smith, G. (in preparation). *Regional changes of cerebral blood flow during increased anxiety in patients with anxiety neurosis.*

Katz, J.L., Weiner, H., Gallagher, T.E., & Hellman, L. (1970). Stress, distress and ego defenses. Psychoendocrine response to impending breast tumor biopsy. *Archives of General Psychiatry, 23,* 131-142.

Klein, G.S. (1970). *Perception, motives and personality.* New York: Knopf.

Kragh, U. (1969). *DMT – the defence mechanism test.* Stockholm: Scandinaviska Testforlaget.

Kragh, U. (1984, May). *Temporally stratified representation of the past in the present: A demonstration by the Defence Mechanism Test.* Paper presented at the 2nd European Conference on Personality. Bielefeld.

Kragh, U., & Smith, G.J.W. (1970). *Percept-genetic analysis.* Lund: Gleerups.

Libet, B., Alberts, W.W., Wright, E.W., & Feinstein, B. (1967). Responses of human somato-sensory cortex to stimuli below the threshold for conscious sensation. *Science, 158,* 1597-1600.

Nachmansohn, M. (1925). Concerning experimentally produced dreams. In D. Rapoport (Ed.), *The organisation and pathology of thought* (pp. 257-287). New York: Columbia University Press, 1951.

Poetzl, O. (1917). The relationship between experimentally induced dream images and indirect vision. *Psychological Issues,* (Monograph No. 7), *2,* 41-120 (1960).

Roffenstein, G. (1951). Experiments on symbolization in dreams. In D. Rapoport (Ed.), *The organization and pathology of thought* (pp. 249-256). New York: Columbia University Press.

Sackeim, H.A., Packer, I.K., & Gur, R.C. (1977). Hemisphericity, cognitive set and susceptibility to subliminal perception. *Journal of Abnormal Psychology, 86,* 624-630.

Schroetter, K. (1951). Experimental dreams. In D. Rapoport (Ed.), *The organization and pathology of thought* (pp. 234-248). New York: Columbia University Press.

Shevrin, H. (1973). Brain wave correlates of subliminal stimulation, unconscious attention, primary and secondary process thinking, and repressiveness. *Psychological Issues,* 8 Monograph, *30,* 56-87.

Silverman, L.H. (1976). 'Psychoanalytic theory: "the reports of my death are greatly exaggerated"', *Amer. Psychol., 31,* 621-637.

Silverman, L.H., Martin, A., Ungaro, R., & Mendelsohn, E. (1978). Effect of subliminal stimulation of symbiotic fantasies on behaviour modification treatment of obesity. *Journal of Consulting and Clinical Psychology, 46,* 432-441.

Silverman, L.H., Ross, D.L., Adler, J.M., & Lustig, D.A. (1978). Simple research paradigm for demonstrating subliminal dynamic activation: Effects of Oedipal stimuli on dart-throwing accuracy in college males. *Journal of Abnormal Psychology*, 87, 341-357.

Smith, G.J.W. (1984, May). *Identification with another person: Manipulated by means of subliminal stimulation*. Paper presented at the 2nd European Conference on Personality. Bielefeld.

Smith, G.J.W., & Carlsson, I. (1983). Creativity and anxiety: An experimental study. *Scandinavian Journal of Psychology*, 24, 107-115.

Smith, G.J.W., & Danielsson, A. (1980). Ideenreichtum, Ich-Beteiligung und Effektivität bei einer Gruppe von Natur- und Geisteswissenschaftlern [Richness of ideas, ego-involvement and effectivity in a group of scientists in the natural sciences and the humanities]. In U. Hentschel & G.J.W. Smith (Eds.), *Experimentelle Persönlichkeitspsychologie. Die Wahrnehmung als Zugang zu diagnostischen Problemen* [Experimental personality psychology. Perception as the entry to diagnostic problems] (pp. 350-371). Wiesbaden: Akademische Verlagsgesellschaft.

Smith, G.J.W., & Danielsson, A. (1982). Anxiety and defensive strategies in childhood and adolescence. *Psychological Issues*, Monograph 52. New York: International Universities Press.

Smith, G.J.W., Sjoholm, L., & Nielzén, S. (1975). Individual factors affecting the improvement of anxiety during a therapeutic period of 1½ to 2 years. *Acta Psychiatrica Scandinavica*, 52, 7-22.

Smith, G.J.W., & Westerlundh, B. (1980). Perceptgenesis: A process perspective on perception-personality. In L. Wheeler (Ed.), *Review of Personality and Social Psychology* (Vol. 1, pp. 94-124). Beverly Hills, CA: Sage.

Spence, D.P., & Ehrenberg, B. (1964). Effects of oral deprivation on response to subliminal and supraliminal verbal food stimuli. *Journal of Abnormal and Social Psychology*, 69, 10-18.

Spence, D.P., & Gordon, C.M. (1967). Activation and measurement of an early oral fantasy: An exploratory study. *Journal of the American Psychoanalytic Association*, 15, 99-129.

Spence, D.P., & Holland, B. (1962). The restricting effects of awareness: A paradox and an explanation. *Journal of Abnormal and Social Psychology*, 64, 163-174.

Spence, D.P., Scarborough, H.S., & Ginsberg, E.H. (1978). Lexical correlates of cervical cancer. *Social Science and Medicine*, 12, 141-145.

Tyrer, P., Lee, I., & Horn, P. (1978). Treatment of agoraphobia by subliminal and supraliminal exposure to phobic cine film. *The Lancet*, 18, 358-360.

Westerlundh, B. (1984, May). *Conflict through subliminal stimulation*. Paper presented at the 2nd European Conference on Personality. Bielefeld.

Wirsching, M., Stierlin, H., Hoffman, F., Weber, G., & Wirsching, B. (1982). Psychological identification of breast cancer patients before biopsy. *Journal of Psychosomatic Research*, 26, 1-10.

Zuckerman, M. (1960). The effects of subliminal and supraliminal suggestions on verbal productivity. *Journal of Abnormal and Social Psychology*, 60, 404-411.

AUTHOR INDEX

Numerals refer to pages; those in italics refer to lists of references.

SUBJECT INDEX

DATE DUE